THE
DARK SIDE
OF HISTORY

To cause things hidden in the dark to appear, and to take away the dark from them, this is permitted to the intelligent philosopher. . . . All these things happen, and the eyes of ordinary men do not see them, but the eyes of the mind and of the imagination perceive them with the true and truest vision.

MICHAEL SENDIVOGIUS
17th-century alchemist

Michael Edwardes

THE
DARK SIDE
OF HISTORY

Magic In
The Making Of Man

STEIN AND DAY/*Publishers*/New York

First published in 1977
Copyright © 1977 by Michael Edwardes
All rights reserved
Printed in the United States of America
Stein and Day/*Publishers*/Scarborough House,
Briarcliff Manor, N. Y. 10510

Library of Congress Cataloging in Publication Data

Edwardes, Michael.
    Dark side of history.

    Bibliography: p. 253
    Includes index.
    1. Occult sciences—History. I.   Title.
BF1411.E33   133.4   76-44265
ISBN 0-8128-2170-3

Preface

Recently, much has been said and written about an "occult revival," as if some Lazarus had been raised from the dead. But the occult has never been dead. It has always been around for those willing to recognize its contribution to the making of our world, though it is a contribution which most historians have either ignored or seriously discounted. However, my intention has not been to write a "history of the occult" or a do-it-yourself manual—a kind of *Joy of Magic*. I have tried to do no more than put the occult where, I believe, it properly belongs—in the mainstream of history, rather than on its manic periphery.

The materials used in this book were found in many libraries and archives, the most important being The British Library, the London Library, and the India Office Library, London; the Bibliothèque Nationale, Paris; the Vatican Library, Rome; and the National Archives, New Delhi.

I am particularly grateful to Sol Stein for encouraging me to begin this project, and to Reay Tannahill, the social historian, whose criticism and advice helped me to finish it.

Contents

vii

CONTENTS

Part Four
Magicians and Machine Guns

Part Five
Worlds of Light and Worlds of Darkness

THE
DARK SIDE
OF HISTORY

Introduction

Magic is a dangerous word. It can conjure up visions of sawing a woman in half or of burning her as a witch, of wondrous wizards commanding mysterious forces, or of the Satanic Church of San Francisco. It is a word that has been so drained of meaning that nothing is left but the smear of guilt by depreciation.

That depreciation has taken many forms and has come from many sources, but the principal one has been the historian, the person on whom we are forced to rely to reconstruct for us the world of our ancestors. Magic—the word is used in this book, as the great Renaissance philosophers used *magia*, to cover all the so-called "occult sciences"—has suffered badly at the hands of the historian. By depreciating and even ignoring its role in the making of man's world, the historian has often consigned whole areas of human history to the dark, abdicating his proper task of explanation and evaluation almost completely to the "occultist" writer, whose contribution adds more dark than light and provides further justification for not giving magic serious study and consideration.

Until very recently, those historians who bothered to consider magic at all could be divided roughly into two schools— the weak-stomached and the embarrassed. The former found some of the practices of magic so revolting that they rejected them completely. Even Lynn Thorndike, whose pioneer *A History of Magic and Experimental Science* is one of the great revealing works of the past fifty years, writing in this case of witchcraft, dismissed contemporary evidence—"the off-scourings of the criminal courts and torture-chamber, of popular gossip and local scandal"—as "certainly beneath the dignity of our investigation." [1] As if *anything* is beneath the dignity of investigation by the historian. A historian overly concerned with dignity is not a historian but a moralist, and there have been too many historians who have been moralists at heart.

Those who have been embarrassed by the apparent absurdities of magical practice have mainly been historians of science. To give serious study to magical beliefs seems, to them, to imply that they also take seriously the absurd pseudosciences often practiced by the men who held such beliefs. Even historians who ought to, and do, know better, have been unable to shed their embarrassment when faced with magical phenomena. Those intellectually honest enough to allow some importance to the role of magic in Western culture have often soothed their consciences by hastening to stress the undeniably intimate relationship between magic and those respectable activities that ultimately led to modern science.

Yet this is all the result of judging past ages by modern standards. In every age men construct their own reality, the scaffolding inside which they live and operate. It is in the nature of things that yesterday's reality should be different from today's, that yesterday's imaginings should not infrequently become today's facts, and today's truths tomorrow's errors. But today's truths *are* today's truths, whatever tomorrow may do to them. As Cornelius Agrippa, the great Renaissance writer on magic, put it: "All sciences are nothing but decisions and opinions of men." [2] The decisions may be wrong, the opinions will certainly change, but to those who make them and hold them they are real, real enough for action, real enough to live a life by. We do not have to be professional historians to understand that.

2

Introduction

Magic was important in ancient, medieval, and Renaissance culture. The heritage of Greece and Rome, on which so much of modern civilization was built, is saturated with magical beliefs. The best minds of the Middle Ages drew on this rich mine and continued to accept the ideas and practices of the various occult sciences without serious question. They may have disapproved of some magical practices that seemed to endanger religion or morality, but they did not deny the effectiveness, the reality, or the importance of magic.

Magic involved not just witchcraft and pacts with the Devil, but also a whole concept of the world and man's relation to it. Thinkers such as St. Albertus Magnus, St. Thomas Aquinas, and Dante believed in sympathetic bonds linking all reality, in the existence of occult qualities, astral influences, and the actions of good and bad demons as described in the books of magic compiled by lesser men. Most historians, particularly those of science, have chosen to ignore this.

The Renaissance carried on without a break this traditional belief in magic. In fact, there was a direct continuity of magical traditions from the Middle Ages right down to the seventeenth century. In the Renaissance, for all its humanist pretensions, magic was considered to be even more important than it had been in medieval times. It was part of the intellectual baggage of any man of culture, whether he was painter or pope, ruler or revolutionary.

By the end of the seventeenth century, it appeared that the new science of such men as Isaac Newton had banished magic to the limbo of peasant superstition. In the eighteenth century, the philosophers of the Age of Reason convinced themselves that magic was dead. The technicians of the first Industrial Revolution did not think about magic at all, and the Victorian empire builder, when he did, viewed it as something objectionable practiced by inferior races. In our own century, magic in the most varied forms has been regarded as the concern of the bored, the affluent, the psychotic, and the cultural anthropologist, all of them peripheral to the mainstream of life.

But, as this book tries to show, magic has never been exiled to the outer limits of the community, to re-emerge only in the form of quaint sayings and folklore remedies. Under the onslaught of reason and science, the occult went underground—but not very far. It reappears, in a manner distasteful to the orthodox liberal historian, in radical and revolutionary political and social theories; in anti-colonialism; in popular education; in efforts to conserve the environment.

The explanation of the persistence of the occult tradition is simple enough. Reason, rationalism, scientific ideas have never been capable of containing either human aspiration or human suffering. Religion for the majority has never been more than a tranquilizer—accept, wait, and on the other side, if you are good, you will find paradise. Magic, on the other hand, has always been activist, a statement of faith in the capacity of man rather than in the compassion of God.

What *is* magic? The once-influential Scottish anthropologist, Sir James George Frazer, called it in *The Golden Bough* "the bastard sister of science," and elsewhere in the same book declared that "magic pulls strings to which nothing is attached." [3] The currently fashionable Belgian anthropologist Claude Lévi-Strauss describes magic as one of "two parallel modes of acquiring knowledge," [4] the other being science. The American anthropologist Weston La Barre, in the shadow of Freud, sees magic as "self-delusory fixation at the oral-anal phases of adaptation, with purely fantasied operation of the omnipotent will." [5] Such definitions, and there are many others like them, are not very helpful. They are not really definitions at all, but judgments of worth, and pretty biased ones at that.

What *is* magic? Is it, perhaps, "the bringing together of practices by which one uses available resources in order to achieve certain valued ends"? [6] That is, in fact, a definition of modern technology by a modern Frenchman, Jacques Ellul, but it fits magic very well—although, like all short definitions of complex subjects, it does not go far enough. Really to know what magic is about, it is necessary to know not only the extent

4

and quality of the "available resources," but something of the nature of the "valued ends."

Like every other work of historical explanation, that is what this book is about—ends and means, and, of course, the people who decided what end they wanted to achieve and what means were available by which they might achieve it.

Prologue
THE MORNING
OF THE MAGICIAN

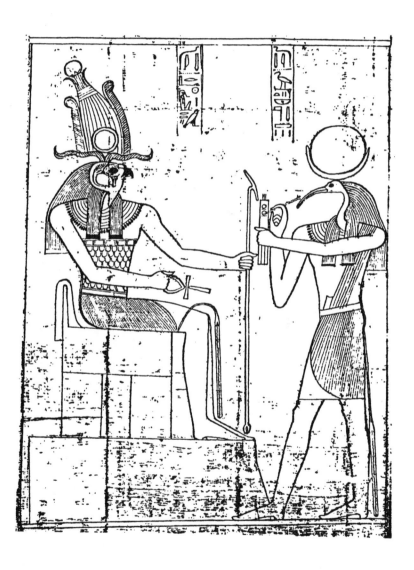

Nestanebanshru papyrus. Thoth/Hermes. Throughout the history of alchemy Thoth was regarded as Hermes Trismegistus.

Certain things are timeless. All the social systems devised by man enshrine his own limitations of development and fulfillment, his inner conflicts, his private rendezvous with death. It is only comparatively recently that he has sought to solve such problems through exclusively secular institutions, to soothe his unease with the exclusively secular myths of perpetual economic growth and the elimination of disease. But, through most of human history, men have tended to project on the screen of the cosmos their ideas of an ideal social system, harmonious between man and man, between man and Nature, between earth and heaven.

Deeply entrenched in all their thinking and feeling was the belief that earth and heaven were vitally interconnected, that they revealed, even in the smallest particular, a limitless series of correspondences. But, as crisis followed crisis, men became more and more aware of the potentialities for change, and as the atmosphere of crisis became more comprehensive and unslackening, they also felt menaced on all sides by ungraspable forces and by a crushing sense of fate. How were they to *know* whether their social structure was indeed a reflection of that of heaven? How, if it was, could they defend it from the forces of disorder? It seemed essential to establish a direct line of communication with the gods.

According to many anthropologists, a medium for such

communication existed even before the gods themselves. The shaman, or medicine man, was portrayed more than ten thousand years ago as a masked dancer on the walls of Lascaux in southern France and other Stone Age caves, and the antiquity of his kind is supported by the worldwide distribution of such images. Early man, preoccupied with hunting, needed little more from the supernatural than aid in hunting, and it was the shaman who had control over animals and over the spirits man believed animated his small world. From long-surviving shamanist cultures such as those of the North American Indian and the Siberian Tungus can be drawn firsthand information on the activist role of the shaman in hunting societies.

The shaman, however, was a figure not only in simple societies. "Civilized" man had need of him too, of someone god-possessed, a god-speaker who was in himself a direct line to heaven. In this extended world the shaman had much greater socio-economic and political power. Sometimes he became part of the apparatus of the state, defending the status quo against the future. Such were the oracles of Apollo in Greece, and the sibyls of Imperial Rome. Sometimes, he was a rebel and reformer. But, whatever his role, every shaman believed—or appeared to believe—that he spoke with the authentic voice, that he was the mouthpiece of god, and articulated divine planning and purpose.

Unfortunately, the statements of the god-speaker were often ambiguous or downright unhelpful. Nor was he always immune to the enticements of bribery or personal ambition. But what was perhaps most unsatisfactory of all was the hallucinatory state itself, the psychic circumstances in which the god spoke. From a mass of available evidence, it seems probable that, initially, the shaman was one who suffered an authentic mental illness—whose symptoms later became the necessary signs of qualification for the job. It was very difficult to know the "real" from the fake, especially since, as a modern American anthropologist, Weston La Barre, has put it, "shamans run the full gamut from self-convinced and sincere psychotics to epileptics and suggestible hysterics, and from calculating psychopaths . . . to plodding naïfs only following the cultural ropes." [1]

Not even in the earliest times, however, did men place their sole reliance on the shaman. Believing themselves part of a living and interconnected universe, they also looked to the world around them for signs and messages that might reveal the pattern of events.

To divine is human. Today, the world has scientific technology and computer sampling. In the millennia before yesterday, there was a somewhat different technology of divination. Different, and vast in its variety. The god-speakers had their place, though it was a passive one since the gods spoke *through* them; so too had the necromancers, who raised and interrogated the spirits of the dead. But the most important and popularly valued side of divination was the interpretation of signs and omens. These could be observed in an almost limitless range of substances and phenomena—the shape of clouds, the pattern of smoke rising from the fire, the colors and deposits of rivers, strange prodigies and monstrous births. One of the most important techniques for observing and interpreting signs was examination of the entrails of a sacrificed animal, particularly the liver, which was believed to be the seat of the soul and the center of life.

The need to organize and classify what had been observed led to the creation of increasingly complex intellectual systems. The struggle to read the will of the gods, the structure of fate, in liver formation and other phenomena, gave birth to subtle disciplines dealing with the interconnection of things and processes, and above all with attempts to control specific events. There was nothing abstract about the diviner's activity. He was not engaged in scholarly research for its own sake. He played an important and often decisive social and political role. And, more than that, for in the *style* of divinatory reasoning—abstraction, analysis, deduction, the search for "laws"—the Mesopotamian diviners created the spirit and method of what we now call science, and bequeathed it to today's world.

11

Mesopotamian thought about omens and correspondences was not unique. There was, for example, a striking similarity between Mesopotamian and Chinese thinking—if not method—in the concept of *feng-shui*, the Chinese system of geomancy, or divination by topographical features. The *feng-shui* (literally, "wind and water") practitioners were perhaps the first environmental engineers, for they believed that good fortune and happiness could result from the particular siting of a building or change in a natural feature. One of the most influential inventions of all time, the magnetic compass, was first developed for *feng-shui* purposes.

It was in Mesopotamia, however, that fundamental ideas on omens and correspondences were first richly developed and elaborated. The reason for this was possibly to be found in social and economic conditions, in the growth of cities with extensive mercantile and industrial activity, and the unease and alienation that fester in urban societies. The area's vulnerability to attack brought disasters, but also new beginnings. A body of established divinatory knowledge, protected by professional magicians, helped to create some social cohesion and stability, even at times of change, while the dangers of change formed an inspiration for further observation and elaboration of divinatory systems. The most exhaustive, the most complex, and the most influential of these was astrology, that study of the stars which ancient Mesopotamians believed formed "the writing of heaven."

The first men had anxiously watched the sky, the source of night and day, of light and darkness, sometimes cool and blue, sometimes angry with wind and water. They learned, in time, to correlate certain happenings in the heavens with happenings on earth, and from their observations produced a simple calendar for hunting and planting.

As observation piled on observation, overwhelming support appeared for the belief that in the heavens resided the powers that ruled all life, whose decrees could be read in the movement of the heavenly bodies. The sun, the moon, and the planets were regarded as divine and given the names of gods and goddesses. These great stars moved against a background of fixed constellations and along a stable path or band. This band we know as the zodiac.

It was the Mesopotamians who first established viable astrological systems, first defined the zodiac, and produced the first horoscopes. But it was the Greeks who gave the names of their gods to the planets, names we still use today in their Roman version—Mercury, Venus, Mars, Jupiter, Saturn. The Greeks also gave precedence to the sun, whereas the Mesopotamians had preferred the moon.

At the center of their world picture, the Mesopotamians had seen mankind ruled by the gods through the celestial elements. The Greeks produced some modifications which vitally affected the development of astrology. About 530 b.c. Pythagoras—popularly remembered, at least during schooldays, for his theorem concerning the square of the hypotenuse—expressed the grand design of the universe in numerical terms, using the mathematical relationship of musical intervals. For Pythagoras, the planets and the stars were living intelligences, their bodies, like those of men, receptacles of a spiritual being. The planets, he said, made music, and man the microcosm vibrated to the tones that they broadcast.

The thinking of the Greeks on astrology—that of Plato on the sun and moon and the sexes, of Hippocrates on its role in medical diagnosis—was the thinking of philosophers and mathematicians, an élite who kept their thoughts to their own class. But in one area the masses met the masters and shared their beliefs, if not the intricacies of their thinking. The souls of men, all classes of men, were believed at birth to enter the body by way of a particular star, and at death to return to the heavens by the same path. Once the position of his star was established for the time of a person's birth, a profile of his personality could be constructed and a prediction made of the pattern of his life. His destiny was there in the machinery of the universe, of which he was a tiny wheel. It was the Greeks who named the tool of prediction; "zodiac" is Greek for "circle of animals."

It took many centuries to build up a pattern which related the twelve signs to human temperament, and to take into account all the influences that might affect a person's psyche. In an interdependent universe those influences were everywhere—in stones and trees, in metals and jewels, in mountains and rivers, in other men and animals. It was essential to establish the relationship of material things to the stars, and the mechanics were supplied by the Greek view of the constitution of matter, which was given its most precise, and most influential expression by Aristotle in the fourth century B.C.

According to Aristotle, the basis of the material world was primitive matter, which in its simplest manifestation took form as the four elements of fire, air, water, and earth. Everything in existence contained these four elements, differences being accounted for by the proportions in which the elements were present. "The kind of reasoning on which this proposition is based may be followed by observing what happens when a piece of green wood is heated; drops of water form at the cut end of the wood, therefore wood contains water; steam and vapours are given off, therefore wood contains air; the wood burns, therefore it contains fire; and ash is left, therefore wood contains earth." [2] On another level, the four elements had other qualities. The earth was said to be practical, water emotional, air intellectual, and fire inspirational. On this level, they corresponded with the four "humours" theory that formed the basis of medicine until the sixteenth century—the psychological categories were phlegmatic (earthy), melancholy (watery), sanguine (airy), and choleric (fiery).

These refinements, as well as systematized observation, philosophical commentary, and metaphysical speculation—all the sophistication of centuries—were assembled in the occult encyclopedia of Claudius Ptolemy, a Greek from Alexandria in Egypt who lived in the second century A.D. His *Tetrabiblos*, the scholarly basis of all later Arab and Western astrology, was a compilation of information on nativities, diseases, marriages, deaths, the signs of nations, weather forecasting, the prediction of future events, length of life, and worldly fortune. Ptolemy also produced, as a synthesis of various models of the universe, one of his own which came to be called the Ptolemaic system and was accepted as the truth for more than a thousand years.

In Ptolemy's explanation, the earth was the center of the universe and surrounding it were the elements of fire, air, and water. Around these was the crystalline sphere of the moon circling within the sun and the five planets. Enclosing the whole were the sphere of the fixed stars and that of the "Prime Mover," while beyond was heaven, the home of the gods. Ptolemy was convinced of the overwhelming influence of the heavenly bodies.

> The sun [he wrote in the *Tetrabiblos*], is always in some way affecting all things on earth, not only by changes that accompany the year's seasons to bring about the generation of animals, the productiveness of plants, the flowing of waters, and the changes of bodies, but also by the daily revolutions supplying heat, moisture, dryness and cold in regular order and correspondence with its position relative to the zenith. The moon, too, as the heavenly body nearest to the earth, bestows her influence most abundantly on earthly things; for most of them, animate or inanimate, are sympathetic to her and change in company with her. The rivers increase and diminish their streams in her light, the seas turn their tides with her rising and setting, and plants and animals in whole or in some part wax and wane with her.[3]

The world of Claudius Ptolemy and that of twentieth-century physics seem very close as modern scientists reveal an earth bombarded by influences from space, by cosmic rays and light rays. It is now possible to hear and measure "the music of the spheres" drifting from the electromagnetic and radio net that shrouds the universe. Modern man is close, too, in his often unstated but no less deeply felt fear of his inability to control his own destiny, in his awareness of being caught in a mechanist society within a mechanist universe.

The astrologers had been quick to allocate three signs of the zodiac to each of the four elements, but they too saw the world of man controlled by the determinism of cosmic law. Man and his earth were at the center of the universe, but it was a powerless center. With submission, however, there had always been hope, hope that the acquisition of knowledge would lead to power, to an escape from fate, to ways of controlling or coercing reality. Dealing, as they thought, with the very stuff of destiny, the astrologers still pursued the knowledge that could save man from fate. Ptolemy, following earlier thinkers, allowed an element of chance to creep in. Others looked for something more positive, for techniques by which to *manipulate* the stars—for magic.

Magic, like the technology of Jacques Ellul's definition, had limited "available resources" but an infinity of "valued ends." The basic resource of early magical technology was the spirits that inhabited the universe and symbolized the parts and motive forces of the cosmic machinery. From the beginning, men had sought to control these forces. The first step toward control is ownership, and the foundation of ownership is understanding. To know a thing is to possess it; to possess a thing is to be able to manipulate it.

To understand something, it is necessary to be able to name it—to give it its true name, the secret essence of the thing. A spirit named could be called and, if properly coerced, made to do what the caller required. (This feeling that knowing the name confers some element of power over the named is still instinctive in mankind; we may still be reluctant to permit someone to use our given name, even though the power it confers amounts only to that of less-than-casual acquaintance).

The very act of calling a spirit was an aspect of the worldwide belief that sound is power, from the Christian *logos*, "in the beginning was the word," to *Om*, the Hindu "sound of creation." Sound is the material of spells and incantations in rituals superficially as different as rainmaking ceremonies and the Catholic mass.

The long morning of the magician was at its brightest between roughly the third century B.C. and the third century

A.D., a period that saw the working out of many ideas, some of considerable antiquity, in magical technology. Among them was what later came to be called (from the Arabic word *alkimia*) alchemy. Writers on alchemy have suggested that the word *kimia* (*al* is the definite article) came from the Egyptian *kēme:* black—as in *kēmet:* Egypt, "the black land," from the black soil of the river Nile—through the Greek *chyma*, meaning to fuse or cast a metal. Whatever the truth, this suggestion at least delineates part of the ethnic route taken by alchemy on the way to its theater of greatest performance, the European Renaissance. It was the Greeks living in Alexandria in Egypt who assembled the basic materials, and the Arabs who refined them, with additions from China, and passed them on, together with the great bulk of the lost culture of the classical world, to a Europe emerging hopefully from the terrors of the Dark Ages.

Alchemy is essentially about transmutation, the change of something coarse into something refined, of something intrinsically worthless into something of great value. These "somethings" could be metallic substances—or human souls. And, indeed, alchemy was to have two inseparable levels of activity, the proto-chemical, dealing with the transmutation of metals (particularly of lead into gold), and the metaphysical, with the search for immortality.

Nearly all theories of metallic transmutation, and there were to be many, had their roots in Aristotle's concept of matter. If all substances contained the same four elements, and if lead and gold, therefore, each consisted of fire, air, water, and earth, transmutation was merely a question of finding the correct process for rearranging their proportions. The search for the answer to this question was to be one of the most fascinating and productive in the history of man. After a life of nearly two thousand years, belief in transmutation was laughed away by the new science of the seventeenth century, only to return in an English laboratory in 1919 when Lord Rutherford, bombarding nitrogen with alpha particles from a radioactive source, turned it into oxygen. The transmutation of metals as well as of gases is now commonplace, but the transmutation of man's soul and the search for immortality continue, with rather less success.

The alchemists' "alpha particle" was the spirit which they saw animating the universe. From the very earliest times, man associated metal with the heavenly bodies—gold with the sun, silver with the moon, iron with Mars, quicksilver with Mercury, copper with Venus, tin with Jupiter, and lead with Saturn. The stars could be involved in alchemical operations, and astrological methods were used to determine the most auspicious times and places for transmutations. This was fairly basic. It was also believed possible to concentrate the universal spirit, the power of the cosmos, into something solid—the philosopher's stone or elixir, a substance that alchemists could use to carry out transmutation.

The first reference to the source of this belief appeared in an Arabic manuscript of the ninth century A.D., which was said, probably based on a Syriac version, itself derived from a Greek original. Both the latter have been lost. This "source," it was said, consisted of the words inscribed on a thin sheet of emerald clutched in the hand of the corpse of Hermes Trismegistus, "the thrice great," which had been found in a cave. Myths soon proliferated about the "Emerald Tablet." According to one version, the fortunate discoverer of the corpse and the tablet was Sara, the wife of Abraham; according to others, it was Alexander the Great, or Apollonius of Tyana, a magician who flourished in the first century A.D. About Hermes himself there was similar imprecision. It was even suggested that there had been three persons of that name. One of these lived before the Flood and was the grandson of Adam and builder of the pyramids of Egypt; he was also the patron of sciences and the first to wear sewn clothes. Another Hermes lived after the Flood, in Babylon; an adept in science and medicine, philosophy and mathematics, he was the teacher of Pythagoras. The third Hermes lived in Egypt, was an expert on poisonous animals, and wrote works on alchemy and town planning. Whoever he was, whether he was any or none of these, Hermes Trismegistus at least achieved some kind of immortality in the modern expression "hermetically sealed."

Hermes also gave his name to one of the descriptions of alchemy, the "Hermetic art." The Emerald Tablet states:

> True it is, without falsehood, certain and most true.
> That which is above is like to that which is below, and that which is below to that which is above.
> And as all things were by the contemplation of one, so all things arose from this one thing by the single act of adaptation.
> The father thereof is the Sun, the mother the Moon.
> The Wind carried it in his womb, the Earth is the nurse thereof.
> It is the father of all works of wonder throughout the whole world.
> The power thereof is perfect.
> If it be cast on to the Earth, it will separate the Earth from that of Fire, the subtle from the gross.
> With great sagacity it doth ascend gently from Earth to Heaven.
> Again it doth descend to Earth and uniteth in itself the force from things superior and things inferior.
> Thus thou wilt possess the glory and the brightness of the whole world, and all obscurity will fly from thee.
> This thing is the strong fortitude of all strength, for it overcometh every subtle thing and doth penetrate every solid substance.
> Thus was the world created.
> Hence there will be marvellous adaptations achieved, of which the manner is this.
> For this reason I am called Hermes Trismegistus, because I hold three parts of the wisdom of the whole world.
> That which I had to say about the operation of Sol is completed.[4]

"All obscurity will fly from thee." But it has never flown from the Emerald Tablet, whose cryptic utterances remain cryptic still. It does, however, indicate the correspondence between terrestrial and celestial affairs that was the basis of alchemy, and it allowed for a wide range of interpretation and commentary. What academic, scientist or literary critic today could ask for more?

Shamanism, divination, astrology, spirit calling, alchemy—such were some of the "available resources" of magic. What were the "valued ends"? The making of gold and the drug of deathlessness might merit the definition, but so too could the individual's desire for power, for personal wealth, for domination over others. Certainly, magical technology could be, and was, used in the hope of satisfying such desires by practitioners who ranged from casters of horoscopes in the market place to para-politicians in the palace, who could decide the fate of thousands or even of empires, and from the constructor of talismans to the sexually deprived who sought to control women. There was also, of course, the show-business end of the magical spectrum, those who turned snakes into staffs, flew in the air, or walked on water, whose acts had the same entertainment value as sawing a woman in half or producing rabbits from a hat. Such uses of magic might offer a way of making a living, but from any other point of view they were basically worthless and unproductive. The nineteenth-century Indian mystic Ramakrishna used to tell his disciples of the man who had spent years acquiring the power of walking on the water. Crossing a river on foot, the man went proudly to his guru, only to be told: "My poor boy, what you have accomplished after fourteen years' arduous labour, ordinary men do by paying a penny to the boatman." [5]

But there were men—there may still be—who were determined that their technology, their science, should be used for socially purposeful ends. For them, magic was man's weapon against fate, against death, against the gods themselves.

One

ALCHEMICAL ARTS
AND NATURAL MAGIC

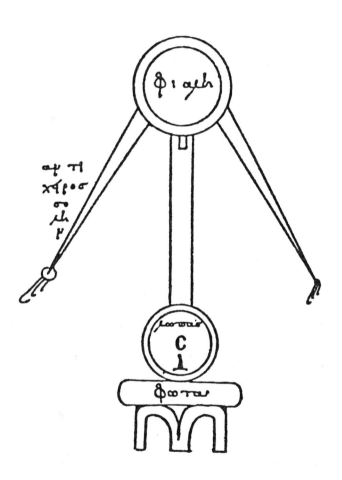

Kerotakis (c. 2000 AD), a boiling device used by alchemists to turn substances such as mercury, sulfur, and arsenic into gold.

1

Magisteries of Gold and Immortality

Silence is golden—especially for anyone who is in the business of *making* gold. Or, if not silence, at least the discretion recommended by Albertus Magnus, the medieval bishop and scholar who was canonized in 1931:

> The alchemist must be silent and discreet. To no one should he reveal the results of his operations.
> He shall live in loneliness, remote from men . . .
> And finally, he will avoid all contact with princes.[1]

Wise advice from someone who knew the nature of princes.

Unfortunately, for most alchemical writers obscurity became the better part of discretion. They disguised their ideas, their experiments and their processes behind a barrier of colorful and confusing imagery, opaque symbolism, and cryptic allusion which left the field open to later scientists, historians, art critics, psychologists, and new occultists to interpret them either as rubbish or revelation, with only the smallest of gaps between. Thus alchemy became "the history of an error," [2] a "mystical superstition," [3] "the earliest phase of modern chemistry," [4] "the historical counterpart of [the] psychology of the unconscious," [5]

23

a "rainbow bridging the chasm between earthly and heavenly planes." [6] All these quotations are from our own century and most of them contain an element of the truth.

The security system of the alchemists was, in fact, not totally impenetrable, though at first sight it must often seem so. A passage in the *Book of Comarius, Philosopher and High Priest, instructing Cleopatra on the Divine and Sacred Art of the Philosopher's Stone,* a work probably from Alexandria in the second century A.D., reads:

> In you is hidden all the marvelous and terrible mystery. Enlighten us, illuminating the elements with your radiant splendour. Make known to us how the highest descends to the lowest, and how the lowest ascends to the highest, and how the midmost draws near to the lowest and the highest so that they are made one with it. Show us the blessed waters come down from above to awaken the dead, who lie around in the middle of Hell, chained in darkness; how the medicine of life comes to them and awakens them, rousing them out of their sleep there; how the new waters that have been produced during their prostration by the actions of the light, penetrate them. The vapour supports them; rising from the sea, it supports the waters. [7]

It is generally agreed that this mystical language contains a description of a process known as reflux (backward-flow) distillation in a *kerotakis* apparatus. The *kerotakis* is said to have been invented by a certain Mary the Jewess who is also credited with the invention of what survives as the *bain-marie* or *double boiler* of the modern kitchen. In the process described, a piece of metal is placed at the top of a cylinder at whose base there is a fire (the "light" of the text quoted above). The fire heats substances such as mercury, sulfur, and arsenic, and the vapors released rise, attack the metal at the top, then condense and run down the sides. The process then begins again and can be continued for as long as is desired.

But for every one of these penetrable pieces of cryptography there is at least one that is not:

> The third day again to life he shall uprise,
> And devour byrds and beastes of the wildernesse,
> Crowes, popingayes, pyes, pecocks, and mevies;
> The phenix, the eagle whyte, the gryffon of fearfulnesse,
> The greene lyon and the red dragon he shall distresse;
> The whyte dragon also, the antelope, unicorne, panthere,
> With other byrds, and beastes, both more or lesse.
> The basilisk also, which almost eache one doth feare.[8]

With such evidence to work on, it is hardly surprising that many writers have been able, without much difficulty, to give alchemy a bad name—and few adequate definitions. But if the fashionable occult jargon is swept aside and alchemy looked at as a this-worldly science based upon "a sublime conviction of the possibility of the control of change and decay,"[9] then the lasting legacies—material and spiritual—come into view. So too does the link between the apparently separate "aims" of alchemy, goldmaking and the quest for immortality, between the philosopher's furnace and the elixir of life.

All That Glitters

Man's fascination with precious metals, with gold and silver, needs no underlining. Desire for them has led to the fall of individuals and empires, to the miser's hoard of Fort Knox, the sovereigns hidden in the mattress, and the Krugerrands in the safe-deposit box. The wedding band still has value as well as symbolism, though the latter may have changed, and the

25

expensive gold wristwatch is advertised, and presumably accepted, as the index of executive success. And if to be "as good as gold" is a rare contemporary ambition, the phrase is at least a memorial to man's long search for substitutes for the precious metals. Out of that search came the false gold, brass, and from China the false silver, cupronickel, first used for "silver" coinage in the second century B.C. and now the most popular coin metal throughout the world.

Exactly when the search for substitutes began, and when a belief in the possibility of producing the real thing emerged, cannot be accurately pinpointed, but both can be seen as quite separate traditions in the city of Alexandria around the beginning of the present era. That vast and splendid city on the Mediterranean, a few miles from the mouth of the river Nile, was the data bank of contemporary knowledge. Its population consisted of a generous mixture of races, its culture was mainly Greek but leavened with ideas and beliefs from all over the known world. Its merchants were rich, for Alexandria was strategically placed to capture the trade of the East, and the rich make the best, if not the only, patrons of philosophers as well as of workers in precious metals. Two of those groups, however, on the strength of the only surviving evidence, never met—the artisans who knew how to make fake golds, and the mystical philosophers who believed they could make real gold.

This division was to remain. The mystical philosopher, the alchemist, never considered the metallurgical craftsman as being in the same social class. Alchemy was for the élite, not the plebs. There was an interchange of techniques and devices, but no more. For one thing, the artisan was a threat to the alchemist since he knew how to test fake gold, a talent which, if called upon, might embarrass the alchemist, to say the least. In fact, one of history's first references to alchemy is contained in an imperial Chinese edict of 144 B.C. which prohibited alchemy and made the manufacture of fake gold punishable by death. The government had in its employ artisans to test the gold.

The literature that survives from Alexandria in the first

26

centuries A.D. is divided into the artisanal and the alchemical. The former contains recipes for artificial golds and silver that are clear and reasonably straightforward. But the recipes for "real" gold in the alchemical manuscripts have already taken on the obscurity, the symbolic character, the macro-micro-cosmic correspondences, that are the essential feature of later alchemy. There are no references to that substance of marvel-ous potency, the philosopher's stone. The Alexandrian alchem-ists—some of whom, like Mary the Jewess, Comarius, and the later Zosimos of Panaopolis, probably used their own names, while others hid their real identity behind such pseudonyms as (the queen) Cleopatra, (the god) Hermes, or (the long-dead Greek philosopher) Democritus—were more concerned with making gold directly than with developing a substance that would turn other metals into gold. The idea of the stone and the search for it that was to become a major preoccupation of *European* alchemy came from the Arabs, who probably got it from the Chinese.

In the seventh century A.D. the Arabs, restless and warlike nomadic tribesmen inhabiting a harsh and arid land, set off to conquer the civilized world. Their stimulus was a new and dynamic religious faith, that of Islam, and their leader the prophet of that faith, Muhammad. By A.D. 629 the Arabs were knocking at the gates of the Byzantine empire, the last fortress of the Roman Empire, which had collapsed in Europe under the attack of other nomads. After the death of Muhammad in 632, the Arabs occupied the outlying provinces of Byzantium, and in 649 conquered Persia. The tide of Arab conquest flowed through North Africa, and by the year 711 Islam was poised to cross the Mediterranean and proceed to the conquest of Spain. Twenty-one years later, only the generalship of Charles Martel prevented the Arabs from overrunning France. Martel's grand-son, Charlemagne, later attempting to restore the Roman Empire in the west, exchanged ambassadors with the caliph Harun ar-Rashid and, according to tradition, received the gifts of a splendid tent, a water clock, an elephant, and the keys of the Holy Sepulcher in Jerusalem. These presents were symbolic of the change that had come over the Arabs since they emerged from the desert. In fact, the empire of Harun was far more civilized than that of Charlemagne. The Arabs, without cultural foundations of their own, had taken the advice of their prophet: "Seek for knowledge, even though it be as far away as China."

The Arabs were fortunate in the materials that lay at their hand. In Persia, they found themselves heirs to the Greek scientific tradition as well as that of Alexandrian alchemy. To the east they were in contact with the Chinese, and to the south with the Hindus. The Arabs were to become the great mediators between Europe and Asia, transmitting Chinese technology, Hindu mathematics, and the ancient wisdom of the Greeks to a West which knew nothing of the first two and had to all intents and purposes forgotten the third.

The principal seat of learning in western Asia, a kind of new Alexandria, was the city of Jundishapur in southwest Persia. To this haven had come Greek exiles and the Christian heretics known as Nestorians. There they met Syrian, Persian, and Hindu men of learning. The Christian heretics translated a number of Greek alchemical works into Syriac, and these in turn were translated into Arabic. Many other Greek works, philosophical, scientific, and medical, were also translated.

Between the eighth and twelfth centuries, the followers of Muhammad held in their hands the knowledge of both the ancient and the contemporary worlds, and the diffusion of that knowledge owed most, if not all, to the Arabic tongue. The prophet himself had said that all believers must know the language of the Koran, the sacred book of Islam, and the Islamic conquerors made Arabic the international language not only of their faith but of the knowledge they had inherited. From Jundishapur and, later, Baghdad, this learning spread to Cairo in the ninth and tenth centuries, and from Cairo to Spain in the eleventh. From there, in a long series of translations into Latin, Greek science and medicine—with Islamic additions—Hindu mathematics, and in particular the so-called "Arabic" numerals, passed into the cultural consciousness of the West. So too did alchemical ideas and practices of considerable sophistication.

One of the most influential of Islamic alchemists was Jabir ibn-Hayyan, whose name was latinized in medieval Europe as Geber. Jabir flourished around the middle of the eighth century and a large number of works bear his name, though he was certainly not the author of some of them. Jabir took Aristotle's four elements of matter—fire, earth, air and water—as a starting point, and added a belief in the existence of four elementary qualities or "natures"—hotness, coldness, dryness, and moistness. In metals, two of the natures were external and two internal. Lead, for example, was cold and dry externally, hot and moist internally, while gold was the reverse. All that had to be done to change lead into gold was to turn its natures inside out. This, Jabir said, could be achieved by altering the proportions of the natures in the substances.

A technique for doing just this was available in the Greek medicine that the Arabs had taken over with enthusiasm. The Greeks, especially Galen, who was well known to the Arabs, attributed diseases to an excess of one of the four "humours." If someone suffered from too much of the dry element he was given treatment with substances which, it was believed, contained a preponderance of the moist element (lamb, for example, was considered "moist"). Jabir tried the same principle, attempting to cure the baseness of metals with medicines which he called "elixirs." According to Jabir, there were specific elixirs for specific transmutations, but there was also an all-purpose substance, the grand elixir. This is the first historical mention of the concept of the philosopher's stone, and it seems likely that Jabir got the idea from the Chinese.

There had certainly been an exchange of information between Alexandria and China, but the idea of an elixir did not appear until after the first Arab ships had begun to trade at Canton, after A.D. 714. The first mention in China of a potent chemical or powder for converting base into precious metals had been before the end of the first century B.C. A gentleman of the imperial court, Cheng Wei, was a great believer in alchemy. He tried to make gold according to the recipes given in *The Great Treasure*, a work said to have been compiled in the fourth century B.C. by a wonder worker named Tsou Yen. Cheng Wei heated quicksilver in a retort, but nothing happened. As he fanned the fire, his wife came to him and said: "I want to try and show you something," and taking some powder out of a bag threw a very small amount into the retort. The powder was absorbed by the quicksilver, and in a short time the contents of the retort had changed to silver. When Wei asked his wife why she had not told him sooner that she had the secret of alchemy, she replied: "In order to get it, it is necessary for one to have the proper fate." [10] In other words, the right destiny and the right astrological circumstances.

The Islamic alchemist Jabir, in the preparation of his various elixirs, used not only metallic substances but animal and vegetable products as well. In the animal category, he placed bone marrow, blood, hair, the urine of lions, vipers, foxes, and domestic or wild donkeys; in the vegetable, aconite, jasmine, onion, pepper, mustard, and pears. Though Jabir's goldmaking recipes often seem ridiculous and highly unlikely to produce the required effect, he also records others that are not. In *The Chest of Wisdom* appears the following formula:

> Take vitriol of Cyprus, one pound, saltpetre, two pounds, and alum of Yemen, one fourth part; extract the water, heating the alembic to redness . . . It is made much sharper if you dissolve in it a fourth part of sal ammoniac; because that dissolves gold, sulphur, and silver.[11]

Vitriol of Cyprus was copper sulfate, and alum of Yemen, aluminum sulfate. This recipe was for the production of nitric acid, and Jabir's process was still in use four centuries after his death.

Practical recipes were not the only ones given in the works assigned to Jabir and other Arab alchemists, but they were the only ones that worked. On the whole, Jabir's writings were clear and free from mystery, but though they became the textbooks of the medieval European alchemist, their very lack of obscurity worked against them. The more mystical alchemists looked down on those who thought they could make gold by laboratory methods from ordinary materials, and dismissed them as "Geber's cooks."

With the goldmaking and other recipes of the Islamic alchemists there came to medieval Europe the suitably mysterious and inspiring statements of the Emerald Tablet of Hermes Trismegistus, a translation of which was available in Latin before the end of the twelfth century.

There were also a number of works skeptical about goldmaking. Doubt appears in one of the texts ascribed to Jabir, though it was not written before the ninth century.[12] One passage denies the possibility of fundamental change in substances, and alleges that each ingredient retains its own "nature." "All that has happened is that their parts have become attenuated and in close approximation to one another, so that to the eye the product appears uniform." This objection bears faint echoes of the Greek "atomic" theory—the belief, first expressed in Athens in the fifth century B.C., that everything was made up of indestructible particles that did not perish when mixed and could be separated afterward. Aristotle's contrary view, however, had triumphed. If it had not, the whole proposition of goldmaking would have been discredited, as it was to be with the revival of atomic theory in the seventeenth century. But, like many another of man's dominating dreams, belief in the possibility of making gold crushed opposition. In fact, even after the revival of atomic theory, one of the "founders of the modern world," Isaac Newton, gave credence to a plan for "multiplying gold." Nothing came of it.

One of the most effective ways of suppressing opposition to alchemical theories was to ascribe the latter to great names

31

from the past. This well-entrenched habit was not only part of the alchemists' security system but an invaluable way of authenticating some new idea or formula. The alchemists never looked forward. Their work was always a search for the secrets that had been known once but had somehow been lost. They did not hesitate to invent a historical work in order to discredit a real one. A case in point relates to the great Persian, Abu Ali ibn-Sina, known in Europe as Avicenna.

Avicenna lived in the eleventh century and was known as the Aristotle of the Arabs. Despite this, he did not believe that it was possible to turn one metal into another. In 1022 he wrote, in the *Book of the Remedy:* "As for the claims of the alchemists, it must be clearly understood that it is not in their power to bring about any true change of [metallic] species." Though they might, he said, be very good at imitations, "tingeing the red metal [i.e., copper] . . . yellow so that it resembles gold," in such products "the essential nature remains unchanged; they are merely so dominated by induced qualities that errors may be made concerning them." In this work, Avicenna did not "deny that such a degree of accuracy be reached as to deceive even the shrewdest," but he believed it to be impossible to carry out a genuine transmutation.[13]

Not so the pseudo Avicenna of the *De Anima in Arte Alchemiae,* a kind of *Reader's Digest* of miscellaneous Arabic originals, probably pasted together in Spain around 1140 and quoted and requoted in alchemical encyclopedias of the thirteenth century and after. Here, Islam's genius comes out in favor of transmutation, and though "he" gives seven tests for real gold, one of which is a good artisan's, "he" comes unequivocally to the conclusion that the best gold is made by the philosopher's stone!

It was little wonder that such contradictions left a feeling of uncertainty among the European inheritors of Islamic alchemy. Even Albertus Magnus, quoted earlier for his advice on security, found himself confused on the matter of goldmaking. He could neither dismiss it nor endorse it. Like many others, he preferred "maybe." In his *Book of Minerals*, in about 1242, he wrote: "The best of all alchemical operations are those which follow the way of Nature herself . . . for what can be done in Nature's case can perhaps be done in the case of Art, and what Nature does by the heat of the sun and the stars can be accomplished [maybe] by the heat of the Art." In effect, what Nature does in the earth to produce natural gold can *perhaps* be done by the alchemist in his retort.

Albertus was a man of genuine knowledge. His curiosity took him to mines and to alchemical laboratories, and he was an enthusiastic field botanist. Sometimes sneered at as the "Ape of Aristotle," he inevitably became encased in a shell of fabulous myth. It was said that he entertained either the Holy Roman Emperor or the Count of Holland (there is some confusion as to which) at dinner in Cologne in the garden of a Dominican monastery in the middle of winter. When the guests arrived, the table was covered with snow, but as soon as they sat down the snow disappeared, the garden was filled with summer flowers, and birds sang in the trees. It seems likely that the miraculous summer of St. Albertus was, in fact, contained within one of the first hothouses. Of such is the kingdom of the alchemists.

The thirteenth-century English Franciscan friar, Roger Bacon, was also a fertile source of legends, most of them less amenable to explanation than the hothouse of St. Albertus. Bacon was said to "make women of devils, and juggle cats into coster-mongers"—though the precise purpose of these activities is not recorded. He had the privilege of being satirized in a popular play by Robert Greene, first performed in 1594. In this, Bacon and his companion—the "wizard," Friar Bungay—made a head out of brass and, with the help of the devil, gave it power of speech. The head was expected to talk within the course of a month, and it was essential that Friars Bacon and Bungay should not miss what was said, for it would not be repeated. Bacon, after staying awake night and day for three weeks, was eventually overcome by sleep and left his servant Miles on watch with instructions to wake him if the head spoke. Soon after, the head did speak. "Time is," it said. Miles felt this was not sufficiently startling to justify waking his master. Next, the head said: "Time was." Then, after a short silence: "Time is past." Thereupon, it broke into pieces with a noise that woke Bacon—but there was nothing he could do, except curse his servant.

Bacon was undoubtedly a practical laboratory worker, and he certainly believed that it was possible to make gold. For him there were two kinds of alchemy, "speculative" and "practical." Speculative alchemy was mainly concerned with the gathering of knowledge, and practical alchemy with the confirmation of that knowledge. It taught "how to make the noble metals, and colours, and many other things better or more abundantly by art than they are made by nature." This type of alchemy, moreover, was socially purposeful, "because it produces greater utilities. For not only can it yield wealth and very many other things for the public good, but it also teaches how to discover such things as are capable of prolonging human life." [14] With those last few words, the idea of the drug of deathlessness entered the European imagination.

In thirteenth-century Europe it would seem that every man with any pretension to scholarship suffered in some degree from the virus of alchemy. Even those who in their writings did not mention the word, or mentioned it only in the most casual way, were infected, men such as the pupil of Albertus Magnus, St. Thomas Aquinas, the great reconciler of Greek and Christian ideas. Aquinas tried to improve on Aristotle, newly revealed through translations from the Arabic, as well as on the fundamental scientific theories of his time. He saw something that Aristotle had missed, that the occult operations of the philosopher's furnace required a component that he called the "celestial virtue." This was the "it," the "spirit" of the Emerald Tablet, the philosopher's stone.

With the support of the greatest scholars—and churchmen— of the day, the practice of alchemy acquired considerable prestige—even, indirectly, the blessing of the church, since it was mainly in the monasteries that suitably educated people with time to spare were to be found. The ecclesiastical authorities frequently issued prohibitions against the practice of alchemy by monks, but these seem on the whole to have been ignored. The attitude of church leaders was dictated not so much by disapproval of alchemy as by the bad reputation given it by a growing number of swindlers professing to make gold. It was no wonder that the genuine alchemist kept his activities and his secrets as close as possible.

What those secrets were we have no idea. From the written word, the key to the cipher is always missing. This, in the proper tradition of secret knowledge, was passed on from master to pupil only by word of mouth. Sometimes the transmission would take no more than a few moments, sometimes considerably longer. Elias Ashmole, the English antiquarian for whom the Ashmolean Museum at Oxford is named, recorded in his diary in 1653 that one William Backhouse, "lying sick in Fleet Street, over against St. Dunstan's Church, and not knowing whether he should live or die, about eleven o'clock told me in syllables the true matter of the Philosopher's Stone, which he bequeathed me as a legacy." [15] What the "syllables" were, Ashmole kept to himself.

But, if the key is missing, there is no shortage of recipes for the making either of gold or the philosopher's stone. Michael Scot, the "wondrous wizard," had one for turning copper into gold. Scot became official astrologer to the Holy Roman emperor, Frederick II, in 1227; Frederick was the grandson of the first Norman king of Sicily, an island where, as in Spain, the West met the Arab East. Scot was given a kind of immortality by Dante in the *Inferno* and, more pleasantly, in one of Boccaccio's tales in the *Decameron*, where he is described as "a great master of black magic." The usual myths gathered around Scot. He flew in the air on a demon horse, and when he arrived in Paris the first stamp of its hooves brought down the bells of Notre Dame and the second the towers of the king's palace. A third disaster was averted only by the king's granting Scot everything he required. Scot also foresaw the way in which he himself would die, as the result of a small stone falling on his head. As a precaution, he wore a steel cap, but removed it in church one day at the moment of the elevation of the Host—and was struck by a stone weighing only two ounces which fell from the roof and killed him.

Michael Scot's recipe called for "the blood of a ruddy man and the blood of a red owl, burning saffron, Roman vitriol, resin well pounded, natural alum, Roman alum, sugared alum, alum of Castile, red tartar, marcasite, golden alum of Tunis which is red, and salt." [16] These ingredients were to be pounded in a mortar, passed through sieves, treated with the urine of an animal called *taxo*, or with the juice of wild cucumber, then dried, pounded once again in a mortar, and put into a crucible with the copper. Another recipe, this time for producing a transmuting powder, began with the shutting up of five toads in a vessel and making them drink the juices of various herbs with vinegar.

There is no surviving record alleging that Scot actually *made* gold, or even any goldlike substance. If he had, it would no doubt have been kept a secret from everyone except his imperial employer. But there had been many men—and were to be many more—who claimed that they had the secret of making gold, and claimed it publicly enough to attract credulous clients.

None of them, however clever, however adroit and convincing, actually produced *real* gold other than by substitution or sleight of hand—by, in effect, salting the goldmine. Some claimants found adequate philosophical and mystical justification for calling any goldlike substance that they made "gold"— as good as natural gold, if not better—in the fact that it was produced by art. Others were mere charlatans, conmen out for a quick profit.[17] The difference between the two types lay essentially in what they *thought* they were doing: indulging in conscious fraud (knowing that there were artisans who could be called in to unmask their fake), or exercising proto-chemical ingenuity sustained by philosophical theory, with no intention of making money directly out of it, and either no knowledge of—or no belief in—the decisive character of the test of the refiner's fire.[18]

The latter, for all their illusions, were not infrequently practical men carrying out actual laboratory experiments and contributing to that growing body of practical and useful knowledge that was to flower into the scientific revolution of the seventeenth century and contribute to the making of today's world.

The discoveries of the laboratory were mundane in comparison with gold, but there was at least one that proved almost as valuable as the precious metal itself. Augustus the Strong, elector of Saxony, who ruled from 1694 until 1733—had a passion for Chinese porcelain and would go to such lengths to obtain specimens that China was said to be "the bleeding-bowl of Saxony." In the first year of his reign Augustus was rumored to have spent more than a hundred thousand *thalers* on porcelain and to have exchanged a regiment of dragoons for forty-eight porcelain vases belonging to the king of Prussia. In his need for money to finance this expensive hobby, Augustus turned to alchemy, employing a succession of experts to make gold. All proved unsuccessful, but a team of two alchemists produced hardpaste porcelain instead. In 1712, Augustus set up the still-famous factory at Meissen, and for some years held a European monopoly. Porcelain was the salvation of the state. In this case at least, the glitter—the sharp white glitter of fine porcelain—*was* the gold.

The Drug of Deathlessness

"That medicine which will remove all impurities and corruptibilities from the lesser metals will also, in the opinion of the wise, take off so much of the corruptibility of the body that human life may be prolonged for many centuries." So wrote Roger Bacon in the middle of the thirteenth century A.D. The philosopher's stone that could transmute lead into gold was also the elixir of life.

The earliest association of gold with immortality is probably to be found in ancient Indian religious texts, but it was the Chinese, more than twelve hundred years before Friar Bacon, who turned that association into a practical search for an elixir and thus became the founders of what today is called chemotherapy.

On its way through Islamic alchemy to the medieval West, Chinese elixir chemistry suffered a number of transformations, but the most important change took place in Europe. The aim of the Chinese was material immortality, of the European, the simple prolongation—not indefinite—of life. When the idea of an elixir arrived in Europe it did so in the cultural context of a Christianity that denounced the world of men as no more than an uncomfortable waiting room for either the delights of heaven or the horrors of hell. For Europeans, the elixir of life was more an elixir of youthfulness, or of a happy and active old age. The Chinese did not believe in other-worldly hells and paradises; for them, immortality was perpetual enjoyment of the world of the senses, with the body retained in some suitably refined form.

The Chinese believed that those who achieved immortality did so not because they were "good"—as a reward for some specific type of behavior on earth—but because they had consumed the drug of deathlessness. Early in Chinese history the drug was thought to be vegetable in origin. In order to discover what it was, it was necessary to find an immortal and question him. At the beginning of the third century B.C., expeditions were sent to the Eastern Ocean in search of the islands of the immortals, the home of the medicine of immortality, and after the unification of the Chinese empire under the first emperor of the Ch'in in 221 B.C., the search was intensified.

This emperor, described not very flatteringly as having a high-bridged nose, long narrow eyes, the breast of a bird of prey, and the voice of a jackal, heard one day that a number of corpses lying on one of the roads to the west had been revived when a bird resembling a crow had placed on their faces a plant that it carried in its beak. A sample of the plant was sent to a wise man named the Devil Valley Master, who lived in a suburb of the imperial capital. "This herb," pronounced the master, "is the herb of deathlessness that grows in the fields among the rose coloured rocks of the island of Tsu-chou in the Eastern Ocean . . . . Its leaves are like watergrass, and one stalk is sufficient to raise a man from the dead." [19] The emperor sent a naval expedition, under one Hsu Fu, to find the island and bring back the herb, but though Hsu Fu succeeded in the first part of his mission, the gifts he carried were thought to be inadequate and he was allowed to do no more than see the herb, not to take any away. He was told that it would only be possible for him to have some in exchange for five hundred young men, girls, and artisans. These were duly dispatched to the island, but none returned to say whether they had reached it or not, and the emperor was forced to continue the search—with no success, and at great expense.

The efforts, and the amount of money spent on them by the first Ch'in emperor, were surpassed by Emperor Wu Ti of the Han dynasty, who ruled from 141 B.C. to 88 B.C. Knowing the emperor's consuming desire to talk with the immortals, charlatans of all types presented themselves at the imperial court. Those who actually reached Wu Ti's presence usually did so through the good offices of a courtier anxious to increase his influence with the emperor. Naturally, these magicians were the most impressive. One, Li Shao-Chun, who was introduced to the emperor in about 113 B.C., demonstrates how ancient is the technique of the occult salesman. Li looked to be an old man, and when he was asked his age replied: "I always say I am seventy." After much persuading, Li explained that he always said he was seventy because he looked seventy, which was the age at which he had discovered the secret of how to avoid becoming older.

"How long ago were you seventy?" inquired the emperor.

"Ah," said Li, "a long time."

"Will you not tell me your real age?"

"If your Majesty will permit, I would rather not say."

"Why not?" demanded the emperor.

"Because I want to prove myself to your Majesty rather than make claims that are difficult to believe. For my age is very great. It is also a long time since I ceased to eat and drink."

The emperor was hooked. Even when Li died some time later, after a short illness, the emperor did not give up hope of using his recipes or of discovering the isles of the immortals.

Other magicians followed Li, and failing to fulfill their promises were executed. The news got about. When Luan Ta was brought before the emperor he refused to make any promises, saying that the fate which had overtaken a certain Chao Wang had "unnerved us magicians. We think it prudent to cover our mouths." The emperor hurriedly explained that he was mistaken about Chao Wang. "He died, in fact, of eating too much horse liver." Luan accepted this explanation—though implying that he had reservations about it—and then embarked on his sensational career. Claiming that he could not contact the immortals without insulting them by his lack of status, Luan Ta received noble titles and honors and was even married to one of the imperial princesses. But the immortals were not contacted and, despite his illustrious connections, Luan was executed.[20]

The intensity of Wu Ti's search for immortality was not a matter for which he was despised. It was thought quite proper for an emperor. What many objected to, however, was the cost, although practitioners of the occult arts were delighted. As Ku Yung put it in A.D. 10, in an address to the then emperor: "There were thousands of magical technicians ... who glared around and slapped their thighs, swearing that they were the real experts in the arts of achieving the life of the holy immortals, making sacrifices, and gaining blessings."[21]

This complaint of a Han statesman indicates that an elixir was not the only method of achieving immortality. There was also that of sacrifice, prayer, incantation, and procession, in special temples dedicated to the worship of gods and the holy immortals. In fact, it seems probable that the incense burner used in temple ceremonies was the ancestor of the Chinese alchemist's furnace, and that the effects on substances burnt in these vessels led to the belief that chemical elixirs would be a more than adequate substitute for the elusive plant of immortality.

Alchemy in China was inseparably entwined with Taoist religion and philosophy. Taoism provided the conception of an earthly paradise, without which there could be no idea of material immortality. Taoists believed that the study of Nature was more valuable to man than the administration of human society, and that human perfection depended rather more on a person's identification with the natural cosmos than on his social relations with other men. This ancient belief has a modern feel about it, and its followers were subjected to the same criticism that is often hurled today at those who have abandoned conventional society for the commune. The Taoists taught that, by withdrawing from society into some quiet place in the mountains and there carrying out various exhausting exercises and meditational techniques, and following a special diet, a man could become a holy immortal. The Confucians who dominated the state regarded this as a dangerous diversion from man's earthly duties. In 60 B.C. a Confucian, Wang Pao, strongly attacked the "immortals" for having "abandoned the common life and cut themselves off from the humanity of their generation." [22]

Wang Pao's complaint was of the same order as "What would happen to the world if everyone acted like that?" or "*Some*one has to stay behind and run the country!" Chinese alchemists accepted this viewpoint; emperors and high officials could hardly spare the time for meditation in the mountains. For those who found the Taoist system impracticable, the obvious alternative was to take an elixir. This was also, in a sense, more democratic. Women and children could swallow an elixir, whereas the Taoist austerities would be beyond their physical powers. By the second century A.D., in fact, the search for immortality for oneself alone, whatever the method, was criticized as selfish, and it was suggested that the highest activity was to bring such salvation to others, even if only to the members of one's own family.

This responsible, almost moral approach to the attainment of immortality was soon reflected in the organization of the immortals themselves. By the end of the third century A.D. it was held that there was a full celestial bureaucracy, with the various categories of immortal properly defined and their habitations fixed. Though there was some disagreement on the exact number of categories, the most generally accepted included the masters of the highest category, who lived in the "aery void" and were known as the "celestial immortals"; those of the second category, known as the "terrestrial immortals," who resorted to the famous mountains and forests; and the lowest category, those who were only able to "slough off the body after death" and were called "corpse-free immortals." [23]

There was certainly, at this time, no shortage of candidates for immortality, many of them helped on their way by elixir poisoning. Cases of elixir poisoning were well known among the Chinese élite. The deaths of large numbers of royal personages and high officials did, as it happened, contribute to the making of a number of major chemical discoveries— including, ironically enough, that of gunpowder—but why did such men continue, over many centuries, to swallow highly toxic substances? Their reasons were very much the same as those of people today who continue to take dangerous drugs that are known to be physically harmful to them. The elixirs at first appeared stimulating, and then became addictive. There was also the insidious effect of the propaganda of immortality. It was very foolish, said the alchemists, to give up taking an elixir just because of a feeling of discomfort. In fact, the discomfort was a sign that the elixir was working!

"If, after taking an elixir," said the compiler of the sixth-century *Records in the Rock Chamber*, "your skin feels as if insects are crawling all over it; if your hands and feet swell like blisters; if the smell of fine food nauseates you and you vomit after eating, and generally feel sick in the mouth; if your four limbs feel weak; if you have to go frequently to the latrine and there is always violent aching in your head or stomach, do not be upset or alarmed. These effects are merely proof that the elixir is expelling all those disorders that had previously remained quiet." [24]

Some of the preparations, especially those containing arsenic, had a tonic effect in the early stages, and a number of others were sexually stimulating—an important property in a polygamous society. Preparations containing arsenic were being prescribed in the West for their aphrodisiac properties until well into the twentieth century. Another metallic substance, iron in various forms, was also widely used in elixirs and did act as a tonic. It is still being offered as such in affluent and well-nourished societies today. The effect of such substances on people living on substandard diets in ancient and medieval times was to confirm the claims of the alchemists that immortality was basically an extension of good health.

One other ancient and continuing Chinese belief was related to the condition of the body after death. There are many stories of corpses reviving and then disappearing into thin air. But there are as many in which the corpse remains undecayed and presumably used by its owner when no one is looking—a proof of the efficacy of the elixir. This explanation had the virtue of some element of truth, for it is a fact that putrefaction is prevented, or at least slowed, by metallic poisons, especially arsenic.

If lack of decay in the body became, at some time in Chinese history, a definite and accepted sign of the achievement of immortality, then it was necessary for the alchemists to devise sure techniques of preservation, to leave nothing to chance. One of the substances said to have preservative qualities was jade. Recently, two complete body cases (discovered in 1968) of

43

this hard and beautiful stone were exhibited in the West. These were made of more than two thousand rectangular pieces of jade sewn together with gold wire. They date from the second century B.C. The bodies inside were certainly decayed, but this was not the case with an almost incredible find made in 1972 when, after the opening of carefully sealed outer coffins, a body was found that had all the appearance of being only a week or two old. Yet it was just over two thousand years since the wife of the Lord of Tai had been placed in her tomb. The body was partly covered by a watery brownish liquid containing mercuric sulfide, and the air in the coffin was almost entirely methane gas under pressure, kept at a constant temperature of about 13° C. (55° F.). The outer coffins were airtight and so was the tomb. The body had not been embalmed or mummified. The skin was soft, and when pressed returned to normal after the pressure was removed. Nor had the Lady of Tai been frozen according to the "cryogenics" or immortality-of-the-icebox principle that recently had a minor vogue in the United States. This provincial noblewoman, who died about 186 B.C., demonstrates the early sophistication of Chinese alchemical techniques, especially as this particular technique has so far defied modern analysis.

The Chinese would not have considered ingesting portions of a mummified body—to do so would have caused problems for the immortal—but the Arabs who accepted Chinese ideas of the drug of deathlessness included it in their pharmacology. They probably took their belief in mummy as a medicament from Egypt; it is hardly surprising that mummified flesh should have been thought to contain some kind of life-conserving essence. The use of mummy substance in medicine was discussed by the Arab alchemist al-Razi, at the beginning of the tenth century, and it was from him and other Arab sources that it passed into Western medical practice, where it survived into the eighteenth century. It was considered then to be particularly effective in the cure of rupture. The Dutch carried on a profitable trade in "a sweet-scented balm from Arabia called mommie." Where they got it from raises some interesting if slightly nauseating possibilities. As late as 1660, Nicolas Lefevre, in his *Traicté de la Chymie*, gave instructions for the preparation of "mumia" from the bodies of young men who had died from natural causes. The flesh could be treated with such substances as alcohol or turpentine, or even smoked.

However, the general belief in Europe, as in China, was that the elixir was a chemical preparation. Roger Bacon had already suggested that it was the same substance that could transmute base metals into gold. Many alchemists were assumed to have discovered how to make the elixir. Ramon Lull, a Catalan philosopher, Christian missionary to the Arabs in Spain and North Africa, and a contemporary of Roger Bacon, was said to have had the secret and even to have produced some twenty tons of gold from base metal in the Tower of London, to help King Edward I finance a crusade against the Turks. Lull, to whose authorship a large number of alchemical works were to be quite falsely attributed, was the first to describe the spirit distilled from wine as *aqua vitae*, "the water of life." It may not have been the elixir of immortality but, as brandy, its restorative qualities can be confirmed in any bar. The effect of it on the cold limbs and failing powers of the men of Lull's time was so impressive that it soon came into use as a medicine against old age.

The contribution of John Dastin, another near contemporary, was not quite so productive or, probably, enjoyable. In a letter to Pope John XXII (1316-34), who had issued a decree against alchemy, he claimed that there was a "most noble matter, which according to the tradition of all philosophers transforms any metallic body into very pure gold," and "makes an old man young and drives out all sickness of the body." Dastin's recipes for what he calls the "red elixir" were, as might be expected, very confusing, but he believed that it could be made from gold and mercury or silver and mercury, and that it possessed a spiritual nature, so that although it could be confined in some sort of matter—otherwise it could not be used—it occupied no space. This view was to be taken up nearly two centuries later by the greatest of all the European pioneers of chemotherapy, Paracelsus.

Dastin may have been confusing about the way to prepare his elixir, but he was quite convinced of its virtues. It was a medicine that "ought to be sought for by all, and before all other medicines of this world. This magistery is for kings and the great of the world, because he who possesses it has a never failing treasure." [25] It is not known whether this blatant appeal to class had any effect on Pope John, though after the pope's death it was said that the enormous fortune he left had been acquired by alchemical means.

Whether Dastin was able to prolong his own life is also not a matter of record, but Nicolas Flamel, a French alchemist born around 1330, was said to be still alive and well in India in the seventeenth century, and to have been strong enough to visit the Paris opera with his wife in 1761. Flamel was supposed to have found the secret of long life in an old book of manuscripts picked up from a bookseller, and to have had advance information (from an angel) in a dream. The first leaf of the book had written on it in large capital letters of gold: ABRAHAM THE JEW, PRINCE, PRIEST, LEVITE, ASTROLOGER AND PHILOSOPHER, TO THE NATION OF THE JEWS BY THE WRATH OF GOD DISPERSED AMONG THE GAULS, SENDETH HEALTH. Unfortunately, Flamel could not understand the text and figures in the rest of the book until it occurred to him that perhaps, as it was a Jewish book, a Jew could interpret it for him. He decided to make a pilgrimage to the shrine of St. James of Compostela in northern Spain, in the hope that he might be granted the favor of finding "some Jewish priest in some synagogue of Spain" who could help him. Once there, Flamel was introduced to a Jewish physician who had become a Christian and was able to give Flamel the secret— before dying of seasickness on the way to France. Flamel claimed to have made the red, or great, elixir on January 17, 1382, though he did not reveal the formula. After his alleged death in 1417 his house was ransacked in case he had left some of the marvelous substance behind, but none was found, although the belief that some of the elixir was still among Flamel's possessions persisted until at least 1560, when a local magistrate impounded, in the name of the king, everything that could be identified as once having belonged to the alchemist.[26]

The story of Theophrastus Bombastus von Hohenheim, self-named Philippus Aureolus Paracelsus, is of a very different character and significance. Paracelsus had something of the old alchemists' love of obscurity—his writings were in a mixture of German, dog Latin, and words of his own invention—but none of the discretion. Modesty was not among his many qualities. Even his assumed name meant "greater than Celsus," the famous Roman physician of the first century A.D. The significance of Paracelsus was that he gave European alchemy a new direction. "Many have said of alchemy," he wrote, "that it is for the making of gold and silver. For me such is not the aim, but to consider only what virtue and power may lie in medicines."[27]

Paracelsus was born near Zurich in December 1493, the son of a local physician. He says he was taught alchemy and medicine by his father and spent at least a year working in the mines and metallurgical workshops in the Tyrol. Before he went there, Paracelsus is supposed to have studied at the University of Basel, then under the occultist abbot of Sponheim, Trithemius. He certainly wandered about Europe, visiting Italy and England, Germany and Sweden. Though restless and unwilling to settle in one place for long, he managed to gain the degree of M.D. at the University of Ferrara in Italy.

On his journeys, Paracelsus searched for knowledge wherever he thought he could find it, among physicians and alchemists, miners and astrologers, even gypsies, and when he finally settled down in Strasbourg in 1526 to practice as a physician, he had acquired a vast amount of curious information. He was fortunate enough to cure an important printer and publisher from Basel, Johan Frobenius, whose illness had failed to respond to treatment by local doctors. On the try-anything principle, Frobenius sent for Paracelsus. While he was in Basel, Paracelsus met many distinguished scholars, including Erasmus, the great Dutch philosopher, then staying at Frobenius's house. Both men were so impressed by the skill and personality of the young doctor that they recommended him for the vacant position of city physician and professor of medicine.

Paracelsus stayed no more than two years in Basel, antagonizing everyone except the people he cured. One of his first acts on being appointed city physician was to burn, publicly, the works of Avicenna and Galen, the gods of orthodox medicine, in a brass pan with sulfur and nitre. He coupled this provocative act with an even more offensive statement about his fellow doctors. "They are nothing but teachers and masters, combing lice and scratching. They are not worthy that a dog should lift his hind leg against them." If they only knew that "their prince Galen—they think none better—was sticking in hell, from whence he has sent letters to me, they would make the sign of the cross upon themselves with a fox's tail. . . . O you hypocrites, who despise the truth taught you by a great physician [he meant himself] who is instructed by Nature. . . . Come then, and listen, imposters who prevail only by the authority of your high positions! After my death, my disciples will burst forth and drag you to the light, and shall expose your dirty drugs, wherewith up to this time you have compassed the death of princes, and the most invincible magnates of the Christian world."

Not surprisingly, the doctors of Basel—one of whom he described in a private letter as a "wormy and lousy Sophist"—reacted strongly against this wholesale accusation of malpractice, but for some time the city fathers defended him. However, Paracelsus went too far when a prominent citizen, Canon Lichtenfels, refused to pay a promised fee. Taking the matter to court, for some legal reason Paracelsus lost his case. He then subjected the startled magistrates to a torrent of filthy abuse. Warned that he would be cited for contempt of court, he secretly left the city.

Off on his travels again, Paracelsus was frequently drunk but always lucid—in his abuse, too lucid. He was so poor that he soon looked like a beggar and was refused admission to the town of Innsbruck because of his condition. As he himself said: "The burgomeister of Innsbruck has probably seen doctors in silks at the courts of princes, but not sweltering in rags in the sun." Finally, he was invited to the court of the Prince-Archbishop of Salzburg, Duke Ernst of Bavaria, who was greatly interested in the occult arts. There Paracelsus appears to have been happy and comfortable. But not for long. He arrived in Salzburg in April 1541, and died in September of the same year.

The real influence of Paracelsus came long after his death with the publication of a collected edition of his writings in ten volumes, between 1589 and 1591. Some of the works included were spurious. Most of these doubtful works deal with alchemy. But from the rest, in spite of their language, his lines of thought were fairly clear.

Paracelsus believed, like so many before him, that there was a unity of earth and heaven and that Nature was a kind of alchemist engaged in operations bringing about life and death, sickness and health in all things. Man as a preparer of medicines could become the alchemist of Nature. Paracelsus also believed that inside man was an "archeus," a spiritual being working in the stomach, which was itself a kind of alchemical laboratory. Sickness and health were, of course, controlled by astral influences, and the function of remedies was to restore harmony between the "astrum," or star, in man, and the star in the heavens. Such remedies had to "reach out to heaven," that is, to be volatile and without form. The actual medicine had to have form, otherwise it could not be taken, but it contained an "arcanum," a spiritual element which was the active ingredient. All the physician had to find out was the "astrum" of a particular disease, and then he could prepare a medicine that would restore the balance with Nature. "Nature and man, in health and sickness, need to be joined together, and to be brought into mutual agreement. This is the way to heal and restore health." That was the theory that really shed light on the matter. "But what light do you shed, you doctors of Montpellier, Vienna, and Leipzig? About as much light as a Spanish fly in a dysentery stool."

Behind the abuse lay a lot of good sense. The medicine of Paracelsus's time was mainly dependent on mixtures of roots and leaves, plants and fruits, the medicine of the village herbalist in a superior wrapping. Medicine needed chemistry to enlarge its range of therapy. Those few physicians who studied chemistry were singled out for praise: "They do not consort with loafers or go about gorgeous in satins, silks and velvets, gold rings on their fingers, silver daggers hanging at their sides, but they tend to work at the [laboratory] fire patiently day and night." They "do not make many words nor gossip with their patients, and do not highly praise their own remedies, for they well know that the work must praise the master, not the master the work."

The formulas of Paracelsus did not in themselves contribute much either to the future of chemotherapy or to the prolongation of life. He really did not know what went on in his chemical experiments, but he did insist that the purer the product the more effective it would be. This led his followers to invent new methods of purification and new tests for purity. At first these were qualitative, leading, as in China, to some fatal consequences for those who took medicines containing arsenic, mercury, or antimony. But later it was realized that, for clinical purposes, purity had to be measured quantitatively.

Because of Paracelsus, chemistry was to become an indispensable part of medical training, and its products, of the treatment of disease. On another level, Paracelsus invented the word *zinc*, and changed for all time the Arabic word for black eyeshadow, *al-kohl*, to alcohol, meaning spirits. Paracelsus believed as passionately as any Chinese alchemist that life could be prolonged, and by very much the same type of elixir. Times change, the hope remains.

2

The Black Dog
of Cornelius Agrippa

Wherever he went he was accompanied by a devil in the form
of a black dog. On his deathbed, he removed a collar bearing
magical emblems from the dog's neck and said: "Depart,
damned beast, who has wholly ruined me." Whereupon the
dog ran out of the house and, leaping into the river, was never
seen again.

This legend about Cornelius Henry Agrippa von Nettesheim,
an almost exact contemporary of Paracelsus and the greatest
occult scholar of the sixteenth century, surfaced within a few
years of his death, and there were others dangerous to his
memory and to his followers. Sixty years after Agrippa's death,
the Jesuit witch finder, Martin del Rio, accused him of having
covered up a murder by occult means. It was claimed that a
man who boarded in the same house as Agrippa, curious about
his fellow guest, rifled Agrippa's possessions and, finding a
magic phrase in one of his manuscripts, foolishly uttered it
aloud. This conjured up a devil which attacked and killed him.
Returning home to find a dead body in his room, Agrippa
summoned the devil back and made him occupy the dead
body, instructing him to go in it to the town's main square,
stroll around for a time, and then collapse as if falling victim to
a heart attack, a natural death. Other legends had Agrippa
conjuring up the shades of great men and, more romantically,

allowing Henry Howard, Earl of Surrey, to see his dead sweetheart in a magic mirror.

The black dog of Cornelius Agrippa was no devil. His constant companions were doubt and intellectual despair, but his style of thinking, magical yet skeptical, was to help create that new sense of mission, of self-confidence, of purposeful striving for progress, that was to lie at the foundations of the modern world. The Renaissance is usually seen as the age of discovery, of a new and splendid Europe, dynamic, flushed with new enthusiasms. But behind the superficial elegance of Renaissance art lay a terrible anguish. The rediscovery of the worlds of classical Greece and ancient Rome, the vocabulary of paganism which painters and poets used to express themselves, the golden light that seems perpetually to illuminate the human landscape—all these have created the impression of a world free from the terrors of darkness. To those who lived in the fifteenth and sixteenth centuries, however, their world seemed in decline. Western Christendom, instead of expanding, was actually shrinking under the assault of the heathen. As the Portuguese navigator Vasco da Gama set his foot upon the soil of India at the end of the fifteenth century, the Turks, at Vicenza, were less than fifty miles from Venice.

A closer look at the new age reveals the despair. The literature of the time was the literature of escape, and the religion that of mysticism. The Dance of Death, that most popular symbol of the fragility of human life, served as a constant reminder that prince and bishop, merchant and soldier, philosopher and artist, inevitably had to take death by the hand. Beside the sculptor's portrayal of fresh and virile youth lay the symbols of death and putrefaction. There seemed little to hope for, and a glance at the profound melancholy of Michelangelo's figures on the tombs of the Medici, in their way the impresarios of the Renaissance, displays the resignation of the times. Conquests beyond the seas seemed of little value when the heart of Europe was crumbling.

As the Turks battered at the gates of Vicenza, doubt battered at the gates of the mind, that one-time citadel of comfortable certainties. The seamless garment of Christendom was fraying in the gale of the Reformation, the traditional balance of social classes was being undermined, intellectual heroes discredited. It was a period not without similarities to our own.

Despair is a natural consequence of loss, and in the anarchy of life in the Renaissance scholars and other intellectuals sought to recover what they believed had been lost, a golden age of purity and truth, above all, of harmony and stability. They did not expect to be able to recreate that world without access to the wisdom, the knowledge, that had vanished. In the literature and monuments of classical antiquity that had been re-discovered they thought they saw the pure gold of a better civilization. They also came to believe, on the basis of new "evidence," that the Hebrew prophets, the Greek philosophers, the founders of the Christian Church—itself now corrupt—had all at one time drunk at one fountain.

This was the Egyptian wisdom of Hermes Trismegistus, reputed author of that alchemical manifesto the Emerald Tablet. Works allegedly by Hermes were already known when in 1460 a monk who was a scout for Cosimo de' Medici brought to Florence a collection of Greek manuscripts, fourteen, in fact, of the fifteen works of the so-called *Corpus Hermeticum*, or works of Hermes. Also in Cosimo's employ was one Marsilio Ficino, a priest, physician, and translator. Ficino was about to start work on a translation of the works of Plato for Cosimo when he was ordered to postpone it in favor of Hermes. It was an indication of the Renaissance respect for the old: Hermes was earlier than Plato, and nearer, therefore, to divine truth. And Cosimo felt that he himself was dying. Ficino produced his translation of Hermes a few months before Cosimo's death in 1464.

The antiquity of the works of Hermes had been proved to the satisfaction of students of the occult, princes and priests; even the fathers of the Early Church had confirmed it. Lactantius, writing in the third century A.D., after quoting Cicero went on to say that Hermes, "although he was a man, yet he was of great antiquity, and most fully imbued with every kind of learning." [1] Lactantius saw Hermes not as a god but as one of the seers of antiquity, who had prevision of the coming of Christianity. St. Augustine, on the other hand, did not approve of Hermes, whom he condemned in *The City of God* for idolatry, but he too confirmed that he was "long before the sages and philosophers of Greece." To a large extent, Augustine's condemnation was ignored. Hermes represented Egyptian wisdom, the oldest of all and because of its age a fountain of truth.

It was not until 1614 that a Swiss, Isaac Casaubon, dated the Hermetic writings not to some Egyptian priest or god in very ancient times, but to post-Christian Alexandria. It was a bombshell that shattered the whole basis of Renaissance magical thought. It also placed the Hermetic writings in a period even more like our own than that of the Renaissance. The world was highly organized and at peace; communications were excellent; the educated class had all current learning available to them. Yet it was a world in which philosophy and science seemed to have reached a dead end, so that men began to seek for knowledge of reality and for an answer to the world's problems that conventional education and establishment learning could not satisfy. The men of the Renaissance, however, were still secure in their error of historical dating, and the works of Hermes Trismegistus were the most important magical writings available to them.

Cornelius Agrippa, during his lifetime and, increasingly, after his death, was seen by many as a symbol of disgust with all orthodox culture and accepted values, with the condition of man in the universe. That he was also a "magician" and Hermetic scholar did not surprise them; in fact, his magical world view was an inspiration to revolutionaries.

Agrippa was born, probably at Cologne, in 1486, into a family either of the upper merchant class or the minor nobility. A precocious child, he received a licentiate in arts from the University of Cologne at the age of fourteen. He later claimed to have been awarded doctorates in canon and civil law, as well as in medicine, but did not say from which seat of learning. He probably did have legal training, and he may have graduated in medicine at the University of Pavia, but there are no records to substantiate his claims. There is, however, no doubt about his learning.

Early in 1507, Agrippa was in Paris studying at the university, though not for long, as he was back in Cologne before the end of the year and then in Spain probably early in 1508. His own account of his adventures is so lacking in definition that none of the place names he mentions can be accurately sited. He was apparently a member of a military expedition dispatched to seize a fortified spot near Barcelona from a band of rebellious peasants. There seems to have been some initial success, thanks to some devices invented by Agrippa, but the force was later scattered.

The friends who took part in the abortive expedition to Spain had formed themselves into a secret society, probably in Paris, with the aim of gaining both worldly and spiritual wealth for its members. Agrippa was certainly considered the leader, and over the years many of the society's members helped him in his efforts to find patrons among princes and others of high rank. One of the members won for Agrippa the opportunity of lecturing at the University of Dôle, in an area which was then part of the Hapsburg dominions and the seat of the governor of Franche-Comté and the Low Countries. It was hoped that Agrippa's lectures at the university would attract the patronage of the governor, Margaret of Austria.

Advised by his friends, Agrippa did not rely solely on his lectures to achieve this end, but composed a remarkable work which, if it did not make him an early exponent of Women's Liberation, at least anticipated some of its feminist writers. In his *De nobilitate et praecellentia foeminei sexus*, he claimed that women were not equal to men but superior. Woman's name, even, was superior, for *Eva* meant "life," and *Adam* "earth." Woman was more perfect than man, as she was created later. A woman's body was more pleasing than a man's, and showed greater modesty in the location of the genitalia. Nor was her face disfigured by a beard. The mother contributed much more to the intelligence of the children than the father. Females were able to conceive without the aid of the male—though Agrippa had to admit that the Virgin Mary appeared to be the only human female who had done so. Women were more eloquent speakers, and there was hardly a single recorded instance of a mute woman! It was Adam, not Eve, who committed original sin; consequently, Christ was born a man, and all priests had to be male. The finest of all creatures was the woman Mary, while men—with the worst, Judas, among them—were first in every sin. When permitted, women had always excelled in all fields, even becoming popes (Pope Joan) and warriors (Joan of Arc). In fact, said Agrippa, it was only masculine tyranny and the male monopoly in education that prevented sixteenth-century women from emulating the exploits of the great women of the past.

Unfortunately for Agrippa, before he was able to present his work to Margaret of Austria, his lectures at the university were denounced by no less influential a person than the provincial superior of the Franciscans. Against such powerful hostility, he had no satisfactory defense—and his praise of women did not reach Margaret of Austria until twenty years later. At the end of 1509 Agrippa considered it wise to leave for Germany. There he visited the famous abbot Trithemius of Sponheim, to whom he dedicated his first major work, On Occult Philosophy (De occulta philosophia).

On Occult Philosophy was not a textbook, a manual for practitioners, for it never detailed the technical procedures— those were left, in the proper magical tradition, for transmission by word of mouth. It took the larger view. The universe, wrote Agrippa, was divided into three worlds, the elemental, the celestial, and the intellectual. Each world was influenced by the one above, so that the power of the Creator descended, through the angels in the intellectual world, to the stars in the celestial, and then to all things, animals, plants, stones, metals, and so on, in the elemental. The magician could make the same progress upward, drawing the powers of the upper world down by manipulating the lower ones. The powers of the elemental could be discovered through medicine and natural philosophy, those of the celestial by astrology and mathematics, and those of the intellectual through a study of the holy ceremonies of religions. Because this was so, Agrippa divided his book into three parts, covering natural magic, celestial magic, and ceremonial magic.

As befitted an encyclopedia, Agrippa's work contained practically everything of interest to the occult student of his times. In the section on natural magic there were chapters on all types of divination, on poisons and philters, and on talismans. A section on psychology was followed by one discussing the passions, their power to produce bodily changes, and how, by cultivating the passions or emotions belonging to a planet—such as the love that belonged to Venus—the influence of that planet could be attracted. Agrippa stressed the power of the emotions, and the use of the imagination in magical technology. He quoted, with approval, the Muslim Avicenna, who believed that "a man could fell a camel, if he but demanded it with his imagination," and commented: "Our soul causes much through faith: a firm confidence, an intent vigilance, and a resolute devotion ... lend strength to the work which we would accomplish. We must, therefore, for every work, for each application to any object, express a powerful desire, flex our imagination, and have the most confident trust and the firmest belief, for this contributes immensely to success." [2] In other words, it was a question of "mind over matter."

In ceremonial magic, Agrippa was concerned "with that part of magic which teaches us to seek and know the laws of religions," and with how, by following the ceremonies of religions, man could learn the truth. Agrippa constantly emphasized the importance of faith. He was very careful to point out that the religions he wrote about were all false compared with the Catholic religion. Nevertheless, all religions had some good in them. God the Creator was the source of all power and the magician had to seek to approach him. This was mysticism rather than magic, but Agrippa saw it as having a practical application through the use the magician made of the knowledge he acquired.

Agrippa was always concerned with practical applications, and particularly so in the second part of his book. There he stressed the role of mathematics, referring to ancient works, the pyramids, great columns, huge artificial mounds, as the products of mathematical magic. He pointed to the wondrous achievements of classical antiquity, the wooden flying dove of Architus, the statues of Daedalus, which moved through the action of weights. Agrippa implied that applied science was part of the general technology of magic, and with his emphasis on number projected himself into the future—for the modern world knows, both to its comfort and its cost, that number is one of the keys to operations by which the forces of the universe are made to work in the service of man.

Agrippa's book was soon circulating widely in manuscript, making friends, admirers, and enemies for its author, in places of power and influence.

The year 1510, in which he completed the first version of his most famous work and dedicated it to the occultist abbot, also saw Agrippa on a mission of secret diplomacy for the Hapsburg ruler, Maximilian I. This took him to London. What the mission actually was is not known; it was either too secret or too unimportant to be written down, though it may have been designed to pave the way for the more open mission sent by Maximilian in September of the same year.

The pattern of Agrippa's life had now been established. He would wander from country to country, from Germany to France, to Burgundy, to Switzerland, to the Low Countries, in search of patrons, and the support of the rich and the powerful. In 1511 he left for Italy in command of a convoy carrying gold for Maximilian's forces at Verona. Once in Italy he was to remain there for seven years, studying the occult arts, lecturing at the University of Pavia, and marrying his first wife, whom he described as a "noble maiden, a well behaved and beautiful young woman."

As before, Agrippa acquired a reputation among those who had become interested in the occult as a result of dissatisfaction with current theology and philosophy. Most looked to the past for some way of purifying their religion; few rejected Christianity, but many wanted reform of the church. The magic they sought was one that had originally come through divine revelation but had since been lost. They wanted to find it again, not for academic reasons but for practical use. Knowledge was power. Agrippa wrote: "The basis of all miracles is knowledge, and the more things we understand and know, the more readily and efficaciously do we work." [3] The enlightened man would not only regain mastery over himself but power over Nature. And enlightenment could not come through reason, "which is hostile to holy faith." Here Agrippa was attacking the rational theology of his day, with its arguments and quarrels as futile as those over the number of angels that could be accommodated on the head of a pin.

In 1518, Agrippa was in Metz, having been forced to leave Pavia after the arrival there of French troops in 1515, when he lost both property and books. At Metz Agrippa soon drew around him a body of like-minded thinkers and admirers. Northern Europe was passing over the frontier of the Reformation, for in October 1517 Martin Luther had nailed his ninety-five theses to the church door at Wittenberg. There were many in Metz who, though not admirers of Luther, hoped for reform in the church as much as did Agrippa's friends at Pavia. Agrippa added to the general atmosphere of questioning and change by reviving an old view that "original sin" had been the act of sexual intercourse between Adam and Eve—thus shocking his friends as well as his enemies. He also defended an old peasant woman against a charge of witchcraft, and procured her release.

Agrippa's defense was not that there was no such thing as witchcraft—such a submission could never have been successful at that time. Instead, he cited legal arguments, questioned irregularities of procedure, the vagueness of the charges, the reliability of the witnesses. There is no evidence that he denied the possibility of witchcraft (he certainly believed in demonic possession), but, unfashionably for his time, he insisted that caution was better than hysteria as a way of approaching the problem.

His success in the witchcraft case earned Agrippa enemies among churchmen and laymen alike. He made many more with his attack on a widely held view relating to the marital status of a saint—no run-of-the-mill saint, but St. Anne, mother of the Virgin Mary. With typical flamboyance, the Middle Ages had embroidered a legend onto the mother of the mother of Jesus. It was said that she had been married three times, and had borne a daughter Mary in each marriage. These three Marys married Joseph, Alphaeus, and Zebedee and bore to them, respectively, Jesus; St. James the Less, Joseph the Just, Simon, and Jude; and James the Greater and the Apostle John. In Agrippa's time, "radical" thinkers insisted that St. Anne had been married only once, and were anxious to clear away all the other legends which had tended to obscure the purity of the Early Church, becoming symptoms of a corrupt sophistication.

If arguments on such subjects had merely been confined to the lecture room and the small world of scholars, they would have been of as little real consequence as any other academic quarrel. But they were not. Religion was of the texture of life. The Church was a great *temporal* power. Religious reform was a matter of secular politics. In Metz, there were factions among the great men of the city; tension and unrest agitated all classes. By inserting himself into a controversy as apparently irrelevant as the marital status of St. Anne, Agrippa was interfering in politics. Very sensibly—if a little too late—he tried to get away, but found difficulty at first in breaking his contract with the city authorities. Get away he did, however, and by February 1520 he was in Cologne.

In the following year he was in Geneva, and married again, his first wife having died early in the year. Agrippa used Geneva as a base while he tried to find another patron. He had influential friends in the city and, as usual, a circle of occult and reform-minded people gathered round him. He received some vague promises of patronage, but at last, impatient with the lack of results, he left Geneva in 1523 for the Swiss city of Fribourg where he obtained the post of town physician. He soon found the requirements of this job too restricting, however, and resigned in July 1523 after only four months.

In spite of his difficulties in finding a powerful patron, Agrippa had not given up hope. His reputation in occult circles was widespread, the secret society of his admirers constantly expanded its membership, and early in 1524 it seemed as if, at last, Agrippa's lofty ambitions were about to be fulfilled. He received a summons to the French court.

France at this time was in turmoil. In the summer of 1524, King Francis had been faced with an invasion, led by the Duke of Bourbon, and had only narrowly succeeded in beating it back. The king was now preparing for an invasion of Italy (which was to lead to his capture at Pavia in February 1525) and the court was on the move, stopping at various places in central France. It was not until September 1524 that it settled at Lyons. While the king was on campaign, the regency was held by his mother, Louise of Savoy, and it was she who was Agrippa's new employer. Whatever the office he might have hoped for, the one he was offered was that of personal physician to the regent. It was a position well placed for gaining influence in affairs of state. Louise suffered constant ill health, and her doctor should have been able to find ways of winning her confidence.

Unfortunately, Agrippa failed to take advantage of his position, or was prevented from doing so by the opposition of powerful courtiers. It is likely, too, that he lost the support of his friends over his constant complaints about money. War drained the state treasury and he, among many others, was often left unpaid. But the others were more discreet. When Louise left Lyons early in February 1526 she did not take Agrippa with her. He further antagonized her by his reluctance to draw up an astrological prognostication for her son, the king. Agrippa thought much of astrology mere superstition, but most rulers of the time did not and astrological predictions were often used by governments as propaganda. Louise was unfortunately shown a letter in which Agrippa not only described her as misusing astrology but remarked that, in any case, the stars favored not Francis but his enemy, the Duke of Bourbon. In 1527, Agrippa was indiscreet enough to tell some friends that the stars menaced King Francis with death within six months, thus committing what Henry VIII of England defined as "constructive treason." No ruler could tolerate prophecies of his death, for they were an invitation to rebellion and intrigue. It was hardly surprising that Agrippa was struck off the payroll.

Without position and without pension, he had to find employment. An offer from two admirers in Amsterdam seemed the only answer, but Agrippa could not get permission to leave Lyons or a passport to cross the frontier. In fact, the French commander in the north tore up papers supplied by Agrippa's friends on the grounds that he was a diviner. Finally, hearing that he was about to be arrested on an order from the regent, Agrippa left Lyons secretly in May 1527 and, after a stay in Paris, succeeded in reaching Antwerp at the end of July.

Here he was joined by his family, and there was a short period of peace and some prosperity. It ended, however, with the death of his second wife in a plague epidemic in August 1529. He received offers of employment from the king of England, from Italy, and from his old patron, Margaret of Austria, still governor of the Low Countries, and accepted the last of these, becoming imperial archivist and historiographer. His work in these high-sounding offices included composing speeches, and a funeral oration for Margaret. He also received an imperial license to print some of his works, including *On Occult Philosophy* and a work composed sixteen years later, in 1526, *On the Vanity and Uncertainty of the Arts and Sciences*, in which he appeared to reject everything in the other work. He decided to print *On the Vanity* first—as, some scholars have suggested, a form of insurance of the kind frequently used by occult writers to avoid theological criticism.

Agrippa attacked all his original sources, from the works of the ancients to the Jewish Cabala, which he declared to be "nothing but a mere rhapsody of superstition." [4] He treated the occult sciences with similar scorn. In fact, he went through his previous beliefs like an intellectual wrecker. But his destructiveness was really selective and conditional. He insisted that there must be some good in all magic, but that it had to be subject to the test of facts. Astrology, for example, was based on the *known* planets. If there were, at present, unknown ones actually in existence, then astrology based on current knowledge would be wrong. "All sciences are nothing but the decisions and opinions of men," [5] and they could change. All interpretations, he taught, were artificial and arbitrary, but that did not mean that they should not be accepted provisionally, as long as they were useful. It sounds very much like the reasoning of modern science.

In another part of *On the Vanity* Agrippa hurled invective at existing institutions, particularly those of the Church. He did not attack religion—which was just as much a part of his skepticism as of his magic—but those who operated it. He told a satirical tale of the origin of the monk's cowl. While he was in Italy, he wrote, the papal authorities had settled the vexing question of the color of the habits of Augustinian monks by reference to ancient paintings and statues. This sent Agrippa to the same sources for the origin of the cowl. Unfortunately, he could not find any Old Testament priests or prophets wearing cowls, or any of the Apostles, or John the Baptist, or Christ himself. Not even scribes or Pharisees. Finally, after much searching, he found a painting of the Devil tempting Christ in the wilderness, and there was the incarnation of evil—wearing a cowl. "I rejoiced very much that I had found in pictures what I had not up to then been able to find in writings, that is, that the Devil was the first author of the cowl, from whom then, I think, the other monks and friars borrowed it under various colours, or perchance received it left to them as if by hereditary right." [6]

Agrippa went further in his denunciation of religious orders. Had you noticed, he asked, that very close to monasteries there were houses of prostitution? Nunneries, he alleged, were often private brothels. As for the churches themselves, the early Christians got on perfectly well without temples; the present kind might be necessary for putting a roof over the worshipers' heads, but they were much too grandiose and costly. The money could have been better spent on the poor, "the true temples and images of God."[7]

Publication of *On the Vanity* aroused considerable opposition and criticism. In fact, Agrippa claimed that if his patron, Margaret, had not opportunely died, he would have been prosecuted for impiety. As it was, he did not receive his pay as imperial archivist, and such was the controversy that even the great Erasmus appealed to Agrippa "not to involve me in this business. I am overwhelmed with more than enough ill will. That would both burden me and harm you more than it would help you."

Agrippa's defense of his book produced no positive results and he began to look around for another patron. Many admirers offered not employment but advice. An old friend, now imperial ambassador in London, praised both books and urged Agrippa to write a defense of the marriage of Catherine of Aragon and Henry VIII, which the king was trying to have dissolved; but though Agrippa played with the idea, he was unwilling to commit himself to either side in the dispute. He did, however, find a patron in the reform-minded archbishop of Cologne, Hermann von Wied. The authorities in Antwerp used a visit to Cologne as an excuse to stop Agrippa's pay altogether and, faced with certain prosecution by his creditors, Agrippa left Antwerp rather hastily in June 1532.

Agrippa's stay at the archbishop's court was pleasant, though not unmarked by controversy. He is said to have repudiated a third wife in Bonn in 1535, and to have made a visit to Lyons, where he was arrested by order of the king for writing libels against the late Queen Louise. Friends at Lyons secured his release, but some months later Agrippa died at Grenoble.

On the surface, Agrippa's achievements may seem few and ineffective. But his influence on thinkers, and even men of power, was both real and difficult to assess—like, for example, that of Che Guevara or translations from the Zen masters in our own times. Every man who claimed to be in touch with contemporary intellectual life in Europe in the sixteenth century had read, in part at least, Agrippa's great occult encyclopedia.

Myths do not grow around the personalities of secondary men, for all myth must have a substratum of truth. Sometimes a poet grasps that essential truth when historians, unnerved by the softness of the available facts, dismiss the truth with the legend. Just over fifty years after Agrippa's death, the English dramatist Christopher Marlowe wrote, in *The Tragical History of Dr. Faustus*:

> Philosophy is odious and obscure,
> Both Law and Physic are for petty wits;
> Divinity is basest of the three,
> Unpleasant, harsh, contemptible and vile:
> 'Tis Magic, Magic that hath ravished me.
> Then, gentle friends, aid me in this attempt;
> And I that have with concise syllogisms
> Gravelled the pastors of the German Church,
> And made the flowering pride of Wertenberg
> Swarm to my problems, as the infernal spirits
> On sweet Musaeus when he came to hell,
> Will be as cunning as Agrippa was,
> Whose shadows made all Europe honour him.

The "shadows" of Cornelius Agrippa von Nettesheim were not those cast by the substance of his life, but by the ideas contained in his two important works, *On Occult Philosophy* and *On the Vanity and Uncertainty of the Arts and Sciences*, both of which were to be reprinted many times after his death.

3

The Pope's Magician

Rome, January 1628. The holy city was full of rumors. Would the pope, Urban VIII, Vicar of Christ, die as the astrologers had predicted? For two years, the pope's horoscope had been the common knowledge of the streets. In fact, he was being paid back in his own coin, for he had had horoscopes cast of the cardinals resident in Rome and had quite openly predicted *their* deaths. Now it was his turn. The Spanish, who detested the pope's pro-French policies, actively encouraged the rumors of his impending death and even made loud preparations for a conclave to elect his successor. It was psychological warfare. The Spanish hoped to frighten the pope to death, and they might have succeeded if it had not been for the counter measures taken by the pope's magician, Tommaso Campanella.

From the beginning of 1628 diplomats and secret agents, their ears tuned to every whisper in the corridors of the Vatican, reported that the pope and Campanella were frequently alone together. The two men were said to be raising the dead, calling up spirits, and celebrating in the dark of the night strange rites with lighted candles. The truth was that an eclipse of the moon was imminent, and Urban and Campanella, far from raising the dead or calling up spirits, were producing a model of the heavens with the planets and stars in favorable conjunctions, as a substitute for the real heavens which were being distorted by the eclipse. It was manipulative magic, right in the best occult tradition. As above, so below; as below, so above.

Pope and magician first sealed a room against the outside air. All the surfaces were then sprinkled with rose vinegar and other sweet-smelling substances, and fragrant herbs, cypress, laurel, myrtle and rosemary, were burnt. The walls were hung with cloths of fine white silk and decorated with branches. Two large lamps, representing the sun and the moon, and five smaller ones for the other planets, were then lit. The signs of the zodiac were also represented in some way, probably by candles. Present in the room with the pope and the magician were a number of other people whose horoscopes had been established as immune to the evil of the eclipse. They were there to play "Jovial and Venereal" music which, symbolizing good and favorable planets, would expel the influences of bad ones and clear the eclipse-infected air. On various tables were stones, plants, perfumes, and colored objects astrologically associated with Jupiter (Jove) and Venus. As the music was played, astrologically distilled liquors were drunk.[1]

Thus an aristocratic and cultivated pope, patron of the arts, and a heretical Dominican friar who had spent half his life in prison for revolutionary activity, came together at the center of the Christian world intent on manipulating the heavens. It was symbolic of the pope's fear, and of his faith in his magician. Urban hoped the favorable conjunction of the planets would permit him to avoid death. He lived. Campanella hoped—with the aid of a grateful pope—for something just as magical. He failed.

Campanella was a magician with a mission. His aim was to create a new world order. Born in 1568 at Stilo in Calabria, then part of the Spanish-Hapsburg kingdom of Naples, Campanella entered a Dominican monastery at the age of fourteen. The people of the south of Italy can be, in temperament, very much like their volcano, Vesuvius, occasionally erupting, threatening beneath the surface even when quiescent. Because of this,

Spanish rule was a harsh and cruel tyranny, and the people who were ruled were prone to revolutionary and heretical ideas. Campanella was no exception. In 1589 he was tried for heresy in Naples and imprisoned.

Three years later he was in Padua, where he met Galileo, then a professor of mathematics at the university. Galileo was another revolutionary, but a revolutionary of science, and he too was to win Pope Urban's friendship if not support for his ideas. At Padua, Campanella's own mind seems to have been as restless and unorthodox as when he was in the south, and after a number of accusations had been made against him he found himself in prison once again. While incarcerated at Padua, he wrote works addressed to the then pope, Clement VIII. For one of these he was again charged with heresy, and was transferred to the prisons of the Inquisition in Rome. His crime was to have taught a doctrine of the world soul, and to have written an impious sonnet. While in Rome, he sent Clement a plan for a world union, with the pope as universal monarch. He also wrote a short treatise advising Italian princes not to oppose the ambitions of Spain. This may have been designed to get him out of prison, though the influence of a powerful protector may have been of more effect in gaining his release in 1595.

Campanella was back in Naples in 1597 consulting astrologers and his one-time fellow prisoner, the geographer Stigliola, who was a follower of Copernicus, the astronomical revolutionary who had placed the sun at the center of the universe, instead of the earth. Campanella seems to have been convinced that there were signs in the heavens predicting widespread political and religious changes, and that he was destined to be the magus of a new age that was about to be born.

Campanella soon gathered supporters, most of them Dominicans. He traveled about the south, gaining adherents and spreading propaganda. Itinerant friars announced, in impassioned speeches, the great changes predicted in the stars, pointing to such things as the decline in charity, the growth of discord among men, as signs of the need for change answered by the heavens. The sun, they said, was descending, coming nearer the earth with its purifying fire. The year 1600 would be particularly important. In numerology, the figures nine and seven were of great significance, and together they made sixteen. Soon there would be a better religion, better moral law, a new harmony. Calabria must prepare the way for the new dispensation by rising up against Spanish tyranny and establishing a new republic, a magical City of the Sun, with Campanella as high priest and prophet.

It was a strange revolution. Christianity would still play a part in the new world, for was not Christ an inspired magus? Campanella quoted widely from Christian saints and scholars, from poets such as Petrarch and Dante, foretelling a new partnership between Christian mystery and natural magic. The cause was preached with wild enthusiasm, but the revolution was not prepared with any understanding of the material weapons of revolt. Campanella seems to have thought that miraculous powers, the signs of the times, and his own charismatic personality would be enough—or almost enough, as some attempt *was* made to involve not only a few disaffected noblemen, but also the Turks. The latter did send a naval expedition to help the rebels, but it arrived too late.

Astrological warfare was no match for the Spanish. The whole affair was easily crushed, and by the end of 1599 the prisons were full of Dominicans and their friends. Many of the prisoners were tortured, including Campanella, and a number were executed. Apparently Campanella escaped this fate by pretending to be mad. Like many another political visionary, he could be cunning in the interests of the cause.

Campanella was to spend twenty-seven years in prison, where he wrote, among other works, his *Città del Sole*, or *City of the Sun*.[2] In this, he set out in great detail the concept of an ideal state which had inspired the rebellion. The work was not to be published until 1623, in a Latin version which differed somewhat from the original Italian one, but the view was essentially the same—of a magical city, pulsating with the machinery of universal harmony.

On a high hill in the midst of a vast plain stood the City of the Sun, divided into seven rings named after the seven planets. Along these divisions, separated one from another by walls, were the houses, the palaces, and the cloisters. Four roads crossed the city, starting from the four outer gates sited at the points of the compass and running toward the center. This center, the summit of the hill, was an immense temple, circular in shape, with a great dome supported on huge columns. On the ceiling of the dome were painted all the greatest stars of heaven, with their names and powers written beside them. On the great altar were two globes, one showing all the heavens, the other the earth. The temple was hung with seven lamps named after the seven planets and always kept alight. The temple, in fact, was a model of the universe.

The walls of the rings of houses and other buildings were also covered with representations. The first wall, nearest the temple, showed all mathematical figures; on the outer side was a map of the earth, listing all the provinces, with descriptions of the rites, customs, laws, and alphabets of each. The next wall showed on its inner surface all the minerals and precious stones, and on the outer, lakes, seas, rivers, wines, and all liquids. There were jugs containing the many different liquors with which all illnesses were cured. The third wall showed, on one side, all the vegetable world, the virtues of trees and herbs and their correspondence with the stars, and on the other all the fishes and their correspondences. On the fourth wall were birds and reptiles, on the fifth animals. The sixth and final wall displayed on its inner side all the mechanical arts and their inventors, and showed the different ways in which these arts were used in different parts of the world. On the outer side were images of the inventors of sciences and laws, including Moses and Muhammad, Jupiter and Mercury, and many others. In the most conspicuous and therefore honorable place on this wall were the images of Christ and the twelve apostles. The city was, in effect, what today is called a memory bank.

The ruler of the city was the high priest, whose name meant the Sun, though he was shown only by the Sun's symbol ⊙ .

He was assisted by three administrators, Power, Wisdom, and Love. Power was in charge of military affairs; Wisdom of the sciences; and Love of the processes of generation, of education and medicine, all that ensured the life, the health, and the intelligence of the inhabitants. There was no evil in the city, for the virtues had conquered the vices and the people were united in brotherly love, holding all things in common without want or competition.

The City of the Sun was not, in any modern sense, a practical plan for a well-governed state. It would have been interesting to see what kind of administration Campanella and his friends would have set up in southern Italy if they had succeeded in overthrowing the Spanish. One suggestion of Campanella's, for example, was for the selective breeding of human beings, though he meant it astrologically rather than genetically. But if the City of the Sun was not an actual blueprint, neither was it madness. Essentially, the city was a manifesto for the social use of knowledge, and a plea for the return of the shattered harmony between man and his environment.

Few things concentrate a man's mind more than the imminence of death. During his long years of imprisonment Campanella always faced the possibility of execution as a heretic, and he concentrated his mind on avoiding such an end, on getting out of prison, and on developing a new strategy of revolution. With the assistance of friends and admirers some of his enormous literary output had a circulation in manuscript copies, but very little ever appeared in print. Nevertheless, copies appear to have found their way into the right hands, for Campanella's reputation as a magician spread. His rethinking on the strategy of revolution, however, developed more into a strategy of reform. Instead of attempting to overthrow the existing power, an infinitely dangerous operation, as the Calabrian affair had proved, he considered the possibility of persuading those already in power to usher in a new world.

As he happened to be in a Spanish jail, Campanella first thought of turning to the king of Spain. If he could persuade the king to take up the tools of reform, these might get him past the prison bars. A manuscript taken out of prison was published in 1620. The *Monarchia di Spagna* prophesied that the Spanish monarchy would become a world monarchy with one ruler, under whom there would be universal peace and justice. The Spanish monarch, however, was unimpressed, and Campanella returned to his old theme that the pope—any pope—could be both spiritual and temporal ruler of a world empire.

Campanella certainly hoped to make use of Pope Urban for these ends. He had already suggested to Pope Clement the role of universal ruler, and Urban was a much more promising target. Cardinal Maffeo Barberini, who became pope as Urban VIII in 1623, was a man out of his time, a Renaissance pope set down in the era of the Thirty Years' War, a scholar and man of letters, who had translated the Bible into elegant verse. Urban had the cynicism, the lust for secular power, of the Borgias, though not the same ruthlessness. He could conspire with the Protestant heretic king of Sweden against the Holy Roman Empire. He could remark, when the great minister of Louis XIII of France, Cardinal Richelieu, died: "If there is a God, Cardinal Richelieu will have much to answer for; if not, he has done very well." When it came to the crunch, Urban's love of the antique gave way to his anxiety about the present. He had cannon cast from the bronze ceiling of that superb Roman monument, the Pantheon, an act which inspired the epigram: "What the barbarians failed to do, Barberini did." Urban was the first pope to allow the erection of a monument to himself in his own lifetime. Urban was also convinced of the truth of astrology, and it was this that got Campanella out of prison. Not in Naples, but in Rome, to which he had been transferred in 1626.

The patronage of princes, however, even—perhaps particularly—princes of the church, is a variable commodity. A work of Campanella's published in Lyons in 1629 contained a description of the procedures used to counter the lunar eclipse of 1628, which had saved the pope's life. Its publication seems to have been a deliberate leak by a highly placed official who hoped to damage Campanella. Urban was so angry at this release of what he must have regarded as important classified material that Campanella found himself not only passed over for the appointment of Consultor to the Holy Office, a post which included censorship of theological publications, but back in jail again.

He succeeded, however, in retrieving the pope's favor. Campanella was even given permission to found a college at Rome, the Collegio Barberini, for the training of missionaries— the first step, he believed, to converting the whole world to his kind of Catholicism.

The magic Campanella had used to protect the pope's life seems to have been specially evolved for the occasion, as there is no trace of any appropriate formulas in the manuscripts he wrote when imprisoned in Naples. Indeed, if he hoped to get himself out of jail, Campanella would hardly have been likely to write about astrology, which had been condemned by a bull of Pope Sixtus V in 1586 that was still in force, despite Urban's known interest in the art. Campanella's magic would seem to have been another of those acts calculated to further his cause. In 1630, however, he used a similar ceremony to help the son of one of the pope's nephews, who was threatened by a dangerous conjunction of the stars. As there was an eclipse of the moon in June 1630, it seems likely that Campanella also repeated the ceremony for Urban himself.

Campanella helped in the drafting of Urban's own bull against astrology, published in the following year. This not only repeated the general condemnation by Pope Sixtus but specifically condemned the prediction of the deaths of princes, and especially of popes, including members of their families down to the third degree of consanguinity, that is to say, nephews and nieces. Such predictions were to be treated as crimes punishable by the confiscation of property and by death.

Through his efforts in preserving Urban's life, Campanella hoped to persuade the pope to back his mystical imperialism, set up the model City of the Sun, and conquer the world for harmony and peace. Campanella was still convinced that the sun was steadily approaching the earth and that preparation could be made, with the aid of missionaries, for the new world that was certainly to come. There seems no doubt that, for a time, Campanella actually did influence policy at Rome; the founding of the Collegio Barberini provides proof of it. But he had powerful enemies, and by 1634 his position at Rome had been so undermined that he was again in danger of arrest.

Like a good revolutionary, Campanella had been preparing his escape. He had had further books published in France and was in touch with the French ambassador in Rome. In 1634 he left Rome for Paris. There he almost immediately published a work glorifying King Louis XIII and his minister, Richelieu, claiming that the French king, like a new Charlemagne, would free Europe from the tyranny of Spain. Some earlier works, newly slanted toward the French monarchy, were also published in Paris, one of them with a fulsome dedication to Richelieu, urging the cardinal to build the City of the Sun.

Campanella's enemies at Rome tried to discredit him in Paris, and they had support from the French ecclesiastical and scholarly establishment. Nevertheless, his ideas struck a responsive chord in French court circles. In September 1638, when a son was born to the king, Campanella looked forward to the coming of a golden age—and in a sense he was right to do so, for the child was to become *le roi soleil*, the Sun King, Louis XIV.

In the year following the birth of the future Louis XIV, Campanella, fearing the consequences to himself of an approaching eclipse, performed the same ceremony as he had used for Pope Urban in Rome, this time in a cell in a Dominican convent in Paris. It was obviously only partly successful, for shortly afterward Campanella died, comforted, or at least sustained, by the last rites of the church.

Campanella's ideas had been welcomed at the French court because they fitted the political ambitions of Richelieu. As in the case of Cornelius Agrippa, Campanella's ideas were often more productive and influential than his actions, though Pope Urban presumably had little to complain of in the latter. Campanella's *City of the Sun* fed the stream of idealism from which utopias are made, while his mystical imperialism was taken over—with suitably cynical adjustments—by Louis XIV. But the men of the new *scientific* future, just over the horizon, considered him a relic and his magic meaningless. One of these men, Marin Mersenne, a French monk, who was already tearing down the grand edifice of the Renaissance magical tradition, wrote to a friend in 1635: "I saw the Reverend Father Campanella for about three hours and for the second time. I have learned that he can teach us nothing in the sciences. I had been told that he is very learned in music but when I questioned him I found that he does not even know what the octave is." He added perhaps the most devastating of criticisms: "But still he has a good memory and a fertile imagination." [3]

René Descartes, the philosopher of the new science and author of that well-known epigram *cogito, ergo sum,* "I think, therefore I am," when asked whether he would like Campanella to visit him, replied that he knew enough about him not to wish to see any more of him. With the authentic accents of arrogant science, the Renaissance magus was consigned to the garbage pile of the dead past.

Two

SUBVERSIVE MAGIC AND THE OCCULT UNDERGROUND

Franz Mesmer

1

An Invasion of Demons

Early in the sixteenth century, Pope Urban had hired a magician. Three hundred years before, a predecessor as Vicar of Christ had been put on trial for *being* one. Pope Boniface VIII was not present in the flesh during the proceedings that began near Avignon in 1310; he had been dead for seven years. But, if the trial had run to a conclusion, his bones would have been dug up and burned. Just before his death, it had been put about that Boniface had, as his personal adviser, a demon whom he consulted on "all matters." By the time of his posthumous trial, this demon had been reinforced by a number of others with wider-ranging and executive functions.

The first demon had been given to him by a woman; a second, more powerful, by a Hungarian; and a third, of even more power, by one Boniface of Vicenza. "Boniface, given by Boniface to Boniface," the pope had allegedly quipped. As an auxiliary, the pope carried around a spirit in a finger ring. When consulting with his demonic aides, Boniface would lock himself in a room from which came sounds as of serpents and cattle; people waiting outside the room would feel the earth shake under their feet.

As if associating with demons were not enough, the pope was also accused of sodomy and murder. For all the alleged crimes there were plenty of witnesses, for Boniface had many enemies. Not least was Philip the Fair, king of France, the instigator of the whole affair. Philip's action was purely political. During Boniface's papacy, the king had tried to tax the French clergy in order to help finance his war with England. This was contrary to the canon law of the time, and Boniface had issued a bull forbidding taxation of the clergy without the pope's permission. Philip's response was to stir up opposition to him.

Boniface replied by issuing bulls excommunicating a number of lesser conspirators, and also the king of France, but when the feud between king and pope was at its height, Boniface died. His successor also died after only a year in office, and was succeeded by a Frenchman, Clement V, who was resident at Avignon and to a large extent dependent on the good will of the king of France.

Philip wanted his excommunication lifted, but Clement proved an unwilling puppet. The king and his minister, de Nogaret, therefore, hit on the idea of discrediting the dead Boniface. If they succeeded, all the acts of his reign would be nullified and the king would be relieved of his excommunication. Success in condemning a past pope would also bring pressure to bear on Clement. Philip had a grandiose plan to make himself ruler of a vast Christian expire centered on Jerusalem, and for this he needed papal approval and support. In 1311, Clement gave in and the "trial" of Boniface was abandoned, there being no further purpose in it.

Unfortunately, attacking a dead pope in order to coerce a living one was not enough for the king. Philip needed money for his imperial enterprise. In pursuit of it, he directed his attention to discrediting the religious military order of the Knights Templars who, having been forced to give up crusading, had turned to banking and other commercial enterprises. Members of the order were accused of the denial of Christ, the worship of Satan, orgies with female demons, and the use of the fat of roasted infants to anoint their idols. Under appalling tortures, the knights confessed to everything.

Satan had been, to the Jews (the name itself is Hebrew for *adversary*), originally an aspect of Jehovah, the God who created both good and evil. Later Satan became the principle of evil, the enemy of Jehovah. And it was this idea that was taken over and expanded by the early Christians, who in their struggle against paganism converted the old gods into demons, the army of Satan. It was not really until the Middle Ages, however, that Christians began to see their world in the grip of demons who had human allies everywhere. Any threat, real or imagined, to the stability of society could be labeled part of the never-ending offensive waged by the kingdom of Satan against the kingdom of God on earth. An accusation of alliance with Antichrist was first directed against unorthodox Christian communities, but Philip the Fair showed that it could also be used for political purposes against men and institutions. What had begun as symbolizing the enemy of the heavenly power of God had become a weapon against the earthly power of men.

On the sound principle of "know your enemy," directories of the leading figures in Satan's kingdom were prepared. Lists of demons described their appearance and their powers.

> Purson *alias* Curson, a great king, he commeth forth like a man with a lions face, carrieng a most cruell viper, and riding on a beare; and before him go alwaies trumpets; he knoweth things hidden, and can tell all things present, past, and to come: he bewraieth treasure, he can take a bodie either humane or aierie; he answereth truelie of all things earthlie and secret, of the divinitie and creation of the world, and bringeth forth the best familiars; and there obeie him two and twentie legions of divils, partlie of the order of vertues, & partlie of the order of thrones.

Reginald Scot, in his brilliant attack on superstition, *Discoverie of Witchcraft*, published in 1584, gave sixty-eight more of these mini-biographies. Other works listed more, but all agreed that such personages existed and could be called up and even controlled by a magician. The trouble was that, once under control, the demon's power could be used either for good or for evil. Some demons specialized in murder, in stimulating wars, and in burning towns to the ground. Others could, in a flash, grant a man all knowledge, or merely help a love affair along. The good or evil was therefore in the mind of the magician—or that of his accuser.

None of the books of magic that proliferated in the Middle Ages, and after, suggested that, by controlling a demon, the magician was worshiping Satan or conspiring to bring to his kingdom the mastery of the world. On the contrary. Demons were there not to be honored but commanded, and this could only be done through the power of God, who had created all spirits. The alliance was with God, not the Devil.

In general, the Church did not accept this view, and it was defined as heretical by a number of papal bulls. In the preface to a fourteenth-century magical manuscript sometimes known as the *Sworn Book of Homorius* it was stated that the pope and his cardinals had sworn to crush the magic art and to kill all magicians, because they were said to have been transgressing the ordinances of the Church, conjuring demons and making sacrifices to them, and deceiving ignorant people so as to drive them to damnation. But, went on the anonymous author, this was not true. It was the pope and the cardinals who had been deceived by the Devil. Magicians forced demons to act against their will, something that could only be achieved by the pure in heart. Wicked men could not practice the art with any success, and that was why the Devil had inspired the pope and others to legislate against the good magician.

A nice reply—but no more. Accusations of commerce with demons for evil purposes were too valuable a weapon against dissent of any kind.

This very sophisticated tool of coercion may seem a long way from the fantasies about illiterate peasant women, sexually seduced by demons and conscripted into the service of Satan, which lay at the heart of the great witchcraft scares. But both were really aspects of a view shared by all—churchmen, magicians, and secular rulers—that evil spirits existed just as surely as did good ones. It was not possible to believe in angels without believing in demons; if there was a kingdom of God, there was a parallel kingdom of Satan. What use was made of this belief depended upon individual megalomania, psychopathology, and ambition. Financial greed, conscious sadism, religious zeal and desire for power, all played their part. Even those who protested against the use of torture as a means of producing confessions of relations with demons did not deny the existence of the kingdom of Satan, or disbelieve in the war against humanity it waged through demons and witches. They had no other doctrine to put in its place. Until the demons could be banished once and for all, any suggestion that they did not exist was seen as coming from Satan himself.

The medieval witch scare had died down by the beginning of the fifteenth century, only to be revived with enhanced ferocity some fifty years later with the coming of the great break in the Catholic Church and the religious wars that followed the Reformation. The magician, the alchemist, the "new" scientist were as much in danger as the witch. Renaissance magic was still a matter of demons and angels, and just as vulnerable as its medieval predecessor. The *Occult Philosophy* of Cornelius Agrippa showed how little the Renaissance view of the world had changed.

Agrippa's universe was permeated by spiritual beings, both good and evil. By careful preparation and use of the correct ritual, man could summon these spirits and the "souls" of everything in the world and force them to do his bidding. There was nothing impious in this, Agrippa said, and then went on to describe the hierarchy of good and bad demons. The good demons were marshaled in three main ranks—the supercelestial, who transmitted divine light to the lower orders; the celestial intelligences, which ruled the planets; and the ministering demons, who watched over men. There were corresponding orders of bad demons. These good and bad spirits struggled for the soul.

The most important thing, Agrippa went on, was to know the names of the spirits. The true names of angels were known only to God, but it was possible to learn them by observing what particular angels, did, or from cabalistic interpretations of passages in the Bible. Agrippa did not discount evil magic and evil magicians, and admitted that the Templars might have been among them, but he insisted that the mind needed the aid of God before it could attain power over the universe.

The danger to the Renaissance magus lay in the matter of which among the world's forces could lawfully be used by man. There could be nothing evil in utilizing such natural forces as fire for cooking. Even some occult forces were irreproachable. The power of magnetism, for example, was not understood, but there could be no objection to using it in a compass. To employ the sun to bleach cloth was hardly a sin. But to employ spiritual beings was a very different proposition.

Clearly, man could scarcely coerce God, but what about angels and demons? Angels were greater than man, so he could not bind them. But he might use them, and what was it lawful to use them for? Even this was a lesser problem than that relating to demons. Agrippa stressed that it was very difficult to get angels to work for man—though, with the aid of God, not impossible. But Satan was the father of lies, and he could deceive the magician with an evil substitute. In fact, whatever the magus said about reliance on God, in practice he could not deny the possibility of an unauthorized and unwanted intervention by Satan.

The magus was an obvious target for attack, but an accusation of commerce with demons could just as easily be made against the "new scientists," the seventeenth-century founders of today's technological culture. René Descartes, the French mathematician whose view of a universe operating within "mechanical" laws made demons (and angels) unnecessary, found himself in just such a situation.

In 1618, fifteen years before he was contemptuously to reject a visit from the "magician" Campanella, the young Descartes left Paris on what was basically a voyage of intellectual exploration. First he went to Holland, then in the next year to Germany. Staying at a place on the Danube for the winter, he had a series of dreams which led him to the conviction that mathematics was the only key to the understanding of Nature. Descartes was a solitary, preferring the company of his own mind to the physical presence of others, but he was not without contacts. From them he heard of a mysterious society called the Brothers of the Rose Cross, who taught a new wisdom and a new science. Descartes spent some time trying to locate the brothers, without success, but when he returned to Paris in 1623 he found himself accused of being one of them, a position that might have led to his arrest, if not worse. Paris was in a state of fright.

The rumors had started when a number of posters appeared on Parisian walls. One read:

> We, being deputies of the principal College of the Brothers of the Rose Cross, are making a visible and invisible stay in this city through the Grace of the Most High, towards whom turn the hearts of the Just. We show and teach without books or marks how to speak all languages of the countries where we wish to be, and to draw men from error and death.[1]

Another stated, in part:

> We, deputies of the College of the Rose Cross, give notice to all those who wish to enter our Society and Congregation, that we will teach them the most perfect knowledge of the Most High, in the name of whom we are today holding an assembly, and we will make them from visible, invisible, and from invisible, visible.[2]

The message of the posters was expanded in a number of sensational pamphlets and books, mostly anonymous. One, with the alarming title of *Horrible Pacts made between the Devil and the Pretended Invisible Ones*, reported that there were thirty-six deputies of the College of the Rose Cross spread throughout the world in parties of six. On June 23, 1623, the Invisible Ones had gathered at Lyons and chosen six of their number as deputies in Paris. The meeting had been held two hours before a Grand Sabbath, which had been attended by one of the princes of the infernal legions, who had appeared shining with inner light.

The deputies had knelt before him and promised to reject all the rites of the church; in return, they were given the power to transport themselves to wherever they wished, always to have money in plenty, and the ability to disguise themselves without fear of detection as natives of whichever country or city they chose. They were also given the power of eloquence, and the ability to attract the wise and the curious.

The brothers, it appeared, were sorcerers, agents of a diabolic subversion, all the more frightening because a man could not distinguish them from his neighbors. Basically, the Brother of the Rose Cross was a contemporary equivalent of the modern "red under the bed." To be accused of membership in this insidious secret society could lead to disaster. No wonder Descartes was alarmed when it was rumored that he had been enrolled.

The six deputies of the Rose Cross College appointed to Paris were said to be living in the Marais quarter of the city, but as Descartes's biographer, Adrien Baillet, reported: "They could not communicate with the people, or be communicated with, except by thought joined to the will, that is to say in a manner imperceptible to the senses." [3] The brothers could neither be seen nor heard, but there was no doubt that they were hatching their plots against Church and state. Descartes, with his habit of solitude, his invisibility, could not clear himself of the accusation without making himself visible. "He confounded those who wished to make use of this conjunction of events to establish their calumny. He made himself visible to all the world, and particularly to his friends who needed no other argument to convince them that he was not one of the Brotherhood of the Rosicrucians or Invisibles." [4] The prophet of mechanism, the most extreme form of reason, was forced to appear frequently in public in order to defend himself against a charge of being a magician! History is full of ironies.

Another was the fact that there was *no* "college" or secret society of Rosicrucians in the early seventeenth century. The Brothers of the Rose Cross were a figment of the imagination of one Johann Valentin Andreae, a Lutheran pastor born in

Württemberg in 1586. He was the certain author of one, and the probable author of the other two "Rosicrucian manifestos" that appeared in print in 1614, 1615, and 1616. The manifestos, and Andreae's later writings, had a strong technical bias and reflected the general atmosphere of the times into which the new science was emerging. But his work amounted to no more than words, though these had a wide circulation.

The Brothers of the Rose Cross, mythical as they were, came to be associated with the rise of Freemasonry, that demonic subversion of later times, and in the middle of the eighteenth century a real secret society, using the name Rosicrucian, appeared. There have been other Rosicrucian societies since then; some still exist today, the most widely advertised being the American Order of the Rosy Cross, which has its headquarters—perhaps inevitably—in California. In order to give these later societies an authentic pedigree, large numbers of books have been produced which claim to prove the existence of the first Rosicrucian Brotherhood. There *is* no such proof, but equally there is no doubt that the accusers of Descartes, and the public of his time, genuinely believed that such a dangerous and diabolic organization did exist.

Nearly forty years later, in 1660, the men who met in London to found the Royal Society, that standard bearer of the new scientific revolution, still feared accusations of witchcraft. The year before, Méric Casaubon had published his edition of *A True & Faithful Relation of what passed for many Years Between Dr John Dee ... and some Spirits.* Dee, by then more than half a century in his grave, had been one of the great figures of the Elizabethan age and the nearest the English had come to a Renaissance magus. He was a mathematician, a practical thinker greatly respected by many of the new scientists, but his ideas were expressed with such supernatural overtones as to raise the frightening possibility that he was in contact with demons.

Casaubon's intention had been to accuse Dee of demonic magic. He succeeded, and smeared Dee's reputation for more than three hundred years. In his preface, Casaubon had declared that not only Dee but such men as Paracelsus were inspired by the Devil. As the major influence in the new medicine was that of Paracelsus, and the new chemistry of Robert Boyle was the offspring of the alchemical movement, the new scientists decided to put up the security fence and wait out the witch scare. One of the Royal Society's rules was that there should be no discussion of religion at its meetings. And its members were very careful what they said in their published works.

Behind the world-changing discoveries of Isaac Newton, a second-generation member of the Royal Society, stretched the "dark" side of magic and alchemy. Newton was not entirely satisfied by the results of his explorations into Nature. One part of him saw, in physical experiment and mathematical reasoning, tools of understanding. But they did not reveal that unity of Nature, the divine Unity, for which another part of him was constantly searching. Newton published works only on physics and mathematics; his alchemical interests remained on the dark side. There is good reason to believe that he was not alone in his desire to keep science within the **micro**-macrocosmic world view, to avoid that separation of science and the rest that has, as we can see today, been so costly to the total environment of man.

Part of the reason for the separation, a separation that hardened with the years, was the understandable reticence of the early fathers of modern science.

Newton lived until 1727. By then the witchcraft scare had been effectively at an end for more than twenty years. In the eighteenth century, the men of the Enlightenment looked back upon it as a folly of superstition from which they, through reason, had gained release. Had they? Or have we, for that matter? Perhaps like the men of the eighteenth century, we have merely changed the names of our demons.

2

Monsieur Mesmer's Revolution

Where was the mecca of the marvelous at the end of the eighteenth century? Paris—not yet the *ville lumière*, the City of Light of the following century, but the City of the Enlightenment, capital of the Age of Reason. A city bubbling with radical ideas and about to boil over into a rebellion against the old world of privilege and exploitation, to create a new one of liberty, equality, and fraternity. And yet on the edge of this great upheaval, the Baronne d'Oberkirch was able to claim, with truth, that "never, certainly, were Rosicrucians, alchemists, prophets, and everything related to them so numerous and so influential. Conversation turns almost entirely upon these matters; they strike everyone's imagination.... Looking around, we see only sorcerers, initiates, necromancers and prophets. Everyone has his own, on whom he relies." [1] The occult underground had surfaced once again—in the service of the revolution.

Police Spies and Celebrated Alchemists

If there was one enthusiasm shared by literate Frenchmen as the eighteenth century came to a close, it was for "science." Its revelations had opened a whole new view of the powerful invisible forces that surrounded man. Voltaire had explained

Newton's theory of gravity, and had not the great scientist himself written of "the most subtle spirit that pervades and lies hid in all gross bodies"? Benjamin Franklin's experiments with electricity had resulted in a cult for lightning rods and electrical demonstrations at the most fashionable places. And in 1783 man had learned to fly when, to the astonishment of all Europe, miraculous gases were used to lift a fragile balloon into the air over the city of Metz.

Man's first flight was received with tremendous excitement. The correspondent of the *Journal de Bruxelles* was almost ecstatic. "It is not possible to describe that moment: the women in tears, the common people raising their hands towards the sky in deep silence; the passengers leaning out . . . waving and crying out in joy . . . you follow them with your eyes, you call to them as if they could hear, and the feeling of fright gives way to wonder. No one said anything but 'Great God, how beautiful!' " [2] When the aeronauts returned, they were feted with public processions and banquets. Their pictures were sold in the streets, and poets composed thousands of verses in their honor. Flights proliferated. A hundred thousand spectators turned up at Nantes; at Bordeaux, two people were killed and the balloon was destroyed in a riot that followed the cancellation of the flight.

Balloon flights brought the wonders of science to the people. Peasants hailed landing aeronauts with: "Are you men or gods?" The intellectual élite saw, opening before them, a vista of man's mastery of Nature. "The incredible discoveries that have multiplied over the last ten years . . . the phenomena of electricity understood, the elements transformed, the rays of the sun condensed, air traversed by human audacity, a thousand other phenomena have prodigiously extended our knowledge. Who knows how far we can go? What mortal would dare set limits to the human mind?" [3] It has a very modern sound, but though eighteenth-century science was separating itself from theology it was not free from fantasy. A respected scientist could claim that Nature marked melons out in sections so that they could be eaten with family or friends. Fully developed donkeys were said to have been seen, under the microscope, in donkeys' semen. Another scientist—long before the author of *The Secret Life of Plants*—had seen plants sleep, breathe, move their muscles voluntarily, and show mother love.[4] The radical novelist Restif de la Bretonne believed that current scientific theory confirmed that the Holy Roman emperor Frederick II had produced centaurs and satyrs by experiments with sodomy.[5] It was an exciting time, and it left a massive door open for the charlatan and the occultist to enter by.

Money was forthcoming for the most extravagant "inventions," ranging from elastic shoes, which—using a newly discovered principle "based on ricochets"—enabled a man to walk on water,[6] to a method of traveling underground which the originator promised to demonstrate by burrowing under the bridge at Avignon. Do-it-yourself experiments of all kinds were carried out for entertainment, but also in the hope of discovering something new to contribute to man's progress.

Electricity was thought to offer cures for practically everything from enuresis to sexual hangups. But another new cure-all was said to be compounded merely of bread and opium. The "wonders of science" were everywhere displayed, from the small-town fair to the most elegant salon. The government and learned societies tried to do something to stem the flood of popular enthusiasm before it reached the uncharted seas of pseudoscience, but without much success. Booksellers sold works on alchemy, promising further wonders, as well as science-fiction journeys to the moon. The poor, unable to afford anyone else, turned to faith healers, those who cured by mystic signs and touches, the vendors of "sympathetic powders" invented in the seventeenth century, and to Leon the Jew, who performed miracles with mirrors. Astrologers, alchemists, and sorcerers had such a firm popular hold that the police found them to be better spies even than priests.

The upper classes shared popular enthusiasms no less credulously but with a little more refinement. Pictures were sold of the *célèbre alchimiste*, the Comte de St. Germain, and one of the most talked-of men in Paris was Count Cagliostro. Both had access to the highest in the land.

Most people have heard of Cagliostro, whose name has the same sinister and dubious overtones as that of Rasputin. But, despite all the books, serious and frivolous, that have been written about Cagliostro since his death at the hands of the Inquisition in 1795, very little is known about him. It is not even certain who he really was, but it is most probable that he was born Giuseppe Balsamo in Palermo in 1743, the son of a poor family.

Balsamo's early life is confused by rumors circulated by his enemies during his lifetime and, particularly, after his death, when an alleged biography was published with the blessing of the Inquisition. But it is certain that he arrived in London in 1776, accompanied by a beautiful wife, and using the title of Count Cagliostro. There he founded a society of Freemasons using the "Egyptian rite," with himself as Grand Copht. Everywhere he went after that, Cagliostro founded a new lodge of the order. The initiation of a new member was reinforced by occult paraphernalia compounded from magical books and his own imagination. Yet Cagliostro was not entirely a charlatan. Being head of a secret society was a good way of earning a living at the end of the eighteenth century, because such an occupation belonged to the general atmosphere of the times. He did, too, express ideas about universal harmony which, as well as having a respectable lineage, were also relevant to his day.

Cagliostro was a man with impressive powers. He was a genuine clairvoyant, though not above giving his predictions a helping hand. His presence was dominating. The same Baronne d'Oberkirch who saw the eve of revolution dark with the powers of the occult and who was hostile to Cagliostro, described her first meeting with him: "While not actually handsome, his face was the most remarkable I have ever seen. His eyes above all. They were indescribable, with supernatural depths—all fire and all ice. It seemed to me that if any two artists sketched him, the two portraits, while having some resemblance, might yet be totally dissimilar. Ambivalent, he at once attracted and repelled you; he frightened you, and at the same time inspired you with insurmountable curiosity." 7

Behind the presence there always lurked, and not too discreetly, the showman. When Cagliostro and his wife entered Strasbourg in September 1780, his coach, covered with magical symbols, was preceded by six servants riding black horses. He did not stay in the fashionable part of town but in poor lodgings over a tobacco shop, where he healed the sick and distributed alms. The rich he refused to see—even Cardinal de Rohan, archbishop of Strasbourg. The two men met only when the cardinal insisted that no one but Cagliostro could cure his asthma. De Rohan, a prince of the blood as well as of the Church, was impressed by Cagliostro, too impressed, according to many. It was at the cardinal's request that Cagliostro made an exception in his attitude to the rich and the aristocratic. He cured the cardinal's uncle, whose life had been given up by his regular physicians.

After this, opposition to Cagliostro began to melt, especially when the cardinal showed one of the more skeptical of his friends a valuable ring which he said Cagliostro had made, before his eyes, from the cheapest of materials. But Cagliostro took no advantage of his new popularity and left Strasbourg because of the hostility of the medical profession there. He did not go to Paris but to Naples, and then to Bordeaux and Lyons. Only at de Rohan's insistence did Cagliostro consent to go to Paris in 1784.

The cardinal's position at court was not happy. He had fallen in love with the queen, Marie Antoinette, when she had first arrived in France from Austria to marry the future Louis XVI. Now she positively disliked him. However, de Rohan allowed himself to be tricked by a plausible young woman, calling herself the Comtesse de la Motte Valois, into buying a valuable diamond necklace, ostensibly on behalf of the queen, who would reimburse him for it. Cagliostro seems to have encouraged the cardinal in his belief that the queen was using him as her front man; either Cagliostro's clairvoyant powers were not functioning, or perhaps the charlatan was uppermost at the time. The cardinal, who sustained a very luxurious life style on a foundation of rapidly diminishing credit, could not pay the first installment on the necklace when it fell due, and asked the queen for cash. The plot was then exposed. The countess, her husband, and the necklace had all disappeared, leaving de Rohan with nothing but a large outstanding debit.

It would have been wiser to pursue the countess, recover the necklace, and clap those involved into the Bastille without any further publicity. But Marie Antoinette insisted on making the affair public. The cardinal and Cagliostro were acquitted at their trials. During his, Cagliostro replied to the judge's request to state who he was by announcing: "I am a noble voyager, Nature's unfortunate child." His reputation disappeared in a flood of laughter. The countess was whipped naked in public and branded, but managed both to escape and to blacken the queen's name abroad. From the beginning, she had claimed to be the innocent victim of the cardinal and the queen, and her allegations—sensationally embroidered in a book published in England and disseminated in France by enemies of the regime—turned the populace against the queen. Whenever Marie Antoinette appeared in public afterward she was almost invariably booed. Napoleon later said that the affair of the diamond necklace was the beginning of the French Revolution, the first milestone on the monarchy's road to the guillotine. Cagliostro's road led to the prisons of the Inquisition at Rome, where in 1795 he was strangled for being a dangerous revolutionary.

The life of the other "celebrated alchemist" whose portrait was hawked through the streets of Paris did not end quite so sensationally. The person who called himself the Comte de St. Germain was probably also an Italian. Casanova, who had a shrewd eye for more than a pretty woman, thought he was a fake, though an extremely intelligent and learned one. St. Germain probably first came to the attention of Louis XV of France through the latter's mistress, Mme. de Pompadour. Certainly by 1758 he was an important figure at the French court and was entrusted by the king with a number of diplomatic missions. Like Li Shao-Chun at the court of the Chinese emperor Wu Ti, some eighteen hundred years before, St. Germain was reluctant to reveal his age, but he talked of having been present at the Crucifixion of Christ, and related parts of a conversation he had had with the queen of Sheba. He never ate in public, merely sitting at table while the others went through the courses and telling stories and anecdotes of great historical figures.

Some thought him "the completest charlatan, fool, rattlepate, windbag and swindler." [8] Others were strongly attracted by this modest, handsome man, whose main interest seems to have been chemistry. Forced to leave France by enemies at court, St. Germain traveled through Europe, including Russia, picking up patrons and being discarded by them. His last was the reigning Prince Charles of Hesse-Cassel who, much against his better judgment, took St. Germain in and later became his friend and admirer. When St. Germain died five years later, in 1784, Charles mourned him as "one of the greatest sages who ever lived." Many people refused to believe that St. Germain was dead. He was reported to have been seen in various places at least thirty years later, and at the end of the nineteenth century he was said to be in Tibet.

Was St. Germain a magician? The mask of the magus has concealed a great many stranger faces. Cagliostro was possibly a revolutionary organizer; St. Germain probably a fine chemist (who lived on a vegetarian diet). Both needed a front, and they chose the one most congenial to the times.

St. Germain left behind a book, the manuscript of which still exists. Whether it is genuine or not cannot be established, but the title has a characteristic ring, *The Thrice Holy Trinosophie*, and the text the authentic obscurity of the great alchemical classics.

Neither Cagliostro nor St. Germain seems to have prophesied the French Revolution, at least in public. But they did contribute to the occult atmosphere that surrounded the bourgeois intellectuals who were to start the movement of revolt.

Not as much, however, as one Dr. Mesmer, by profession a German physician and the discoverer of animal magnetism.

Magnetic Massage and the Fall of the Bastille

Franz Anton Mesmer, armed with introductions to some highly placed persons, arrived in Paris in February 1778. He was then forty-four years old and had studied medicine at Vienna before opening a clinic in collaboration with a Jesuit professor of astronomy. Mesmer claimed to have discovered a fluid that was so fine that it could not be seen, but penetrated and surrounded all bodies. This "primeval agent of Nature" bathed everything in the universe. It was the medium of gravity, and it could be brought down to earth to give Parisians the marvelous benefits of heat, light, electricity, and magnetism. But the real value of the fluid was in the treatment of sickness, for illness was just an obstacle placed in the way of the free flow of the fluid. The human body was like a magnet. The north pole was at the head, and the south pole was at the feet. The fluid's action could be controlled by "mesmerizing" or massaging the "poles." The obstacle would be removed and a "crisis" would be caused which could be seen in the form of convulsions. After the crisis, health was restored as was the "harmony" of man with Nature.

Mesmer set up his first Parisian clinic in an apartment in the fashionable Place Vendôme. Gossip was soon going the rounds. There was a room lined with mattresses designed for the more violent convulsions of patients in crisis. And there were the magnetic tubs. These were usually filled with iron filings and mesmerized water in special bottles arranged like the spokes of a wheel. The bottles stored the mesmeric fluid and passed it on through movable iron rods which patients applied to their afflicted areas. Sufferers would sit round the tubs in circles, joined by pieces of rope. Mesmer did offer portable tubs for patients who preferred privacy, but communal treatments were much more effective because of the power generated.

Mesmer also treated patients outdoors. His usual method was to mesmerize trees and then attach groups of patients to them with ropes—tied without knots, as knots would block the flow of the fluid. But it was the indoor clinic that produced the best effect. The floors were covered with thick carpets, the walls decorated with strange signs; heavy curtains were drawn to shut out the day. Somber mirrors reflected dull candlelight, and soft music played on wind instruments, on the pianoforte, or on a glass harmonica filled the air, accompanied by muffled screams and bursts of hysterical laughter. As the invisible (and totally imaginary) fluid struck the patients, some would fall writhing on the floor, to be carried away by Antoine, Mesmer's valet and assistant, into the crisis room.

If a patient failed to feel the fluid at work, if there was no tingle in the spine or tremble in the hand, Mesmer himself would approach, wearing his lilac-colored taffeta robe and carrying his mesmerized wand. He would place the patient's knees between his own and run his fingers over the patient's body, searching for the poles of the magnets that together made the great magnet of the body. They were not easy to find, as they had a habit of shifting around. Some, however, such as the fingers and the nose, were stable, though the balance of the latter could be seriously upset by taking snuff. The poles at the top of the head and in the feet were usually avoided as they received, respectively, mesmeric influence from the stars and from terrestrial magnetism. The best place was around the abdomen and, because of this, gossip was quick to talk about sexual magnetism.

Not every patient had a crisis in convulsions. Some fell into a deep sleep and, while in it, experienced communications from the dead or other spirits.

Altogether, mesmerism had a great deal going for it. Mesmer's patients were cured of such varied afflictions as blindness, sexual incapacity, and boredom. Mesmerism was both scientific and magical, reason taken to the extreme. And its influence so penetrated into the subconscious that we still speak today of some great actor or politician "mesmerizing" his hearers with his "magnetic personality."

But Mesmer hit the conscious first, and his reputation grew quickly enough to threaten more respectable practitioners of science. He was invited to expound his theories before the Academy of Sciences, but its members were not impressed, and ignored him. He then retired from Paris to a nearby village, collected a number of patients, and invited the Royal Society of Medicine to investigate his cures. The society agreed, but Mesmer refused to accept their findings and turned next to the medical faculty of the University of Paris. There he had better luck, converting Charles Deslon, an important member of the faculty, who was also principal physician to the king's brother, the Comte d'Artois. But even such a powerful advocate could not swing the other members of the faculty to Mesmer's side, and they even refused to accept a copy of the first French edition of his book on animal magnetism. The doctors believed Mesmer's cures to be entirely natural and coincidental. But they, and all the others who published pamphlets attacking Mesmer and his ideas, only contributed to his increasing success. The scientific establishment published its attacks; the mesmerists replied. The war of words became so violent that the faculty used it as an excuse to expel Deslon from their ranks. This created even more trouble, and a split in the faculty between the younger doctors and the old guard.

The mesmerists now had a martyr, though Deslon was rather an awkward one, since he quarreled incessantly with Mesmer. (Even when he died, in August 1786, he was tactless enough to do so while receiving the mesmeric fluid.)

Mesmer decided that he would leave France to take the waters at Spa, to recover, he said, from the wounds he had received at the hands of the establishment. In fact, feeling as he did, it was highly probable—he conveyed—that he would never return. The response was instant. Queen Marie Antoinette intervened and the government opened negotiations with Mesmer. He was offered a pension of twenty thousand livres for life, and ten thousand a year to set up a clinic. For this, he would have to agree to some kind of supervision. He refused— in a public letter to Marie Antoinette, in which he lectured the queen on the "austerity" of his principles. He did not take bribes, and in any case the offer was not substantial enough. He wanted a country estate, and the queen could well afford to give him one.

Just the same, Mesmer did stay. He received what was potentially a better offer and one that was almost free of strings. A rich hypochondriac and lawyer with philosophical leanings, Nicholas Bergasse, had founded a Society for Universal Harmony with Gustave Kornmann, a banker from Strasbourg. Both had received treatment from Mesmer, and it was they who came to his rescue. In return for financial support, Mesmer was to give the society his secrets, and they were to release them for the benefit of mankind. There was a lot of hard bargaining—to Mesmer's advantage, for by June 1785 he was living in luxury in the rue Coq-Heron, traveled about Paris in a magnificent coach, and had collected nearly 350,000 livres. The society, too, did rather well, expanding its membership and setting up branches in provincial towns.

Of course, there were leaks. Defectors from the cause published what they alleged were Mesmer's secrets. Fake magnetic tubs were soon on sale, and drawings for do-it-yourself versions were on the bookstalls. Other practitioners set up in business, and tales of miracles performed were part of common conversation. Mesmerism was no passing fad. Its supporters included not only the naïve but the intellectual, for mesmerism seemed to be a new *scientific* explanation of the invisible forces of Nature, and "man, with his liberty, walks only to the cadence of all Nature, and all Nature moves only to that of a single cause; and what is this cause if not a truly universal fluid, which penetrates all Nature?"

Not all Mesmer's supporters allowed themselves to think as far as that, but even enemies had to take the subject seriously. Especially since, at a time when all authority was being questioned, mesmerism offered a challenge not only to established science and its institutions, the academies and royal societies, but to the government itself. The Paris police, through their informers, learned that during mesmerist meetings radical political ideas were being discussed.

The government decided to crush mesmerism once and for

all. For that purpose they chose to set up a commission, whose members were to be the most prestigious—and anti-mesmer-ist—they could find. There were to be four prominent physicians, from the university faculty, and five members of the Academy of Sciences, of whom one was Benjamin Franklin. As a backup, the government also set up a separate commission of members of the Royal Society of Medicine. The ostensible target was Charles Deslon, who, after a more than usually acrimonious quarrel with Mesmer, had set himself up in separate practice. In a letter to Franklin, Mesmer rejected Deslon's interpretation of his theories, but his protestations were ignored.

The major commission carried out a series of investigations, watching, with some distaste, mesmeric "crises." "The commission has seen them last for more than three hours; they are accompanied by expectorations of a viscous matter, torn from the chest by the violence of the attack. Sometimes there are traces of blood in the expectorations. The convulsions are characterized by involuntary spasmodic movements of the limbs and of the whole body, by contraction of the throat, by spasms of the hypochondriac and epigastric regions; their eyes are watering and distracted; there are piercing cries, tears, hiccoughs, and extravagant laughter." [9] A hundred years before, it would probably have been taken for demonic possession. The commission, representative of the Age of Reason, came to the conclusion that the effects of the mesmeric fluid were the results of an overheated imagination.

The mesmerists replied with a flood of pamphlets accusing the commission of ignoring the well-authenticated cures and of failing to investigate Mesmer himself. Commission members were attacked as defenders of orthodoxy and of their own self interest. So too were the physicians of the Royal Society of Medicine who, predictably, also produced a negative report. Satire was brought in to reinforce reaction. Mesmer was caricatured in a popular play as a shameless swindler—which inspired more pamphlets and more publicity. An attempt was made to break up a performance of the play, but the man employed for the purpose got the wrong one on a double bill. More significantly, Jean-Jacques d'Eprémesnil, who was soon to attack the government in the Parlement of Paris, tried to pressure the king, the Parlement, and the police to ban the play as an outrageous slander.

But the establishment was winning. Thomas Jefferson, then the United States representative in France, thought so. "Animal magnetism dead, ridiculed," he wrote in his journal on February 5, 1785. But, if mesmerism had been severely injured in Paris, it was alive and well in the provinces, and in 1786 Mesmer made a triumphal tour of the Societies of Harmony in southern France.

Not all the pro-Mesmer majority accepted his theories *en bloc*. Some more spiritual characters, such as Louis-Claude de Saint-Martin, mystic and founder of the secret brotherhood of the Elus Cohens, felt that Mesmer's fluid might be used to let in evil influences from "astral intelligences," a more contemporary way of saying "demons." Saint-Martin helped to "spiritualize" mesmerism, and it was this variety that was to become the vogue in the nineteenth century.

Mesmer was also having more personal trouble with his old savior, Nicholas Bergasse. With Kornmann and d'Eprémesnil, who had been an early member of the Paris Society of Harmony, he wanted to revise the society's rules to allow, at last, for the *public* propagation of Mesmer's secrets. Mesmer fought this, as he had done from the start, and at a general assembly of the society in May 1785 defeated his opponents and had them expelled. They failed in an attempt to set up a rival society, but continued to meet and develop the social and political aspects of mesmerist theory. In doing so, they broke away from what was, despite the reaction of the scientific establishment, an essentially conservative movement.

Membership in the society, though open to all, was restricted by a large entrance fee of one hundred louis, which allowed in only the wealthy bourgeoisie and the aristocracy. At Mesmer's house, where the society met, a magnetic tub reserved for the poor was seldom used, and Mesmer's German doorman was said to announce the social status of patients with the aid of a set of whistles. In fact, it was a club for gentlemen and gentlewomen, not a revolutionary cell.

Bergasse, like some early Trotsky, immediately attacked the purity of the society's gospel. Mesmer was accused of being interested only in financial gain and of failing to pass on his secrets for the benefit of all suffering humanity. Mesmer had betrayed the original idea of the fight against the "despotism of the academies," and had deliberately restricted the implications of his theories for the important problems of morality, education, the arts, and suchlike. Bergasse's group, which included among its members the Marquis de La Fayette, attracted a number of important supporters. One, Jacques-Pierre Brissot, wrote later that Bergasse had not hidden from him that he was really concerned with liberty. "The time has now come for the revolution that France needs. But to attempt to produce one openly is to doom it to failure; to succeed it is necessary to wrap oneself in mystery, it is necessary to unite men under the pretext of experiments in physics, but, in reality, for the overthrow of despotism." [10]

Brissot was a radical by nature, a follower of Rousseau, whose book *The Social Contract* is often said by historians to have been the inspiration of the French Revolution. It was, in fact, a crashing failure and was read by very few Frenchmen. What Brissot saw in the mesmerism propounded by Bergasse was a way of transmitting radical ideas to a very large audience.

The radical element had been there from the beginning; Mesmer was portrayed in pamphlets as coming to Paris with a discovery that would bring an end to suffering, but being betrayed and persecuted by the scientific establishment and the government. He was a threat to vested interests which did not care about the sufferings of the many. Mesmer had then rejected the professionals. "It is to the public that I appeal." It was this, in fact, that had frightened the government, which gave its approval to attacks on Mesmer and mesmerism and even distributed twelve thousand copies of the report of the commission and other attacks by other bodies. The establishment could be seen closing ranks against the rest.

In 1784 Bergasse had persuaded the Parlement of Paris to set up its own investigation into the claims of mesmerism. But the inquiry was never completed. The Parlement hesitated to attack the government, even indirectly. But Bergasse had won publicity for his case and that, in itself, was enough to make the government cautious. The king's ministers, on the basis of extensive police reports, had considered expelling Mesmer from France and prosecuting mesmerist societies. That they did not do so was a victory for mesmerism against despotism.

It was a strange alliance of dissenters. La Fayette, for example, was anxious to export mesmerism to the United States. In May 1784 he wrote to George Washington: "I will obtain permission to let you into Mesmer's secret, which, you can count on it, is a great philosophical discovery." When he sailed for America in the following month, he took with him Mesmer's cure for seasickness—grasp the mainmast, which will draw away the sickness by acting as a mesmeric pole. Unfortunately, the base of the mast was heavily coated with tar, and the fluid did not flow. But La Fayette, after his arrival, was a very active missionary, and so successful that Jefferson sent off a large number of anti-mesmerist pamphlets and copies of the commission's report to friends. La Fayette does not seem to have been among those who connected mesmerism with radical political ideas. Before 1789 his radicalism was chic rather than sure.

The occult atmosphere of pre-Revolutionary France has been largely ignored by political historians. Even those revolutionaries upon whom it appeared to have no influence were not immune. Robespierre, the sea-green incorruptible, took his first step into public view by speaking up in defense of electricity and the general science of his time. Marat, fixed for all time not only by the dagger of Charlotte Corday but by the art of Jacques-Louis David, demanded that French youth should ignore politics in favor of physics.

Marat's interest in science was intense. Brissot first met him in 1782 and they became great friends. Marat had tried to break into the scientific establishment three years earlier with a work on electricity, and the claim that he was greater than Newton. But his theory of the origin and nature of light, heat, fire, and electricity was rather like Mesmer's; they were produced, he said, by invisible fluids. The Academy was initially more friendly to Marat than to Mesmer, but by the time of the Commission on Mesmerism, Marat was convinced that he too was being persecuted by the establishment. If Mesmer and Marat were not exactly allies—there is no evidence that Marat supported Mesmer—at least they had the same enemies. There is a certain aptness in the fact that Marat was assassinated in his tub, even though it was not a magnetic one.

It was ambition frustrated that thrust both Marat and Brissot into revolutionary activity. But unlike Marat, Brissot saw in mesmerism the ideal anti-establishment cause. He discovered occult messages in the works of Rousseau and in mesmerism "a way to bring social classes closer together, to make the rich more humane, to make them into real fathers of the poor." Brissot's attacks on members of the scientific élite became more and more violent. They were "base parasites," "oppressors of the motherland," enemies of free and independent men, and fit only to "amuse ladies of fashion and bored young men." [11] Above all, because they were frightened of progress their answer was persecution.

If Brissot had been alone, he might be dismissed as an isolated crank, but he was not alone in his ideas. Politics are often fiction, but rarely science fiction. It was as if the mad scientist was out, not to conquer the world, but to change it into one of harmony and brotherhood. The plea was basically one for acceptance of merit rather than of privilege, for equality of opportunity. "Our liberty must be given back to us," wrote Bergasse. "All careers must be opened to us." [12] It was the cry of the democrat—and of the bourgeois intellectual.

The ideas of the radical mesmerists may seem, almost two

hundred years later, rather pointless, but they were considered by police and government to be a threat to the state, and regarded by those who propagated them as a true political ideology.

It was Jean-Louis Carra who perhaps gave mesmerism the appearance of being a scientific approach to politics. He, like Marat and Brissot, was a professional outsider who found in mesmerism a revolutionary cause. Carra maintained that there were various "atmospheres" surrounding bodies, which were penetrated by interrelated fluids connected, in some vague way, with Mesmer's universal fluid. Such things as unjust legislation upset a man's atmosphere and led to sickness. During the Revolution, Carra was to claim that a republic was the ideal form of government, "because the great physical system of the universe, which governs the political and moral affairs of the human race, is itself a veritable republic." [13] Politics and medicine were so closely related that both physical and social sickness could be cured by a combination of cold baths, dieting, head washing, and reading philosophical books. Carra saw the future in signs and omens. In 1783 Europe had heavy fogs, an earthquake, and a volcanic eruption. The winter of 1783-84 was so severe that marauding wolves were a danger to life. The following spring there were disastrous floods. The revolution, according to Carra, was surely on its way, for the harmony of the universe was being disrupted.

Bergasse was not so sure about the imminence of revolution, but he believed that France could be revolutionized. He attacked the decadent society of his time by contrasting it with primitive nature, through which the universal fluid flowed without obstacle, bringing health to man and society. Mesmerism, he claimed, offered "simple rules for judging the institutions to which we are enslaved, certain principles for establishing the legislation appropriate for man in all given circumstances." [14] Mesmer revealed lost worlds free from the prejudices of civilization. Bergasse, like Rousseau, thought that the new harmonious society could be brought about through education. Rousseau had believed that a child's moral development depended upon the sensations it received, but he had died without knowing that Mesmer's fluid was the means of transmitting sensations. Luxury, debauchery, even political institutions, interrupted the flow of the life-giving fluid. "We owe almost all of the physical ailments that consume us to our institutions." [15] Bergasse may have had the better plan, but it was Carra who was to be proved right in his prediction.

"It was about half past three," wrote one who was there. "The first bridge was lowered, the chains severed. But the portcullis barred the way; people were engaged in getting the cannon in by hand having unlimbered them first. I crossed by the little bridge and helped on the inside to get the two pieces of cannon in. When they were remounted on their carriages ... we formed up [and] we marched as far as the drawbridge of the château ... The cannons were levelled; the bronze one opposite the large drawbridge and the little iron one, damascened in silver, opposite the little bridge." [16]

Inside the great fortress the governor panicked. Promised a safe conduct, he surrendered, only to be seized by the mob and lynched. The attackers had expected to find the dungeons stuffed with state prisoners, but they discovered only four forgers, two lunatics, and a young nobleman. It did not matter. The Bastille, that symbol of despotism, had fallen to an enraged people. It was July 14, 1789. The Revolution had begun.

Monsieur Mesmer was not in Paris on that great day. He had left France to seek further fortune in England, Austria, Italy, Switzerland, and Germany, where he died not far from his birthplace in 1815. But it had been his Revolution, too.

3

The Magician
at the Barricades

The nineteenth century was the age of the Industrial Revolution, the time when the machine appeared to be omnipotent. But it did not bring the golden age that so many of its defenders announced. Dissatisfaction with man's situation remained, especially as, for the majority, it appeared to get worse. For many, industrial progress became not only the engine of a more efficient despotism than any known before, but seemed to bring a diminution rather than a fulfillment of man's aspirations. Machines destroyed the harmony of man with Nature, for technology and science were the instruments of man's growing domination over his environment, weapons in a war *against* Nature. Men turned again to the irrational, to the occult tradition—and, as others had done before, brought the occult into their politics.

The Occult Conspiracy

It is difficult today to understand the depth of the emotional and psychic shock of the French Revolution. It opened up the era of revolution in which we still live. The modern West has been bludgeoned by repetition and television into indifference to any suffering and violence other than its own, but for the men of the late eighteenth and early nineteenth centuries the experience was novel and frightening—and they needed an explanation.

What they got was what they wanted, something simple and tidy. Today, it is easy to take the words "Communist" and "Capitalist," add the word "conspiracy" to either—according to personal taste—and have a full explanation of the ills of the world. After the French Revolution, most people were satisfied that it had been the result of a conspiracy of secret societies. It is an old, undying technique. Invent a conspiracy, whether by Satan or, as in present-day China, a "gang of four" aided by "capitalist roaders," and anyone you care to name can be made party to it. Once give form to a conspiracy and there is nothing that cannot be made to fit. Heads I win, tails you lose.

The Abbé Fiard, who had been warning his fellow Frenchmen since 1770 of the dangers of harboring wizards and magicians like Cagliostro and Mesmer, was convinced that the Revolution had been the work of demons.[1] Many agreed with him, but preferred to attach to the conspiracy the general name of Freemasonry.

In Britain, as later in America, Freemasonry was what it remains today, basically a charitable organization maintaining the exclusiveness of its membership behind a barrier of secret rites and rituals. Even in eighteenth-century England, it was probably no more than that. But in eighteenth- and nineteenth-century Europe, Freemasonry was considered—and in many cases actually was—something very different, and less easy to define. Because of this, it was a very convenient term. As "Christianity" can cover everything from the Church of Rome to the Diocese-Vicariate of Niagara Falls, and "Communism" everyone from Vanessa Redgrave to the hard men of the Russian Politburo, so the term "Freemasonry" was wide enough to contain every secret society formed for political, religious, occult, or private drinking purposes, if it appeared to threaten the established order.

The origin of Freemasonry is one of the most argued-over

subjects for historical inquiry. According to Masonic legend, it is as old as architecture, going back to the building of the Temple at Jerusalem by Solomon. But the earliest-known facts about the mystical secret society rather than the craft union are dated 1641, when Robert Moray joined a Masonic lodge in Edinburgh. Moray did more than anyone else to persuade Charles II to become patron of the Royal Society, and there are suggestions that Freemasonry eased the king's return to his throne.

To fit the conspiracy theory, Freemasonry had to be associated with the Enlightenment and with radical ideas. This was easy enough. The eighteenth century was the age of secret societies, and there was a great deal of cross fertilization. There were orthodox Masonic lodges whose members were of the utmost political and social respectability, but there were also breakaway lodges, new lodges, often hard to distinguish from the orthodox, as well as some that were distinctly different. One such was founded in 1776 by a professor at the University of Ingoldstadt in Bavaria, Adam Weishaupt.

Weishaupt called his new society the Order of the Illuminati, and its purpose was to infiltrate the orthodox Masonic lodges, take them over, and use them for political subversion. Sensational rumors were followed by police raids and the publication of even more sensational revelations. The order was ruthlessly suppressed in Bavaria in 1785.

The Order of the Illuminati was the perfect stereotype of a secret conspiracy. It was intimately connected with Freemasonry, which it had taken over as a front. Its declared purpose was to overthrow existing society, and it was opposed to religion. Its ceremonies were full of occult overtones, and its members were bound by the most fearsome oaths of secrecy. When the French Revolution broke out, the danger that had been bypassed by the suppression of the Illuminati seemed only too obvious, and the Bavarian ruler remained so scared that he threatened anyone caught recruiting for the order with death.

The influence of the Illuminati had already spread all over Europe, *except* to France. There, on the eve of the Revolution, in 1788, the French public was warned of the danger of a "reactionary" conspiracy, threatening them and the rest of Europe. The conspiracy was that of the Order of the Illuminati, supposedly suppressed nearly three years before in the country of its birth for being "radical." The Marquis de Luchet, who revealed this, had been campaigning against "man's weakness for the extraordinary" for years. He had written about Cagliostro and condemned the "shameful fruits of credulity." [2] Luchet's Illuminati were not specifically Adam Weishaupt and his supporters; the marquis merely made use of a convenient name for all those who had been, according to him, seduced by the occult. He called upon men of good will to rally round the banner of reason and enlightenment. Luchet showed not only that anything could be made to fit a conspiracy theory, but that a conspiracy theory could be made to fit any point of view, radical or conservative, left or right.

To those who held the view that the French Revolution was the product of an occult conspiracy, the revolutionaries themselves gave support, although Jacques-Pierre Brissot, mesmerist radical, once he reached the center of power turned against the mesmerists. Two men, alleged Brissot—now leader of one of the major revolutionary parties—had tried to communicate a reactionary program to the king by means of mesmeric fluid. The message was said to have come from the Virgin Mary by a rather roundabout route, and the men were engaged in "imprinting" it on the king's mind when they were arrested—much to their astonishment, as they had thought they were invisible. It was all a part, said Brissot, of a counterrevolution. He too saw a conspiracy in the Illuminati, whose sects were "increasing instead of diminishing" and whose mysterious doctrine attracted men "who are unhappy with the new order of things." [3]

In 1792, a friend of Carra, Nicolas de Bonneville—certainly a member of the real Order of Illuminati—assisted the radical attack on Freemasonry by claiming that "of all religious or federative systems, Freemasonry is the most general; as nothing must be secret among a free people and they have now attained their object in France, let the Freemasons now open up their temples." [4] When this advice was ignored, the leaders of the Terror claimed the temples were hotbeds of aristocratic reaction and instigated the mobs to attack them and murder their members. By 1794 there was no longer an open Masonic lodge in France, and many of those who had spoken out for the mesmerist radical view had been guillotined in the Terror.

The conservative attack on Freemasonry was supported by a letter that had been written by the late Queen Marie Antoinette to her brother, the Austrian emperor Leopold II, in August 1790: "Take great care over any associations of Freemasons. You should already have been warned of this; it is by means of masonry that the monsters in this country count on succeeding elsewhere. May God keep you and my native land from such miseries!" [5]

A wave of conservative criticism began in the same year with a publication in Rome which warned that all the general movements labeled, for convenience, Freemasonry, were "working more or less blindly towards the ruin of the human race." [6] This pamphlet did not specifically accuse the Masons of starting the Revolution, but it prepared the way for another, that did, in 1791. After that, the full flood of anti-Masonic publications began, greatly helped by the printing of Cagliostro's alleged confessions, written in his prison cell in Rome in the hope of buying his freedom from the Inquisition. He "revealed" the monstrous conspiracy of Illuminati and Masons of various kinds, claiming to know all their secrets, including the fact that after the overthrow of the Bourbons in France the next victim was designed to be the papacy itself. To finance their activities, vast sums of money had been deposited in banks in Holland, Italy, and England. The publication of these "revelations" was designed not to damage Cagliostro—who was already as good as dead—but to use the tremendous publicity value of his name as a weapon against the Masons.

The advantage of the Cagliostro revelations was that they could be used by either branch of the conspiracy theorists. Outright papal condemnation of Freemasonry would be accepted by the faithful, while revolutionaries could stress the obscurantist and antirational elements introduced under the name of orthodox Masonry. The French translator of the "confessions" added a preface in which he associated Cagliostro with "the gloomy follies of the German Illuminati, about whom one may read in M. de Luchet's book . . . . The sect of maniacs now surrounds thrones, blindfolding sovereigns with error, keeping away from them men of talent and virtue . . . . Thus it threatens to destroy the states where it has power. It detests equally the religion which condemns it and the philosophy which fights against it." [7]

This was all good stuff, but the references were to comparatively recent times. What was needed to make the present conspiracy clear was to show how such organizations as the Illuminati were merely contemporary expressions of a long-standing conspiracy. Past events could then be brought in as historical proof. There was already a legend that Freemasonry was connected in some mysterious way with the Templars, who had been destroyed by Philip the Fair in the fourteenth century. And there was another tale that the Templars had sworn vengeance for the suppression of their order, no matter how many centuries it might take. These two traditions were brought together in a pamphlet, *Le Tombeau de Jacques Molay,* published in 1796. The story it told was quite simple and devastating.

In prison, while awaiting execution at Philip the Fair's order, Molay, Grand Master of the Templars, had founded four lodges, one of which was at Edinburgh. Its members were to carry out the vengeance of the Templars and "to exterminate all kings and the Bourbon line; to destroy the power of the pope,

to preach liberty to all peoples, and found a universal republic."
The members of these lodges eventually became the secret
controllers of lodges of Masons who did not know the secret
design. Over the centuries, the controllers had carried out their
work, penetrating all kinds of organizations. They had even
infiltrated the Society of Jesus and supplied the murderer who
killed Henri IV of France and the man who had attempted to
assassinate Louis XV. They gave their support to Cromwell in
England. They were responsible for the education of revolutionary leaders and had financed Cagliostro. Gustavus III of
Sweden had been removed, also by assassination, so that he
could be replaced by one of their own number, and they had
chosen to start the French Revolution with the attack on the
Bastille because it stood on what had been the site of Molay's
confinement.

All the Revolutionary leaders were in the conspiracy, from
Philippe Egalité, the renegade Duc d'Orléans, to Robespierre,
though they often did not know that they were being manipu-
lated by secret controllers (of whom there were only 108). But
they were all "united over the tomb of Jacques Molay." [8] Some
other works introduced the Protestants, behind whom was the
wicked hand of England, but this was just extra embroidery for
Catholic readers. The real culprits were the Masons, their occult
allies, and their secret controllers.

In the mass of conspiracy literature, the most outstanding
was the work of the Abbé de Barruel, who did more to create
the image of secret societies that dominated the nineteenth
century than anyone else. Barruel, born in 1741, was a priest
who had been tutor in a great aristocratic household and later
almoner to the Princesse de Conti. As a writer, he was a
persistent critic of the Enlightenment and a thorough believer
in the reality of intellectual subversion in France. He did not
leave France until after the September Massacres of 1792, when
he fled to London. There, in 1797, he published the first two
volumes of a book that was to make him famous and set the
final pattern of the conspiracy theory. In 1802, he returned to

France—though he does not seem to have approved of Napoleon—and it was rumored that he had been offered, and refused, a cardinal's hat by the pope. He was friendly with Fouché, the minister of police, and also with the director of the secret service, a former priest, but friendship did not save him from being arrested on a charge of supporting the pope against Napoleon, though he was held only briefly. After the restoration of the monarchy he was much in favor at court, and died in 1821.

For all his activities, Barruel's claim to fame rests on his *Mémoires pour servir à l'histoire du jacobinisme*. It was an instant bestseller, being translated into English, German, Italian, Spanish, Portuguese, and Dutch. It was last reprinted in 1911, but is still being quarried by writers on secret societies. The secret controllers are there in Barruel's book, manipulating the innocent and the not-so-innocent alike, arranging assassinations, planning rebellions, fomenting peasant uprisings in Bohemia and Transylvania. According to Barruel, the front men numbered more than six hundred thousand in 1789, and were led by La Fayette among others. At their head was that arch villain, the Duc d'Orléans. In Barruel's full five volumes there is practically everything. The horrifying details of initiation rites in underground caverns, with altars of skulls, terrible oaths, and ritual murder, are given in lip-licking detail. Nearly a whole volume was devoted to the Illuminati, though Barruel admitted that he had been unable to get hold of an account of their ritual. He had discovered that the supreme rank in their infernal hierarchy was that of magus, followed by that of man-king. Barruel might not be sure of the ritual, but he was convinced of the intention—it was to create universal anarchy and the destruction of property. The final details of the plot which resulted in the French Revolution, Barruel said, were discussed in Paris in 1787, when Cagliostro and the Comte de St. Germain helped in the briefing of the "heads of the conspiracy." Among the plans—Barruel knew his readership—was one to expropriate private property.

Barruel's book contained many errors of fact. Any tale he

heard, any piece of nonsense, was packed in, usually without being checked either for truth or plausibility. The shape of the guillotine blade, for example, was said to have been dictated by the Masonic triangle. Some of his extravagances even offended his admirers—but his critics, although condemning his overuse of the imagination, accepted that he had proved his case. No propagandist could have asked for more.

The rulers of Europe, who had first viewed the Revolution in France as an opportunity to make profit from that country's troubles, soon began to worry about their own stability. Most of them were already convinced of the existence of subversive organizations in their own countries. Once the Revolutionary armies were on the move, it seemed that they were the spearhead of a universal conspiracy. Some rulers took defensive measures by creating their own secret organizations to counter subversion.

One of those who had already reacted to the threat of the Enlightenment and, therefore, responded even more strongly to the Revolution itself, was Frederick William II, king of Prussia. He called himself a Rosicrucian. An "Order of the Gold and Rosicrucians" had been founded by unknown persons in Regensburg in about 1755. They claimed a connection with the original and wholly fictitious Brothers of the Rose Cross. The order had an elaborate hierarchy of nine degrees, with that of magus as the *highest*. The members met in what was known as a "circle" of nine. The initiate swore "freely and voluntarily, and after careful consideration" to follow the rules:

1. To live constantly in the fear of God.
2. To be guided in conduct by the love of my neighbor.
3. To maintain the utmost discretion.
4. To be attached to the order with unshakable fidelity.
5. To show perfect obedience to my superiors.
6. To have no secrets from my brothers in any matter which might interest them.
7. To devote myself completely to my Creator, His Wisdom, and this order.[9]

Many members of the order spent their time trying to make alchemical gold, or in medical experiments to prolong life (which resulted in a number of recorded deaths). The rituals of the order, its claim to possess secrets, attracted astrologers, alchemists, and even Mesmer himself, who was a member at least for a time. Many enlightened Germans thought the order was a front for the Jesuits, whose society had been suppressed by Pope Clement XIV in 1773. But, to many conservatives, its support of authority had great attraction in a disintegrating world. "It is one of our foremost duties," wrote a prominent Rosicrucian, "to serve the state in which we have been placed by Providence."[10]

The new order was, in fact, a valuable weapon against political subversion, and it had, as well as Frederick William, other powerful supporters. In Austria, its head was one of the emperor's closest friends, who persuaded him to authorize close government supervision of Masonic lodges in 1785. In Warsaw, the king of Poland was the order's most prominent member.

So the occult confronted the occult. But the decisive battle was between armies. Frederick William had neglected his, and so had many other rulers. But perhaps Napoleon had superior occult support as well as superior troops and weapons? It was said that he consulted a mesmerist fortuneteller before a battle, and there were many who believed, when the French emperor was finally defeated, that occult forces had turned against him. The secret controllers had used him, but were not defeated with him. They had retired into an even deeper obscurity from which they would certainly re-emerge. And re-emerge they did.

As the century moved on into more and more revolutions, the conspiracy theory hardened. The secret controllers were often given different names, and their front organizations became societies of socialists and democrats. But the longest-lasting name for a continuing and general conspiracy, at least as far as the papacy was concerned, was the original one of Freemasonry. As recently as October 1975, the Rome correspondent of the London *Times* reported that a letter had been circulated by the Vatican advising bishops that Catholics who became Masons need not consider themselves excommunicated—but only in those countries, like Britain and the United States, where the society did not "conspire against the Church."

Mystical Socialists and Utopian Democrats

In the year of Napoleon's defeat and the death of Franz Mesmer, the Society for Universal Harmony was re-established in Paris under the name of the Société du Magnétisme. And Alexander, tsar of all the Russias, visited Nicholas Bergasse. Bergasse had survived the Revolution, but his radicalism had not. He was no longer wealthy, and received the tsar in a badly furnished gardener's cottage on the outskirts of the city. Alexander was accompanied by the Baronne de Krüdener, a mesmerist mystic who had gained the tsar's confidence by revealing to him that the campaign against Napoleon was really one against the Antichrist. She had also helped to put into Alexander's mind the idea of a Holy Alliance of the kings of Europe against revolution. Alexander saw this as a brotherhood of Christians, and consulted Bergasse several times on the form this new universal harmony should take. It is possible that Bergasse actually produced a draft of the Holy Alliance.

Madame de Krüdener stayed on in Paris and, attaching herself to the novelist Benjamin Constant, adapted her prophecies to reflect his liberal views. Unfortunately, the most important of them, the apocalypse, did not arrive on schedule, and the fashionable world of Restoration Paris turned to other, more attractive mesmerists, such as the Abbé Faria, who could make water taste like champagne. As for the ordinary people, they used the dubious services of a horde of mesmerist fortunetellers, though the better off could now afford the very low fees charged by the new mesmerist society.

As with the old society, the new one attracted the abuse and hatred of the medical and scientific establishment. An anti-mesmerist satire was put on the stage in 1816, and nine years later the Academy of Medicine began a series of investigations which revived the old war of pamphlets. But some concession was made. One commission actually agreed that mesmerism had some therapeutic value. A few years later, however, another report was openly hostile. The Academy offered a prize of five thousand francs to any mesmerist who could read without using his eyes. One of the current mesmerist claims was the ability to do so. When all the contestants failed, the Academy declared that it would never investigate mesmerism again, for it had proved itself to be rubbish. This was in 1840.

Just as medical mesmerism survived the Revolution, so did its political aspect. The conservative strain that had so attracted Tsar Alexander never lost its appeal to supporters of authority and theocracy, but it was the old radical strain that was to have more effect. In France, it appeared in the ideas of the mystic opponent of capitalism, Charles Fourier. Though Fourier had stolen many of his ideas from Bergasse, he foretold that at the arrival of the millennium he would burn every book except his own. "It is necessary to throw all political, moral, and economic theories into the flames and to prepare for the most astonishing event ... FOR THE SUDDEN TRANSITION FROM SOCIAL CHAOS TO UNIVERSAL HARMONY." [11] Away with civilization. Back to a primitive, "natural" society.

Fourier strongly denied any mesmerist influence in his ideas mainly because he maintained that he had discovered everything himself; but the evidence of his own writings condemns him. The mesmerists considered Fourier one of their own, even though he had added a number of strange ideas, such as that planets copulated, and that civilization would be transformed when the male electricity of the North Pole arced over to join the female electricity of the South Pole.

Fourier projected the establishment of ideal communities—he called them "phalansteries"—with a maximum of eighteen hundred members. These would be the cells of the new world, as Campanella had hoped his City of the Sun might be. Several such cells were actually established. Among them was the Brook Farm Institute, founded by George Ripley, the New England Transcendentalist, in 1841 and converted to a Fourier-type community three years later. It collapsed in financial ruin in 1847, proving, as so many utopian communities have done since, that though riches do not purchase happiness neither does poverty purchase harmony, even on the most limited scale.

Radical mesmerists had considered for some time that it was a pity Mesmer himself had written nothing to support their views. Providentially, there was discovered in 1846 a manuscript said to have been written by Mesmer during the Revolution and sent to the French National Convention. Published in serial form in the *Journal du Magnétisme* over the next two years, it revealed that the master had been a radical after all, advocating popular democracy, equitable taxation, laws subject to the "general will," and one novel idea—"It will be proved by the principles that form the system of influences or of animal magnetism, that it is very important for man's physical and moral harmony to gather frequently in large numbers . . . so that all intentions and will should be directed to one and the same object, especially toward the order of Nature, while singing and praying together; and that it is in these situations that the harmony that has begun to upset some individuals can be re-established and health fortified." [12] The battle cry was "liberty and health," and the result of victory would be a democracy that would live forever.

Such an appeal could not, since 1789, have come at a better time. There had been another revolution in France in 1830 when the last of the Bourbons had been overthrown and replaced, ironically, by the son of Philippe Egalité, that Duc d'Orléans, Mason and occultist, whose pretensions to the throne had perished with his own death in the Terror. But the new king was no radical, and his reign saw the triumph of the landlords and the bourgeois capitalists. When Mesmer's radical views were "revealed" in 1846, people were ready for revolution once again.

The poets, writers, and painters who made up what is known

as the Romantic Movement in France were obsessed by the occult, the exotic, and the radical. The mesmerist influence had come mainly through a German physician, Doctor Koreff. He had known most of the principal Romantic writers in Germany, where he had been a professor of psychology at the University of Berlin and an influential member of the royal Council of State. When Koreff's influence had declined in Berlin he had left for Paris and, with his presence and wit, had soon become the darling of the fashionable salons of the Restoration and the bourgeois monarchy.

Koreff introduced to Paris the tales of another mesmerist, E. T. A. Hoffmann, and the poems of Heinrich Heine. For writers, he became a kind of impresario of the fantastic. The Romantics lapped up everything he had to offer. Highly commercial writers like Alexandre Dumas incorporated mesmerism into their novels. Dumas was constantly carrying out experiments in hypnotism. His play *Joseph Balsamo* had the Cagliostro-style hero projecting mesmeric fluid through mirrors and pianos, as well as his eyes. The novels of Balzac were full of mesmerist references, and one, *Ursule Mirouet*, had a mesmerist as its principal character. For Balzac as for Dumas, mesmerism was no literary device, no attempt to cash in on a popular fad. It was an essential part of the psychic atmosphere in which they lived. Mesmerism was there too in the works of Victor Hugo, that archetype of Romanticism and rebellion. And, as with the mesmerist radicals of the 1780s, the rallying cry was for liberation from the tyranny of the establishment, for a new social order, for the restoration of harmony.

A bad harvest and potato blight in 1846 led to bread riots and famine. An industrial crisis brought many bankruptcies and soaring unemployment. The government did not seem to know what to do, and the king would not give in to demands that he dismiss his reactionary prime minister, Guizot. The pressure was building up from all sides. Moderate parliamentarians held a series of banquets—political rallies, in effect—and when these were finally banned by the government the organizers substituted a great procession through the streets on February 22, 1848. The king ordered out the National Guard, which turned against the government, and he then abandoned his minister. But too late. The mobs were in the streets, and in the evening of the following day there occurred an incident that turned a riot into another revolution.

Victor Hugo was there.

> The crowds which I had seen start cheerfully singing down the boulevards, at first went their way peacefully and without resistance. The regiment, the artillery, the cuirassiers opened their ranks everywhere for their passage. But on the boulevard des Capucines a body of troops, both infantry and cavalry, was massed on the two pavements and across the road, guarding the Ministry of Foreign Affairs. Before this impassable obstacle, the head of the popular column tried to stop and turn aside; but the irresistible pressure of the huge crowd weighed on the front ranks. At this moment a shot rang out, from which side it is not known. Panic followed, and then a volley. Eighty dead or wounded remained on the spot. A universal cry of horror and fury arose: Vengeance! The bodies of the victims were loaded on a cart lit with torches. The cortège moved back amid curses at a funeral pace. And in a few hours Paris was covered with barricades.[13]

Hugo did not know who fired the fatal shot but it seems to have been a young man, "nervous and delicate," named Marie-Joseph Sobrier. It was he who had organized the procession and headed it with a drummer at his side and a pistol in his belt. By the time the march had reached the waiting soldiers, Sobrier and his escort were no longer at the head of the procession, but, according to at least one source, it was he who fired the shot that released the revolution. Sobrier was a radical, a mesmerist, follower of a mystic messiah named the Mapah. The magician was at the barricades, and when the monarchy fell a day later it seemed that the millennium had arrived. But once again the Golden Age was to be postponed. The men were there and so were the plans, but they were defeated by the very instrument they had hoped would provide them with the franchise for change. One of the first acts of the new government was to bring in universal suffrage. The mass of the new electorate, mainly illiterate peasants, voted in a conservative assembly. A workers' rebellion in Paris in June 1848 was savagely suppressed and the mystical socialists and utopian democrats either ended up in prison or fled abroad.

Yet they had helped to change the world. The revolution was betrayed by the very people it was intended to release from serfdom and suffering, but the repercussions in Europe were profound. The long, dark tragedy of democracy had begun.

The Holyeyed Figure of Mananan MacLir

In the cone of the searchlight behind the coalscuttle, ollave, holyeyed, the bearded figure of Mananan MacLir broods, chin on knees. He rises slowly. A cold seawind blows from his druid mantle. About his head writhe eels and elvers. He is encrusted with weeds and shells. His right hand holds a bicycle pump. His left hand grasps a huge crayfish by its two talons.

MANANAN MACLIR

(With a voice of waves). Aum! Hek! Wal! Ak! Lub! Mor! Ma! White yoghin of the God. Occult pimander of Hermes Trismegistus. (With a voice of whistling seawind). Punarjanum patsypunjaub! I won't have my leg pulled. It has been said by one: beware the left, the cult of Shakti. (With a cry of stormbirds). Shakti, Shiva! Dark Hidden Father! (He smites with his bicycle pump the crayfish in his left hand. On its cooperative dial glow the twelve signs of the zodiac.

That was James Joyce, mischievously attacking the Irish poet and novelist George Russell in *Ulysses,* and with him the whole occult infrastructure of Irish nationalist politics at the turn of the nineteenth century. And not only Irish politics, but the politics of all the rest of the area often called the "Celtic fringe"—Scotland, Wales, Cornwall, and Brittany.

First mystic socialism, then mystic nationalism. And, if a nation is primarily a collection of racial myths surrounded by customs posts, then those myths have to be established. The Celtic nationalists found them in folklore. The expression "folklore" was first used in 1846, but the urge to collect fairy tales and stories from the peasant unconscious came from Germany with the Romantic movement, and particularly with the works of the Brothers Grimm. Sir Walter Scott was its pipeline, and Anne Macvicar Grant its outlet; in the second decade of the nineteenth century she published a two-volume collection of the superstitions of the Scottish Highlands. The other two great collections appeared in 1860 and 1900. A similar attempt was made in Wales, but there, in a country with an integrated and living language and culture, there did not seem to be the same demand for the comforts of myth. In Ireland, however, always consciously aware of English rule, the folklore movement was dominated by such men as Douglas Hyde, the founder in 1893 of the Gaelic League, and first president of the Irish Republic.

The material that was collected contributed much to the powerful external myth of the Celtic peoples, the inevitable association with witches, hobgoblins, the evil eye, and second sight—the latter investigated in Scotland on behalf of the Society for Psychical Research in 1894 by a lady who soon acquired the Gaelic nickname of *Cailleach bheag nam Bocan,* "the little woman fascinated by ghosts." The "hidden wisdom" of peasant cultures was extracted for the benefit of those who had been "spoiled by civilization." This whole highly misleading impression of the Celtic peoples received powerful reinforcement in Ireland from George Russell and the poet William Butler Yeats.

It was second sight that stimulated Yeats's interest in the occult. A female servant of his uncle, George Pollexfen, possessed this faculty to a surprising degree. One morning, she was about to bring Pollexfen a clean shirt when she stopped, saying there was blood on the front and she would bring another. Stepping over a low wall on his way to the office that day, Pollexfen fell and cut himself, getting blood on his shirt. On other occasions, the servant would lay extra places for dinner without being warned that her master was bringing guests. She was a valuable and valued domestic asset.

Yeats joined a new lodge of the Theosophical Society, founded in Dublin in 1886, of which George Russell was also a member, but soon left theosophy behind and became a member of The Hermetic Society of the Golden Dawn in London in 1890. The visible head of the society was one Liddell Mathers, whom Yeats first saw in the reading room of the British Museum wearing a brown velveteen coat and "a gaunt resolute face." Mathers referred mysteriously to "secret chiefs" he had met in Paris, one of whom seems to have been the Comte de St. Germain on a short visit from Tibet. Later, Mathers created himself Count MacGregor of Glenstrae and appeared at meetings clad in kilt and doublet.

Yeats was not entirely convinced by Mathers and tended to think of him as a charlatan, but through him he was introduced to the Cabala and other occult traditions which fitted very well with his cast of mind. Yeats was certainly taken with the idea of a spiritual élite, and proposed a project for a "Castle of Heroes" to be set up on an island in a lonely lake, where the exhausted fighters for Ireland's freedom could refresh themselves with occult rituals. Yeats's Ireland was an Ireland of the imagination. As was George Russell's.

Russell, who wrote under the pseudonym AE, made things quite clear. "A nation exists primarily because of its own imagination of itself. It is created by the poets, historians, musicians, by the utterances of great men, by the artists of life." [14] By the last he seems to have meant some type of magician. "Ireland was known long ago," he wrote in *The Irish Theosophist* in 1895, "as the Sacred Island. The Gods lived there ... men who had made themselves Gods by magical power ... Dear children of Eire, not alone in the past, but to today belong such destinies .... The Gods have not deserted us. Hearing our call they will return. A new cycle is dawning and the sweetness of the morning twilight is in the air. We can breathe it if we can but awaken from our slumber."

Yeats thought Russell was "the one masterful influence among young Dublin men and women who love religious speculation but have no historical faith," because he had "taught many to despise all that does not come out of their own minds, and to trust to vision to do the work of the intellect." But Yeats was not being fair to Russell and he knew it. Russell could drop much of his occult candyfloss when it came to practical matters. His imagination, Yeats admitted, could become vivid in the service of something he had not created. In his paper, *The Irish Homestead*—ridiculed by Joyce as "the pig's paper"—Russell showed his practical side by advocating the setting up of agricultural cooperative banks, as well as other ideas designed to help the Irish farmer to stand on his own two feet. He was also a great supporter of Irish writers and Irish literature.

If there was any sense of a "national spirit" at the time of the Easter Rising of 1916, it had its origins in the occult elements gathered round Russell and Yeats. They created an Ireland of dreams for the men with guns to convert into reality. The state, wrote Russell at the time of the Rising, "is a physical body prepared for the incarnation of the soul of the race." That state came into existence, partly, in 1922, but the Ireland of dreams is still being fought for today. Behind the terrorist on the streets of Belfast lies the long tradition of the occult underground.

In Scotland, nationalism has not yet followed the same path as in Ireland. Power is coming, not out of the barrel of a gun but out of a barrel of oil, from the diminution of Britain's status in the world, from the pressure of inflation, the energy crisis, and the dubious bonanza of the North Sea. The occult plays no open part today in the propaganda of the Scottish National party except perhaps in the irrationality of its economic projections for independence. But it was there at the beginning, and remains deep in the belief that Scots are different from the rest of the people of the United Kingdom. That belief was the product of exile, and exile is not simply a matter of being away from one's homeland, though there are many thousands of Scots distributed about the world and millions of second-, third-, and fourth-generation émigrés who still feel they have Scottish roots. There is a much more potent exile of the mind, a separation from psychic foundations that has nothing to do with physical actuality. The Scotsman, wrote Lewis Spence in 1927, "creates for himself ... a spiritual fatherland, the microcosm of the Caledonian scene. He is a Faust, or shall we say ... a man of alchemies and druidism, a man of magical ancestry." [15]

Agitation for Scottish self-government was contemporary with that of the Irish. In 1885 the first Scottish Office was established under a government secretary of state, and in the following year the first Scottish Home Rule Association was founded. Among the generally Liberal founding fathers was Theodore Napier, who worked for the restoration of the Stuart monarchy, a cause moribund since 1714 and dead since 1746. Napier helped to create that nostalgia for the Jacobite cause which is so valuable a tourist attraction in the Scotland of today.

The most important figures in the creation of a Scotland of dreams, that mental structure that is so essential to any successful nationalism, were not crackpot royalists or Liberal politicians, but a professor of botany and a writer who divided himself, professionally and successfully, into two persons.

William Sharp, born in 1855, was a friend of Dante Gabriel Rossetti, of the Pre-Raphaelite movement, and of the American poet Walt Whitman. Sharp was interested in the occult and corresponded with Yeats. As his alter ego, Fiona Macleod, he also corresponded with Yeats (and with George Russell), disguising his handwriting. Fiona Macleod was one of the great figures of the Celtic revival in Scotland, though Sharp would never publicly admit his connection with her. It was only on the verbal assurance of a friend that Sharp was granted a small government pension toward the end of his life—for being Fiona.

As Fiona, Sharp published a number of romances with titles like *From the Hills of Dream* and *The Immortal Hour*. Turned into an opera by Rutland Boughton, the latter achieved considerable popularity in the 1920s and has been recently revived. In 1895, ten years before his death, Sharp met Patrick Geddes, professor of botany at the University College of Dundee and now hailed as one of the pioneers of sociology and town planning. Geddes was a fervent Scottish patriot, anxious to provide his patriotism and that of others with a psychic foundation. His thought, which on a practical level was concerned with slum clearance, soon acquired mystical overtones; town planning became for him an instrument for the recreation of the organic unity of human existence. Geddes ran summer schools for like-minded people and set up a publishing house to issue the works of Fiona Macleod. The group was also responsible for publishing an influential, if short-lived magazine, *The Evergreen*, decorated with astrological signs and containing the work of Celtic writers from Brittany, Ireland, and Wales, as well as Scotland.

Geddes and Fiona Macleod created the imaginative image of Scotland. It was left to others to provide the political vehicle for Scottish nationalism, which survives today. A number of groups came together in 1928 to form the Scottish National party. Its first president was R. B. Cunninghame Graham, writer and traveler, who had also been first president, in 1888, of the Scottish Labour party. His only obvious occult connection was the preface he wrote in 1897 to a work by William Stirling called *The Canon, an Exposition of the pagan mystery in the Cabala as the rule of the arts*, in which the Cabala appeared as the basis of a rule of universal proportion. The vice-president, however, was Lewis Spence, journalist and poet, who claimed to hear "faerie singing, wordless and of wonderful harmony" in the small hours of the morning. While on a walking tour through the mountains, he had had revealed to him "the great soul-drama of Scotland's fate." Spence belonged to a German occultist order, wrote exhaustively on the lost continent of Atlantis, and produced a work on *The Mysteries of Britain*, with illustrations by another well-known Scottish nationalist, Wendy Wood.

So the magicians helped to create a nationalism of dreams for the harder men to shape and form. Some were frightened at what they had done. In 1900, Fiona Macleod created an uproar by writing: "It is time that a prevalent pseudo-nationalism should be dissuaded. I am proud to be a Highlander, but I would not side with those who would "set the heather on fire." [16]

Three
INDUSTRIAL REVOLUTION
AND SCIENTIFIC MAGIC

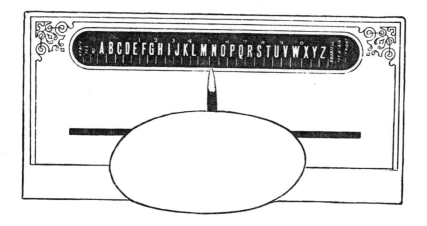

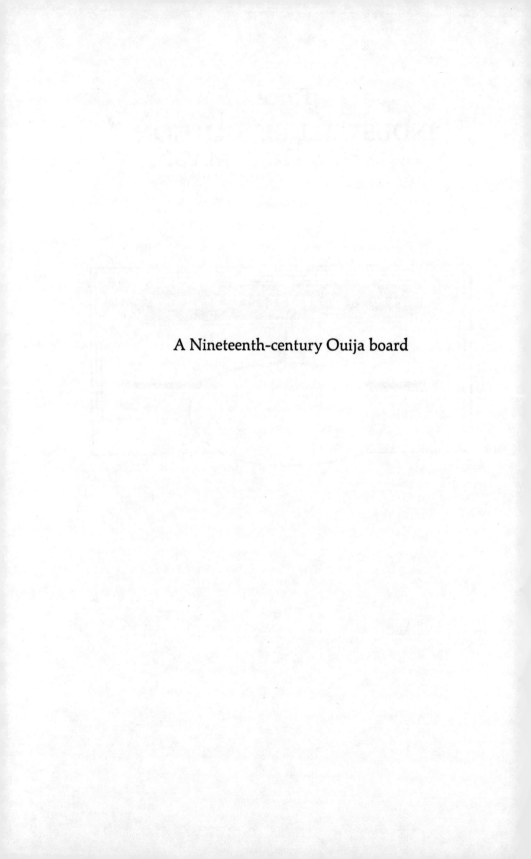

A Nineteenth-century Ouija board

1
The Medium
and the Message

The public in nineteenth-century Europe and the United States was as fascinated by the wonders of science as it had been in the eighteenth century. And with more justification, for science appeared to conquer all—at least on the material plane. The railroad, the steamship, the telegraph, as well as advanced weaponry, spread Western culture throughout the world, creating empires part of whose justification was the pushing of primitive peoples—often against their will, if not their better judgment—into the bright light of the modern world. But there were other realms than the material. Could science also provide answers about the immaterial, the world of the spirit? The law of supply and demand, far older than the industrial capitalism that worshiped it, operated there, too.

To satisfy the demand for explanations of death and the afterlife, which orthodox religion failed to give, there came spiritualism. It claimed to demonstrate the survival of human personality beyond death and to establish, scientifically, the validity of the subjective experiences of the medium by showing that they gave access to information that could be checked.

The demand for a synthesis of scientific information and general wisdom which promised to deliver scientifically based answers to the age-old problems of human *life* produced phrenology, "the science of the mind."

A Bump on the Head

Samuel Taylor Coleridge wrote: "There is in every human countenance either a history or a prophecy"; [1] Balzac of "the imperceptible fluid, the basis of the phenomena of the human will, from which the passions, habits, and the shape of the face and the skull result." [2] Both were influenced by the "science" of phrenology, invented by Franz Joseph Gall in 1796.

There had been other attempts to read faces. Giambattista della Porta, a Neapolitan physician, produced a system in the late sixteenth century for classifying features and complexions. In 1775, John Caspar Lavater, a mesmerist-mystic of Zurich, began publishing his many volumes on physiognomy. There had been a method of divination based on the distribution of moles on the human body, and another on lines on the brow. Gall's system was divination by bumps on the head.

Gall, of course, did not call it divination, but a scientific analysis of the external features of the skull as an index of the mind and character. Gall believed that the configuration of the skull corresponded closely with that of the brain, and that mental characteristics were recorded, like a relief map, on the outer surface of the cranial bones. He defined thirty faculties of the human mind; his disciple Spurzheim added five more, and constructed a chart of the scalp showing the areas associated with special faculties, among them conjugality, parental love, acquisitiveness, and ideality.

Gall's lectures on phrenology in Vienna were banned by the government in 1802 as being hostile to religion. A commission of Paris physicians investigated his system in 1807 and, characteristically, reported that it was worthless. Spurzheim's Paris lectures, however, attracted large audiences. At one given in 1817 an Edinburgh lawyer named George Combe was totally converted, and returned to Britain to spread the gospel through lectures, books, and the British Phrenological Society, which he founded in 1830. After Spurzheim's death in 1832, Combe became the leading international advocate of the science, and exponent of its wide social and philosophical implications.

Phrenology was to have a long run—the Phrenological Society survived until 1967—but its real influence lasted only for as long as it could be considered a science rather than what it genuinely was, a branch of fortunetelling. Phrenology penetrated the newly forming theories of human evolution. Herbert Spencer's first book, *Social Statics*, which appeared in 1851, was really a work of phreno-mesmerism, and Alfred Russel Wallace, who quite independently produced a theory of natural selection almost identical with that of Charles Darwin, was still maintaining as late as 1898 that the greatest error of "the Wonderful Century" was its neglect of phrenology.

Combe was determined to maintain phrenology's status as a science, though its tenets demanded from followers more faith than reason. Because Combe's ideas seemed to elevate reason over the supernatural world of Christianity, his enemies saw phrenology as a threat to orthodox religion, or as an alternative to it. In 1840, the Unitarian minister James Martineau, brother of the abolitionist and advocate of mesmerism Harriet Martineau, was one of phrenology's attackers. "There is," he wrote in 1840, "a set of mere anti-supernaturalists chiefly proceeding from the phrenological school or from the numerous ranks of thinkers indirectly created by it. ... I believe they are very numerous among us and likely to increase." [3] He was right on both counts.

Phrenology, despite its occult origins, was by implication materialist and secularist. The Scottish Association for Opposing Prevalent Errors, and similar bodies, always gave Combe top billing. The pope put his works on the index of books prohibited to the faithful. But among ordinary people as well as "thinkers" phrenology was enormously popular. It carried the warranty of famous names—Goethe and Karl Marx, and the novelists George Eliot, Charlotte Brontë, Charles Dickens, and

Bulwer Lytton. Combe was even invited by Prince Albert to examine the royal children, and one of the tutors of the future King Edward VII was sent to study phrenology under him before taking up his appointment. Combe even examined Queen Victoria herself, though only from a distance. Seeing her at the theater he trained his opera glasses on the royal cranium and was pleased to report that she would be more likely to favor reform if her organ of causality were better developed. This could be achieved by a study course in chemistry, he advised.

The great advantage of phrenology was that it was easy to understand and needed no special equipment except a head, and everybody had one of those. Public demonstrations were not inhibited by problems of modesty; the head was readily visible. The lecture programs of Mechanics' Institutes, those founts of popular knowledge, always included one or more on the subject. At a time when knowledge was both power and entertainment, a whole, comprehensive history of mankind could be found in Combe's book *The Constitution of Man,* based on phrenological principles, first published in 1828 and consistently reprinted. There were chapters on planets and fishes and the strange beasts that had preceded mankind. There were excursions to the lands of primitive peoples. But there were also sections on crime and punishment, education, religious observance, and good government.

There were, of course, those who mocked. As early as 1817 the anonymous authors of *The Craniad* had laughed at phrenology's claim to help not only in the choice of profession (or of a servant) but in avoiding possible disasters.

> Soft simple maids may sly seducers shun
> By simply taking care of *number one.*

Number one was the area of amativeness.

Nevertheless, phrenology did suggest that if character deficiencies could be discovered and defined, they could be corrected, perhaps by a change in environment. This was particularly relevant to the treatment of criminals. *The Craniad* might sneer at the "craniological paradise" to come—

> When thieves and murd'rers all will know, to be
> Afflicted with a sad calamity!
> And learned doctors of the law shall then
> Labour to cure, but not to kill such men.

—but it has a very modern penological ring about it. Phrenological ideas were on the side of penal reform, that notion of prisons as "moral hospitals" which reflected radical thinking in the nineteenth century. But phrenology also, and more positively, backed more widely held opinions. No wonder a new popular radical journal declaimed, in its first issue in 1850, that not only would it strike at the heart of both monarchy and aristocracy, but it would do everything in its power to further whatever made for "Progress and Improvement in all things . . . Teetotalism . . . Phrenology, Reform in Theology, Dietetics, and the Healing Art." [4]

The current virtues were supported by phrenology, and its ungodliness could be ignored. Most propagandists for the cause kept this latter aspect as quiet as possible anyway, but even so, its secularism seemed to give a great deal of intellectual comfort to those who had been brought up in the more repressive and narrow-minded Christian sects. Phrenology also gave "scientific" backing to such beliefs as that in national superiority, which most people favored instinctively. British brains were undoubtedly, and provably, the best, so there was really nothing to be surprised at in the existence of the British Empire. The colored races were just unfortunate. Their "organs," as the phrenological areas were called, were inferior. So too were those of Frenchmen and other foreigners, and, of course, those of the Catholic Irish.

Nearer home, the position of the lower classes was perfectly judged; their skulls were the skulls of people of the lower rank.

At Cambridge University, however, the mathematical dons had heads that appropriately displayed noble qualities of weight and number. The higher the status, the more bumps. Women's unfortunate propensity to an over-prominent organ of love of approbation was balanced by equally prominent ones of philoprogenitiveness and amativeness.

On the whole, the phrenological paradise was here on earth, with something for almost everyone—foreign policy, class, race, sex, even the problems of scholars. Statues and portraits could reveal the true source of the greatness of the men and women of the past. Homer had an enormous bump of ideality; Columbus, as one would expect, a substantial protuberance of locality (even if it was the West Indies he discovered, rather than the East). Literary criticism could be served by phrenology. Francis Bacon's head, "as given to us in the well known bust by Roubiliac," wrote one of the most active of phrenological propagandists, Charles Bray, was the only one "out of which Shakespeare's plays could have come." [5] In art, there was no need even to look at the work of sculptors and painters, but only at representations of the artists themselves. If art were graded by bumps, Leonardo da Vinci and Raphael easily came out tops.

In private, Combe seems to have rejected all forms of supernaturalism and even immortality, although in public he frequently referred to the Supreme Being.

> Dr Gall observes that this organ of Veneration is an indirect proof of the existence of God. Destructiveness is implanted in the mind, and animals exist around us, to be killed for our nourishment; Adhesiveness and Philoprogenitiveness are given, and friends and children are provided as objects on whom they might be exercised; Benevolence is conferred upon us, and the poor and the unhappy, on whom it may shed its soft influence are everywhere present to us; in like manner, the instinctive tendency to worship is implanted in the mind, and

conformably to these analogies of nature, we may reasonably infer that a God exists whom we may adore.[6]

Careful stuff, especially as veneration could also be directed to earthly things—to parents, for example, though children generally had small bumps of veneration and large ones of self-esteem, a dangerous and unpleasant combination. Genuine Tories had a large veneration, radicals small, as it should be. The simple arguments, anecdotal "evidence," naïve explanations piled up on one another in the phrenological books. Both Combe and Bray were serious men, believing implicitly in their "science of the mind" as "the only scheme of Human character which has hitherto [until 1861] been elaborated in a manner proportioned to the subject." [7] But it was just the comprehensiveness of phrenology—not to mention the general mediocrity, even hilarity, of its arguments—that repelled such men as John Stuart Mill, one of the most influential radical thinkers of the century.

The French philosopher Auguste Comte, who was a firm believer, had urged Mill to take it up in 1842, but Mill replied that phrenology in England seemed to be dominated by men of inferior intellect. Mill had, in fact, been examined by a practitioner and had been given a grossly obvious misreading. He refused to reconsider his unfavorable opinion, to the intense annoyance of Combe and Bray, who blamed the lack of headway made by their creed in the important areas of politics and intellectual studies not only on incompetent practitioners— "ignorant professors"—but on men like Mill who, by failing to contribute their great authority to the furtherance of the cause, were, according to Bray, "principally responsible for turning a whole generation out of the way."

The phrenological movement in Britain was tattered by internal frictions. It never achieved its long-standing hope of getting a champion in Parliament for its views of popular education. Yet it fixed itself deeply in the popular consciousness, sanctifying class divisions with its pseudo-science, while offering the placebo of a radical reformist program in many sectors of human society.

In the United States phrenology took a different course, leading to another profoundly influential movement, spritualism.

A Voice from Beyond

In December 1847, John Fox, a Methodist farmer, with his wife and two daughters, Margaret, aged fifteen, and Kate, twelve, moved into a little frame house in Hydesville, a village within the township of Arcadia, Wayne County, New York State. For their first three months in residence, the Fox family were regularly disturbed by mysterious noises which, occurring only at night, prevented them from sleeping. There seemed no adequate explanation. Though the house was made of wood, it was not the cracking of beams or movement of the floors.

Then, on a Friday night in March 1848, the source was revealed. The family had gone to bed early to catch up on their lost sleep.

> My husband had just gone to bed [Mrs. Fox later explained], when I first heard the noises. . . . I had just laid down when it commenced as usual. I knew it from all the other noises I had ever heard in the house. The girls, who slept in the other bed in the room, heard the noise and tried to make a similar noise by snapping their fingers. The youngest girl . . . is the one who made her hand go. As fast as she made the noises with her hands or fingers, the sounds followed up in the room. It did not sound different that time, but it made the same number of raps the girl did. When she stopped, the sounds would stop for a short time. The other girl . . . then spoke in sport, and said: "Now do just as I do. Count one, two, three, four etc., at the same time striking one hand in the other."

138

The blows which she made were repeated as before. It appeared to answer her. She only did it once. She then began to be startled and I said to the noise: "Count ten" and it made ten strokes or noises. Then I asked the ages of my different children successively, and it gave the number of raps corresponding to the ages of each of my children.

I then asked if it was a human being making the noise, and if so to manifest itself by the same noise. There was no noise. I then asked if it was a spirit?—if it was, to manifest it by two sounds. I heard two sounds as soon as the words were spoken.[8]

With the help of neighbors, a system of communication was established, and it was learned that the source of the tapping was the spirit of a peddler who had been murdered in the house some four or five years earlier. When digging began in the cellars of the Fox home in search of his remains, the excavations filled with water, but later some human bones and hair were alleged to have been found. The first reaction of the public was curiosity, and the Fox family had to suffer a stream of inquirers. They moved to Rochester—and the tapping followed them. A number of clergymen attempted to exorcise the spirit. Others condemned the whole thing as the work of the Devil.

Whatever it was, the people of Rochester demanded some kind of proof. In 1849, the first public investigation of spiritualism took place in the largest hall in the town. A committee of responsible persons could detect no fraud, but the audience was not satisfied and another inquiry was convened. This also reported in favor of the Foxes. A third committee, made up of the most skeptical, was also forced to admit that it could discover no imposture. The final meeting broke up in a riot.

All this was reported in the newspapers in the East, which gave the Foxes splendid publicity, though much of the reaction was of dubiety. Mediums, the white man's shamans, appeared in response to the publicity in a number of widely scattered places. There had been those who claimed to talk with the other world before the Foxes had been heard of, and they now joined the spiritualist movement. So too did some men of distinction and influence. Horace Greeley, editor of the New York *Tribune* was one, and the first New York circle numbered among its founders a former judge of the State Supreme Court. By 1850 spiritualism had acquired its own paper voices in such journals as the *Spiritual Messenger* of Springfield, Massachusetts, the *Spirit World* of Boston, and the *Light from the Spirit World* of St. Louis.

If the non-spiritual press was often hostile, it was still happy to print accounts of the sensational phenomena produced by mediums. And sensational they usually were. The Boston *Post* reported in 1853 that after a séance room had been darkened,

the table was forcibly drawn up to the ceiling, leaving the dents of its legs on the ceiling; it then came down, having adhered to the ceiling with such force as to drag down the plaster dust with it. It was raised some twelve or fourteen inches from the floor whilst the whole party had their hands on its upper surface. Whilst six of our party strove to hold it by main force, it was wrenched from our grasp and thrown some six or eight feet upon the bed. The medium was lifted bodily from the floor at various distances, whilst we held him by either hand. He was lifted from the floor and placed, standing, on the center of the table and again stretched upon his back thereon. Being seated in his chair, himself, chair and all, was elevated several inches and hopped about the room like a frog. Suddenly it was lifted, medium and all, into the center of the table. Again it was drawn up so high that the medium's head touched against the ceiling; and finally the medium was thrown out of it upon the bed, while the chair was hurled upon the floor.[9]

The wide publicity given to these spiritualist performances naturally inspired opposition from the more orthodox members of society. The churches were often highly critical, and their congregations sometimes violent. In 1850, Margaret Fox was attacked by a mob of Irish Catholics on a visit to Troy. Three professors from Buffalo tried, in 1850, to catch the Fox sisters out by declaring that the raps were made with their knee bones, but failed to prove their case.

Ex-Governor Talmadge of Wisconsin joined the movement, and his signature was among the thirteen hundred on a petition to the U.S. Congress requesting the setting up of a scientific commission to investigate spiritualist phenomena. Senator James Shields made a long and obscure speech in the Senate in which he referred darkly to Cornelius Agrippa, Cagliostro, and Dr. John Dee, names no doubt utterly familiar to his fellow senators. It was a speech "listened to with much attention, but frequently interrupted by laughter."

> *Mr. Weller:* What does the senator propose to do with the petition?
> *Mr. Pettit:* Let it be referred to the three thousand clergymen. [Laughter]
> *Mr. Weller:* I suggest that it be referred to the Committee on Foreign Relations. [Laughter]

The petition was shelved, but spiritualism went on spreading, in city and village, in the settled states of the Union, and in the lawless frontier territories of the West. It reached the Pacific as early as 1849 and settled comfortably into the feverish camps and rough mining towns of the Gold Rush. Clementine might be lost and gone forever on the physical plane, but it was highly likely that she could be contacted on the other side.

There were a wide variety of ways in which this might be done. The techniques were there even before the philosophy had been fully propounded. *The Spiritual Magazine*, in 1860, listed all the methods then current:

1. The Rappings, Table-tippings and other sounds and movements of ponderable bodies
2. Spirit Writing and Spirit Drawings
3. Trance and Trance Speaking
4. Clairvoyance and Clairaudience
5. Luminous Phenomena
6. Spiritual Impersonation, or the representation or reproduction in a medium of the actions and manner, gait, deportment, and other peculiarities which distinguished the actuating spirit in his earth-life
7. Spirit Music—represented both with and without the instruments
8. Visible and Tactual Manifestations, such as the appearance and touch of Spirit-Hands
9. Spirit intercourse by means of the Mirror, Crystal, and Vessel of Water

Less common were:

10. Apparition of the Departed
11. Visions and Previsions
12. Dreams
13. Presentiments
14. Spirit Influx by which ideas and sentiments are infused into the mind
15. Involuntary Utterance, including Speaking in Tongues
16. Possession

And, in tune with the Age of Science, the medium could have the assistance of such magical machinery as the planchette and the ouija board (whose name was taken from the French and German for "yes"), which spelled out the spirit messages.

The purpose of it all was to prove one thing and to prove it scientifically—that there was life after death. Communications with spirits, even with gods was nothing new. The god-speaker, in forms of varying refinement, had been around since man first lived by hunting. But to be able to communicate, oneself, with men and women one had once known and loved was something very different. Intellectuals might find the idea of communicating with the great minds of the past fascinating—and they did—but the opportunity for ordinary people to talk with their own dead was the real gift of modern spiritualism. In any case, the great dead seemed to have lost much of their genius during the passage to the Beyond. Victor Hugo, who contacted Shakespeare during a séance in 1854 was answered by the playwright with some pious verses (in French!) which ordered his characters to bow low before God: *"Hamlet, Lear, à genoux! A genoux, Roméo!"* [11] Such disappointments led Thomas Henry Huxley, the evolutionist, to remark that it was: "Better to live a crossing sweeper than die and be made to talk twaddle by a medium hired at a guinea a séance." [12]

Patient researchers into the origins of modern spiritualism in America have come up with a bewildering array of sources, ranging from phreno-magnetism, through the works of the eighteenth-century Swedish mining engineer and mystic, Emanuel Swedenborg, to Amerindian shamans in the newly settled districts of New York State, where the phenomenon of the talking dead first occurred. All probably contributed in some way, but the most important factor was the social and psychic atmosphere of the time.

Oscar Handlin has written of the "preoccupation with bodily ills" and "a shuddery fascination with death" that went with it in the America of the 1840s.[13] It was a time of unease and anxiety, of personal loneliness and search for identity. Tensions were increased by a great flow of foreign immigrants, Irish refugees from famine and German refugees from religious persecution. The majority of these immigrants did not go to the expanding frontiers. They were too poor for that. They stayed in the Eastern cities, expanding the slum areas instead. Their poverty drove them to accept lower wages during the American Industrial Revolution, antagonizing the longer-settled Americans and creating further tensions.

America in the mid-nineteenth century was a land of opportunity and fear, optimism and insecurity. Old World landmarks had been left behind, and the New World had few that could be recognized by the immigrant. America was a melting pot in which nothing seemed to coalesce. Yet one problem united all. The problem of death seemed not to be satisfactorily answered either by imported or native religion. The thought of a life after death was in itself a powerful tranquilizer. Proof that there actually was one was a prophylactic against fear.

In America, spiritualism was a cult of social change, an easing of the harassment of everyday life in a society changing from the traditional to the modern, from rural to urban, from agriculture to industry. Its proposition of a life after death was essentially religious, its insistence on proof essentially scientific. It held both worlds together and made them compatible and dependent. The messages from Beyond were often trivial but they were always soothing. Yet spiritualism did not simply offer an insurance policy that paid off in the hereafter against the premiums of suffering paid in the here and now. That was the orthodox religious approach which was so unsatisfying in a world of terror and unease. The here and now needed something too.

The trouble with spiritualism was that it had no coherent philosophy. Its followers shared only one belief, that in life after death. The most important, Andrew Jackson Davis, had already had his trance experiences before the events at the Fox farm. He tried to push the movement in the direction of his own rather muddled social thinking. This was influenced not only by Swedenborg, but by the French mesmerist-radical Charles Fourier.

Before he attached himself to spiritualism, Davis had a distinctly socialist bias. In a book published in 1848, which enjoyed an immediate success and went into thirty-four editions in thirty years, he divided society into three parts: "The poor, ignorant, enslaved, oppressed, and working classes.

The semi-wealthy, learned, enslavers, oppressors and dictating classes. The rich, intelligent, enslaving, oppressing, and idle classes. The poor are the *sustainers*, because they are the *industrious*. They are the producers of wealth and of all the blessings that circulate through other and higher societies, and yet they are the forgotten, the despised, and the uneducated." [14]

Davis put aside his socialism, perhaps because the seer saw that American individualism did not mix well with socialist principles or community living, but he never lost his belief that the poor remained poor because of lack of education. In 1863, at a meeting in New York, Davis described the methods used for the education of children in the Spirit World. Spiritualists believed, he said, that when children die and pass Beyond, they continue to grow on the Other Side and must, naturally, be educated. Davis called the other world "Summerland." The schools there were called Lyceums—a remembrance, perhaps, of other lyceums, the adult-education centers of the twenties and thirties. The Lyceums of Summerland were beautiful halls surrounded by gardens, and there the children were instructed by the leaders.

Some of Davis's audience were so impressed by his description that they decided to form a lyceum for the education of earthly children on Summerland principles. The essence of Davis's teaching, spread by a growing number of admirers, was that "a child is the repository of infinite possibilities. Enfolded in the human infant is the beautiful image of an imperishable and perfect being." And he went on: "It is the end of true education to develop that image, and so truly, too, that the child's individuality and constitutional type of mind shall not be impaired; but rather revealed in its own fullness and personal perfection." [15] In that statement can be found many of the principles of modern educational theory. Davis thought that conversation and discussion were the ideal methods of teaching, that making a child think was preferable to stuffing his mind with facts.

The lyceums, or spiritualist Sunday schools, as they were

more often called, had a limited but real success and were copied in England, using Davis's *Manual* as a guide to teaching methods. Spirtualism in its new American form had arrived in Britain in 1852, when a Mr. Stone, an American lecturer on animal magnetism, brought the medium Mrs. Hayden to London. There had been some indigenous mediums in Britain before the arrival of Mrs. Hayden. One, Georgiana Eagle, had given a demonstration before Queen Victoria in 1846. But no groups had formed. American spiritualism first attracted the English middle classes more than the workers. There was already a great interest in the supernatural, and a great willingness to accept scientific proof of any of its phenomena.

Orthodox scientists, however, were skeptical, even though a professor of mathematics at London University had found his own investigation of Mrs. Hayden startlingly convincing. He published his conclusions anonymously! The critics of spiritualism, in contrast, were quite happy to have their names known. Michael Faraday, in a letter to the London *Times* in June 1853, advanced the explanation that rappings were an unconscious muscular movement, and there were other scientists anxious to agree with him, and in public. This did not halt the spread of the movement—the publicity may even have assisted it. Mediums sprang up all over the country; table rapping became a favorite after-dinner entertainment; the dead were pursued and their messages demanded on an ever-increasing scale.

Some of the mediums were tricksters, clever conjurers making a swift killing out of the dead. But others were not, or at least not provably so.

Perhaps the most famous, and certainly the most remarkable medium of the nineteenth century was an American, born in Scotland, Daniel Dunglas Home. He claimed that his father, who spelled his name Hume, was the illegitimate son of the tenth Earl of Home. Daniel's parents had emigrated to America in 1840, leaving their seven-year-old son with an aunt in

Edinburgh. Two years later, Daniel and his aunt also left for America. Daniel's mother was said to have second sight, and her son began to see visions at the age of four, though it was not until nine years later that he had his first important psychic experience. He saw the spirit form of a friend who had, it was learned later, died just three days before. Other experiences followed, and his aunt, finding the local ministers unable to exorcise the devils so obviously occupying her nephew, threw him out of the house.

Home spent the next few years with friends and the spirits he constantly saw before him. He often brought the two together in séances, which were soon extended to include outsiders interested in the subject of communication with the other world. A committee from Harvard testified that a table they had been sitting around, with Home, moved about and actually rose into the air. Others, less academic but no less influential, confirmed that similar manifestations took place in Home's presence.

By the time Home returned to his native land in 1855, his reputation was such that he was welcomed into the houses of the rich and the aristocracy. Writers, too, found him attractive, the poet Elizabeth Barrett Browning so much that her husband, Robert, later satirized him as Mr. Sludge the Medium. On his first return visit to Britain, Home stayed only for a short time before leaving for Italy. In Florence, the English community welcomed him and the letters of introduction he carried. He made Countess Orsini's grand piano rise in the air while the countess was actually playing it. Spirit hands appeared and played the concertina, then shook hands with the guests. Some of the hands were pleasant to the touch, some were not. In the bedroom of a villa in which a man had been murdered several hundreds of years before, the hand was thin and the fingers skinny and yellow. But the ghost agreed to stop haunting. In a monastery rented by the American sculptor Hiram Powers, a séance was interrupted by the ghosts of twenty-seven rowdy monks, who tore at Mrs. Powers's skirts. Perhaps they were the sexually deprived ones attacked by Cornelius Agrippa three centuries before!

The effect on Florentine society of these startling performances was sensational. Home became the lion of the season, and was actually "kidnapped by a strongminded society lady of title, an Englishwoman living apart form her husband," who installed him in her villa. The resulting scandal got back to England and inspired Elizabeth Barrett Browning to remark in a letter that Home "gave sign of a vulgar Yankee nature, weak in the wrong ways."

Home was threatened by rather more dangerous things than sexual gossip. He was in a Catholic country with strong views about sorcery. An Italian official warned him, probably humorously, that he should keep away from windows in case someone shot at him with a silver bullet, the only sure way of killing a sorcerer. Home was advised not to go to Rome, but go he did—to become a Catholic. His voices had told him that he would lose his powers for a year, and he wanted to visit Rome. His accommodation with religion won him an interview with the pope, which he could hardly have had otherwise, and the papal recommendation of a confessor when Home arrived at the next place on his itinerary, Paris.

As it had been well publicized that his powers would return on February 10, 1857, the confessor's assurance that they would not in fact do so was of no consequence. They did return, in the presence of the confessor and an emissary of the emperor, Napoleon III, exactly on the stroke of midnight. Séances followed at the imperial palace of the Tuileries, with Home's powers operating at full strength. A spirit hand formed, and held that of the Empress Eugénie. Another held one end of a concertina, while the emperor held the other, and between them they played tunes, which included, suitably enough, "Home, Sweet Home." At one séance, the hand of the first Napoleon was made to appear and sign its name. It disappeared after being kissed by the empress.

The emperor, who was himself something of an amateur of the occult, was greatly impressed, and so was Eugénie, who had at first been less than enthusiastic. Home's influence with the imperial family became such that enemies began to attack him—mainly by exaggerating his powers. Wisely, he left for America, returning a few months later with his sister Christine, who became a protégée of the empress. Home, who was tubercular, found his powers weakening as his body did, and he decided to return to Italy to recuperate. In Rome, he was invited to dine with a Russian count, and found the count's seventeen-year-old sister-in-law, Alexandrina de Kroll, so attractive that his second sight told him they would be married within the year. The wedding was in St. Petersburg, and Alexandre Dumas was best man. After the marriage, the Homes were often guests of the Russian imperial family, the kind of interest that opened many doors, but in August 1859 they left for England. On the whole, it was thought that Home's "vulgar Yankee nature" had been much improved by his marriage into the Russian aristocracy.

The spirits were active in London. During a lecture on Cagliostro, Home was surprised to find the spirit of Cagliostro entering the hall and sitting next to him. A little later, he also appeared in the Homes' bedroom and spent some time sitting on the bed gossiping. There is no record of what Alexandrina Home thought of this. In any case, she died in 1862 from tuberculosis, probably contracted from her husband. With her went Home's regular income, for she had been an heiress and her relatives fought the terms of her will. Home produced an autobiography to finance his current needs while the legal arguments moved tediously and expensively on. But the proceeds were not sufficient to sustain his extravagant lifestyle. He stayed with friends, and then decided to leave for Rome. Once there, he was summoned by the police and ordered to leave the papal territories within three days for being a sorcerer.

His enemies used Home's expulsion from Rome as a weapon to discredit him. His royal patrons did not seem to have much interest in his problems; Napoleon III appeared bored, and the king of Bavaria had an attack of deafness. But Home was solidly supported by a wide variety of people, including, in England, some leading Protestant clergymen. Another visit to St. Petersburg was as successful as the first, but essentially unsatisfying, and Home returned to London. There he became associated with a wealthy widow aged seventy-five, Mrs. Jane Lyon. But while Home was away taking a hydropathic cure at Malvern, Mrs. Lyon acquired another medium, under whose influence she set out to recover, by means of legal action, a sum of money she alleged she had given Home.

The prosecution's case displayed Home as a charlatan, and a greedy one, too. Mrs. Lyon deposed that Home had produced messages from her dead husband instructing her to give him money. The money, however, had been given not to Home himself but to a society called the Spiritual Athenaeum, and the judge felt compelled to say that donations made to a properly constituted religious body were perfectly legal, and people should not be allowed the privilege of changing their minds. Though it was blatantly obvious that Mrs. Lyon had given false evidence in court, the judge—who openly condemned spiritualism as a delusion—ordered Home to refund the money while instructing Mrs. Lyon to pay not only her costs but Home's as well. For Home, it was a shattering defeat disguised as a vindication. Not only did he have to produce money already spent; the whole spiritualist movement suffered too. The decision of a hostile judge left legal innocence with the appearance of guilt.

Home, himself, does not seem to have suffered too much. He began a very successful lecture tour and in 1870 was once again the subject of controversy. In that year a young man, Lord Adare, privately—though not privately enough—published an account of his experiences with Home. Adare was not a spiritualist. On the contrary, he was the type of caricature English nobleman whose life was normally bounded by the trout stream, the hunting field, and the grouse moor. But the phenomena he recorded were not record bags of game shot or weights of fish caught. They were of conversations with the dead, of furniture being moved around by unseen hands, of visible hands scattering flowers and lighting the gas. On one occasion, he claimed, in the presence of himself and two other impeccable witnesses Home had floated out horizontally—the window was opened only a foot—from the third story of a house in Buckingham Gate, London, and back in through another window seven feet away. The range of Home's activities seemed limitless: using red-hot coals to wash his face; increasing his height, while the witnesses held his feet; materializing the spirit of the recently dead American actress, Ada Mencken. On one occasion Home provided an object lesson in the dangers of abusing alcohol.

Partially covering himself with the window curtains [wrote Adare], but holding the glass with the brandy in it over his head, between us and the window so that we could see it, he was lifted off the floor about four or five feet. While in the air, we saw a bright light in the glass; presently he came down and showed us that the glass was empty, by turning it upside down; he also came to us, turned it upside down upon our hands; then going to the window he held the glass up and we heard the liquid drop into it. He began talking about the brandy, and said, "It is under certain circumstances a demon, a real devil, but, if properly used, it is most beneficial." As he said this the light became visible in the glass, and he was again raised in the air. "But," he said, "if improperly used, it becomes *so*" (the light disappeared) "and drags you down, down, lower and lower," and as he spoke he sank gradually down till he touched the floor with the glass. He again raised the glass above his head, and the liquor fell over and through my fingers into the glass, dropping from the air above me.[16]

151

It was all very impressive, as were most of Home's performances. They could have been produced fraudulently and it is possible that they were, but they were never proved to be. In 1871, after the furore raised by Adare's book, Home agreed to be investigated by a distinguished young physicist, William Crookes. To the surprise of other scientists, Crookes reported that though his rational mind told him that the phenomena produced by Home must be fraudulent, he could not discover them to be so and was convinced that they were genuine psychic manifestations. This did Crookes a great deal of harm with the scientific establishment. As for Home, he decided to retire, and died fourteen years later after a comfortable life in Russia and on the French Riviera, living with a second wife on his first wife's money, which had finally been awarded to him by the courts. Home was never a part of the spiritualist movement. His career gave it both a high gloss and a dark smear. Yet he put spiritualism into the palace of the ruler as well as the front parlor of the bourgeoisie.

Tsar Alexander II showed interest in spiritualism, as did Napoleon III. Spiritualists also claimed Queen Victoria as a convert. After the death of Prince Albert, the queen's seclusion and known concern with the afterlife allowed the most extravagant rumors to circulate. Her servant John Brown was said to be a medium who materialized the spirit of the dead prince consort. But there was no evidence to back the rumors. In Austria, the Archduke Johann thought Spiritualism might be subversive, for "this modern superstition flourishes not only among the weavers . . . or among the workmen and peasants . . . but it also has its fixed abode in numerous palaces and residences of our nobility, so that in many cities of the monarchy, and especially in Vienna and Budapest, entire spiritualistic societies exist, carrying on their obscure nuisance without any interference." [17] In Berlin, Kaiser Wilhelm II attended a séance at the house of General von Moltke and was so upset when the medium began to prophesy bad luck for the imperial house that he banned any public reference to such matters.

In the United States it was the aristocracy of politics and wealth that felt the need for the solace of spiritualism. Perhaps for the self-made millionaires there was a feeling that "from rags to riches" implied a converse of "from riches to rags," and the other world might have some valuable advice to rap out to them. Commodore Vanderbilt, in his eighty-third year, took up the investigation of spiritualism and switched his erotic interests from housemaids and the ladies he met at trotting races to female mediums. They put him in touch with the dead as well as with their own living bodies. Two of them, Tennessee Claflin and her sister Victoria Claflin Woodhull, not only produced occult phenomena and satisfied the Commodore's aging erotic fancies but publicly advocated such highly spiritualistic ideas as free love, feminism, and socialism. The Commodore set them up as stockbrokers, at which they did remarkably well despite their disapproval of capitalism, and he even wanted to marry Tennessee. But the two lady mediums were disposed of by a southern girl fifty years younger than the Commodore, who married him, led him back to religion, and even persuaded the man who hated philanthropy and mistrusted education to found Vanderbilt University. If he had married Tennessee, he might have put his money into spiritualist Sunday schools instead. The sisters' association with Vanderbilt, however, gave them great publicity, especially in the women's rights movement, and Victoria was actually nominated as a candidate for the U.S. Presidency.

Away from the palaces of railroad kings and European rulers, spiritualism did help to provide a sense of community for people disoriented in times of social chaos and uncertainty. It also offered the means of revolt against established Christianity, which appeared to have no answers to the problems and strains created by technology and science. This was particularly obvious in France, where Léon Hippolyte Denizart Revaille, who called himself Alan Kardec, had discovered a "perfectly coherent picture of the universe" through the mediumship of two young girls. Kardec's views were strongly anti-Catholic, but even in the atmosphere of the times his ideas had very little influence in France. After his death in 1869, however, his writings filtered to Brazil, where they gained considerable popularity.

In Kardec's system, the mediums received the spirit of light in their being, and through them advice and counsel were transmitted. The spiritual power was seen as fluid which could be transferred as healing, both psychic and physical. The process of communication was also said to be beneficial to the dead, helping them, as well as the living, toward perfection. Men were believed to live in a number of habitable worlds, and their passage through them was dependent on merit, not on grace. Though the movement respected God and considered Jesus as a spirit guide, it also believed in reincarnation.

Kardecism in Brazil was established on a properly organized basis in 1884. Unlike spiritualism in America and Europe, it set up social institutions, hospitals, clinics, asylums, shelters, and schools on a scale which is today very impressive, considering the size of the movement, which may have a membership as low as six hundred thousand. The movement has almost as many welfare establishments as the Catholic Church. Kardecism expanded when spiritualism was declining in the West. In Brazil, it emerged at a time when Church and state were separating, and may have offered some kind of religious liberation in an age of change.

In the United States spiritualism declined for a variety of reasons, ranging from its advocacy of free love and of socialism to the obviously fraudulent activities of many mediums. But its main failure was due to the lack of a coherent philosophy, organization and doctrine. Yet it still survives, as it does in Europe, helped along by the dead of two world wars and the desire of relatives to communicate with their loved ones. Spiritualism is no longer *socially* significant in Europe and the

United States as it is in Brazil, but it had its historical function. It was a magical view of the other world, offering in the language of science a continuity with one's ancestors in a world whose foundations—personal, familial, and environmental— were crumbling away.

2
Wise Men
from the East

"The departure of the wise men from the East," remarked the English wit Sydney Smith in 1835, "seems to have been on a more extensive scale than is generally supposed, for no one of that description seems to have been left behind."[1] Smith's witticism had the same ring of Western cultural arrogance as the words of Lord Macaulay, historian and law minister in the government of British India, when in the same year he dismissed the whole of Indian culture as basically without value—"a single shelf of a good European library [is] worth the whole native literature of India and Arabia."[2]

But there were others, less imperially minded, who did not agree and were prevented neither by humor nor rhetoric from making their own investigations. They contributed not only to Oriental scholarship but to some of the wilder reaches of the Western imagination.

The Fatal Ring

It was the Crusades, in their alliance of faith and force, greed and ambition, the first of Europe's colonial wars, that released the exoticism of the Muslim East into Europe. The influences were essentially superficial, a reference here and there in

156

literature or art, a motif in architecture, the home comforts of sugar and spices, elegant silks and carpets. The great Arabic contributions to European culture, in alchemy and medicine, in engineering and the rediscovery of the ancient worlds of Greece and Rome, though not entirely independent were barely assisted by the activities of the Crusaders, who were for the most part men of little learning but vast material ambition. Nor were the Crusaders interested in any spiritual wealth they might acquire; they had their own religion and, in theory at least, it was their ideology as well. Even the men of the eighteenth century did not think much about the spirit. They, in turn, were attracted by the sexual customs of the Muslims and by the richly colored background of the tales brought to them by Antoine Galland when he produced the first translation from *The Thousand and One Nights* in 1704. But even if the alleged delights of the harem and the idea of a heaven populated with beautiful girls whose virginity was miraculously restored every day—an idea which had the authority of that holy book, the Koran—had considerable appeal, no one seems to have turned Muslim in order to enjoy them.

It was, in fact, China that first exercised an intellectual force upon the European mind. Its exotic elements influenced art and literature so extensively that around the middle of the eighteenth century, an English poet complained:

> Of late, 'tis true, quite sick of Rome and Greece,
> We fetch our models from the wise Chinese.
> European artists are too cool and chaste,
> For Mand'rin only is the man of taste.[3]

But philosophers found the Chinese sage Confucius more to their taste. Voltaire, that merchant of the exotic, made him into the archetype of the eighteenth-century rationalist. Confucius, he wrote, "appeals only to virtue, he preaches no miracles, there is nothing in his books of religious allegory." China, Voltaire believed, was ruled by philosophers and scholars under a philosopher king and, as a philosopher himself, he thought European monarchs should follow the Chinese example. Unfortunately, no eighteenth-century ruler would have dreamed of employing a professional philosopher in an important office of state. Frederick the Great of Prussia, of whom Voltaire had great hopes, dismissed the idea simply and brutally: "I leave the Chinese to you," he wrote to Voltaire in 1776, "along with the Indians and Tartars. The European nations keep my mind sufficiently occupied." [4]

The legend of China was destroyed by the experiences of Europeans who visited the country and found that the "philosopher" officials were, in the words of Captain George Anson, "corrupt, their people thievish, and their tribunals crafty and venal." The eighteenth century knew nothing of other Chinese beliefs such as Taoism or Buddhism; those were to be a later revelation. When the "rational" Confucius turned out to be something of a letdown, China was abandoned.

The end of the century saw both a revival of interest in the Muslim East and a new interest in India, usually shared by the same people. By 1775 Voltaire was convinced that Western astronomy and astrology had come from the country of the river Ganges. The astronomer Bailly, who was guillotined in the Terror for other reasons, maintained that the Brahmins, the Hindu priestly class, had been the tutors of the Greeks and therefore of Europe. But, though both men were convinced of the great antiquity of Indian culture, they did not have access to its equally ancient literature. The existence of the literary language Sanskrit had been known for many years, but it was difficult to find a Brahmin willing to teach a European this "holy language." Nevertheless, Europe was being prepared for an important revelation when the wonders of Sanskrit literature were finally exposed to view.

The revelation came from William Jones's translation in 1789 of the play *Sacontala* [*Sakuntala*], or *The Fatal Ring*, by the dramatist Kalidasa who had lived around A.D. 400. The play, which mixed the supernatural and the ordinary in a manner comparable with the idyllic comedies of Shakespeare, was originally translated into Latin, as Jones maintained that that language "bears so great a resemblance to Sanskrit, that it is more convenient than any modern language for a scrupulous interlineary version." He then translated out of Latin into English. It was from the latter version that translations into other European languages were made.

Despite Jones's pioneer work, Indian philosophy hardly penetrated the consciousness of English writers and thinkers. In Germany, however, the Romantics grasped at India and its philosophy. Their enthusiasm owed much to Johann Gottfried von Herder. Herder's reverence and adulation—

O Holy Land, I salute thee, thou source of all music
Thou voice of the heart

—helped create the Romantic image of India. Although his view was originally derived from travel books, his attention was later drawn to Jones's *Sacontala*. In his preface to the second German edition of this work, Herder warned his readers not to be disturbed by the marvelous elements, by gods walking the earth, or the personification of Nature. These were, he maintained, records of authentic experiences. Here on the Ganges, said Herder, on that river of Paradise, the Golden Age existed. Nothing could have been more appealing to the young Romantics. "It is to the East," wrote Friedrich Schlegel in 1800, "that we must look for the supreme Romanticism."

In the reaction of German writers to India there were two distinct strains. Schlegel represented a longing for harmony between the arts and sciences, for that unity of religion, philosophy and art that had been broken by the progress of Western civilization. Those who followed him thought they saw, in the inextricable mingling of the human and the divine, of all wisdom in the everyday which is the essence of Hinduism, the presence of the Golden Age. Through a synthesis of the cultures of East and West, it seemed that the profoundest revelation of the human spirit might be attained. To a politically divided Europe and a nationally divided Germany, the legendary Hindu world seemed to offer a concrete ideal—the integration of personal, social, and political life.

The Romantic image of India had a comparatively short life in German literature, but the vision of India, had, in fact, satisfied a particular longing in the minds of the German Romantics. They were searching for a means by which to shake themselves free from the cultural disintegration of Europe; basically, they were looking for that unity of art and religion which they believed had existed in the Middle Ages, for an identity of man with Nature. Their aim was even bolder—it was to discover the unity of all mankind. "Asia and Europe," Schlegel claimed, "together make up a single indivisible whole." The myth of India was thus part of a primal myth, saturated with lost innocence, enriched by the unselfconscious dialogue of God and man.

In France, by contrast, the first impact of India on literature and literary thought was almost entirely superficial—a touch of color, an exotic phrase, an occult thought, but very little more. This was so even though a growing number of French Oriental scholars were in close and personal contact with the poets and writers of their day. To the French, in fact, India was, and remained, only one of several sources of exoticism—fascinating, certainly, but no more so than the Muslim East or North Africa.

India was, however, to have rather more influence on American writers and poets. The Transcendentalist school of American literature, which included Ralph Waldo Emerson, Margaret Fuller, and Theodore Parker, and influenced such other writers as Hawthorne and Thoreau, was a reaction against puritan prejudices, materialistic philistinism, and utilitarianism. Its sources were a mixture of Plato and Swedenborg, German idealism, the Scots essayist Thomas Carlyle, English poets such as Coleridge and Wordsworth, and translations of Oriental literature. Emerson, the movement's principal figure, was well acquainted with Sanskrit texts, and his idea of an omnipresent deity and of the human personality as a passing phase of the universal Being is contained in what is almost a paraphrase of part of the Hindu epic, the *Bhagavad-gita*, his poem "Brahma."

> If the red slayer think he slays,
> Or if the slain think he is slain,
> They know not well the subtle ways
> I keep, and pass, and turn again.

The American Transcendentalists were, in effect, the true heirs of the early German Romantics. Unlike their French contemporaries, they were immensely serious and humorless in their search for universal truth. It was perhaps because of this, as well as for other reasons, that India and its philosophies scarcely ruffled the surface of American culture.

A new era in oriental scholarship began in London in 1874 with publication of the first volumes in the series *Sacred Books of the East*. The editor was a German, Friedrich Max Müller, who had settled in England and was mainly responsible for rehabilitating Indian ideas and creating the myth of "spiritual India" which still exercises its power today.

At the same time as the renewed interest in Hindu literature and philosophy, there emerged an interest in Pali, the language of the Buddhist scriptures. It was a British civil servant in Ceylon, George Turnour, who was responsible for the first important Pali text in 1836, but it was French Orientalists who produced the first works on the philosophy of Buddhism. Yet the most active interest in Buddhism was displayed by Christian missionaries, on the sound principle that it was good battle tactics to know one's enemy. The missionaries decided that, as they had been told in Ceylon that Buddha was not a god, Buddhism was an atheistic creed. Western rationalists were delighted.

In the climate of questioning that suffused the nineteenth century, men subjected their traditional beliefs to a variety of tests. One was to ask about the nature and very existence of God himself. Was God a myth, a disposable empty? Was the universe a machine, and God the great mechanic? Above all, in a world of expanding technology, what possible relevance could the ideas of a Galilean carpenter's son have for the men of the modern age?

The first offensive against Christianity was aimed at disproving its uniqueness. Buddhist scholarship helped considerably. In 1877, T. W. Rhys Davids, probably the most influential Pali scholar of modern times, published his *Buddhism*, stressing the rational elements.

But the secularists and the free thinkers were in a minority. The greatest demand in the materialist West was not for more materialism, but for spiritual solace. And the West was prepared to pay for it. As Swami Vivekananda, one of the most articulate of the early propagandists for Indian spirituality, put it on a visit to the United States in 1892: "As our country is poor in social virtue, so this country is lacking in spirituality. I give them spirituality, and they give me money." [5] The same might have been said of Helena Petrovna Blavatsky—but she gave them magic as well.

The Teacup Creed

Once upon a time some people in India made a new Heaven and a new Earth out of broken tea-cups, a missing brooch or two, and a hairbrush. These were hidden under bushes, or stuffed into holes in the hillside, and an entire Civil Service of subordinate gods used to find or mend them again; and everyone said: "There are more things in Heaven and Earth than are dreamt of in your philosophy." Several other things happened also, but the Religion never seemed to get much beyond its first manifestations; though it added an airline postal service, and orchestral effects, in order to keep abreast of the times and choke off competition.[6]

Rudyard Kipling being funny, and not altogether fair, about what he called the "teacup creed" and others called the Theosophical Society.

The society had been founded in the United States in 1875 by a gentle American lawyer, Henry Steel Olcott, who was also an honorary colonel, and Helena Petrovna Blavatsky, daughter of a real colonel in the Russian army. As Helena von Hahn, she had been born in Ekaterinoslav in the Ukraine in 1831, but from this point her biographies diverge, though most agree that at the age of eighteen she married Nikifor Blavatsky, vice-governor of the province of Erivan, whom she left soon after, returning to her grandfather's house. He sent her back to her father, but she never arrived. At the port of Poti on the Black Sea she made the acquaintance of an English sea captain and was taken by him to Constantinople, where she joined a circus in a riding act. Picked up by a Hungarian opera singer, she disappeared only to resurface in Paris as an assistant to Daniel Dunglas Home. Later, she managed an artificial flower factory in Tiflis, occasionally visiting home, and looking fatter each time—by middle age she weighed 232 pounds—but still, if rather strange, sweetly feminine.

According to her own account, HPB, as she came to be called, traveled widely in Mexico and Texas, India and Tibet, as well as Europe and Russia, where she is said to have achieved some reputation as a medium. In 1873 she went to the United States and found the psychic climate ready for her peculiar talents. During a séance at a farm near Chittenden, Vermont, she met Colonel Olcott.

Olcott was immediately attracted by HPB's occult powers, and the two set up house together in New York. There was no question of a sexual relationship. HPB seems to have done herself an irreparable injury during her circus days which made intercourse not only inadvisable but painful; besides, she

163

thought sexual love "a beastly appetite that should be starved into submission." This did not prevent her from marrying several times, though her first husband was still alive.

In the New York apartment the Theosophical Society was born. At the beginning, the society had no precise doctrine and was mainly a gathering point for various people interested in various strands of the occult. In the main, the society was to be a vehicle for the often-changing ideas of Helena Petrovna Blavatsky. While living in the New York apartment, HPB produced a voluminous and incoherent work, *Isis Unveiled*— thirteen hundred pages of occult compilation, tall stories, and archaeology. But on almost every page there were hints of hidden knowledge. The book was a great success, its comprehensiveness and obscurity providing a mine for interpreters then and now. At that time, HPB tended to emphasize Egypt as the source of secret wisdom. Why, she asked, could not the modern world, with all its scientific wonders, "give us the unfading colors of Luxor—the Tyrian purple, the bright vermilion and dazzling blue which decorate the walls of this place and are as bright as on the first day of their application? The indestructible cement of the pyramids and of ancient aqueducts . . ." As for those who, "infected by the mortal epidemic of our century—hopeless materialism—will remain in doubt and mortal agony as to whether, when man dies, he will live again," there was the message that the problem had been solved long ago. "The answers are these. They may be found on the time-worn granite of pages of cave-temples, on sphinxes, propylons and obelisks," but, she added, no one "except the initiates" was able to understand "the mystic writing."

Egypt was soon to give place to India or, rather, Tibet, after Olcott and HPB arrived on the subcontinent. Olcott, who seems to have abandoned his wife and three children, arrived in India with HPB in 1878 after a brief visit to London en route. They settled at Adhyar near Madras, and there set up the international headquarters of the new society. In the warm climate of India, HPB's occult powers blossomed ever brighter, though on a more everyday level she found some things, including child marriage, objectionable—and said so, loudly. She soon attracted a following among the expatriate British, bored perhaps with the effort of sustaining the empire and anxious to be entertained. HPB was ready to oblige.

She visited Simla, the summer capital of the government of India, notorious (among the envious) as the "Capua of India," where picnics and adultery whiled away the time for refugees from the harsh imperial duty of the plains below. Simla stood on a ridge in the lower Himalayas on the road to Tibet, where Madame Blavatsky now placed the *mahatmas*, the occult masters behind the Theosophical Society. For some reason, very strong efforts were made to attract followers in Simla, especially among high government officials. It was rumored that HPB was a Russian agent and that she had been kept under constant surveillance ever since her arrival in India, but her host in Simla was indifferent to such slanders.

Allan Octavian Hume was not a transient visitor to Simla but a permanent resident. He had retired from government service after a distinguished, if unspectacular career, and built himself a luxurious house called Rothney Castle. One of his first interests had been bird collecting, and his collection ended up in the Natural History Museum in London. After birds came theosophy, and HPB was a welcome and frequent guest at Rothney Castle. There she would receive regular communications from her spirit guide, Kut Humi, in the form of letters written on palm leaves. One such letter, which floated down from the ceiling at nine o'clock on a July evening in 1879, was handed by HPB herself to a skeptic.

I read it. Addressed to Madame, the purport of it was that she need not trouble herself with attempts to make proselytes of the incredulous. Enough that those who believed and practised should gain the higher plains of knowledge and power. What mattered it to them that the rest of human kind wallowed in ignorance. The adepts could smile at them in contempt from their superior height! The text of the letter might indeed have been that to preach to the ignorant would be to "cast pearls before swine." Reading through the letter it struck me that Kut Humi must have had considerable intercourse with America, as more than one of the phrases appeared to savour of the Yankee dialect.

HPB could produce more than palm-leaf airmail. At the dinner table, with a carefully selected body of believers and potential believers, she could be prevailed upon to give an example of the power "which the true Theosophist acquires by ascerticism, faith and self denial." First she would protest, like a young lady asked for a song: "It is very trying to me; it exhausts much; no, no, I cannot, I cannot"; but further pressed, at last exclaimed,

> Well, then, I must, but it is hard, it is hard! Mrs Hume! (turning to her hostess) what is there that you would like? You shall say. Have you lost anything that you would find?
> *Mrs Hume*—Yes. A year or more ago I lost a brooch. Find that and it will be indeed wonderful.
> *Madame*—It is hard but IT SHALL BE DONE! Khitmatgar [butler]! Bring me one lantern! The lantern brought, Madame rose, led the way through the opened doors leading to the garden; there halting, she pointed to a bush and commanded, Dig there!! A spade produced, earth was removed, and lo! there was the brooch. The guests wonderstruck and, some of them at least, convinced, returned to the table where a succinct account of the miracle was drawn up and signed by all present.

On another occasion, HPB, finding that there were not enough cups at a picnic, discovered by her incredible powers of divination that another cup of exactly the right design had been buried under a bush.

166

These activities caused a considerable stir in certain sections of Simla society, a stir which even survived a number of exposures of Madame's conjuring tricks. Mr. Hume himself had the best of both worlds. He described her as the most marvelous liar he had ever met, but excused her on the grounds that her lies and her tricks were designed with the honest object of converting people to "a higher faith." [7]

Everything HPB did, of course, however trivial, she claimed was really the work of the *mahatmas*, particularly the Masters Morya and Kut Humi, who had taken the society under their occult protection and had been the teachers of HPB during her stay at some notably imprecise location in Tibet. At Adhyar, the masters on one occasion caused to materialize a view of the secret valley in which they lived. In the center of the valley was a lake in which stood the Master Djwal Kul; only his back was visible as he thought "his Mongolian features not worth recording." To the left of the picture, and less reticent, was the Master Morya, on horseback. Unseen in the picture, but described by HPB, were the vast underground halls that stretched for miles and contained a museum—under the curatorship of Kut Humi—in which there were models of every important or significant work of art or architecture produced by man. The museum seems to have been a kind of economy version of the memory banks of the ideal cities of Campanella and Andreae. There were also books containing all knowledge, which HPB read with her occult eye. These included the oldest book in the world—*The Book of Dyzan*—from which HPB later claimed to have extracted the true story of the Creation, revealing it in her own work, *The Secret Doctrine*, which was published in 1888.

The *mahatmas*—one of them was later said to be the Comte de St. Germain—were actually present on earth and could therefore be seen. One obsessed Indian follower actually trailed HPB when she said she was on her way to visit the secret valley, in the hope of seeing them for himself. HPB contrived to give him the slip, but he was not to be put off. Armed only with an umbrella and a fixed determination to find the *mahatmas* or die, he pressed on and arrived in the little hill state of Sikkim. Assured that he would have no difficulty crossing the Tibetan frontier in the guise of a pilgrim, he was making his way along the road when he saw a solitary horseman galloping toward him. At first, he thought it was some soldier of the raja, who would ask for his pass and on finding that he did not have one would probably arrest and deport him. But no! "As he approached me, he reined up. I looked up and recognised him instantly. . . . I was in the awful presence of him, of the same *mahatma*, my own, revered *guru* whom I had seen before in his astral body on the balcony of the Theosophical headquarters. I knew not what to say: joy and reverence tied my tongue." [8] This story was well received by theosophists.

Europe received advance warning of HPB's revelations in a more popular style than that of the great woman herself, through two works of A. P. Sinnett, editor of one of the most influential English-language papers in India, *The Pioneer* of Allahabad. That newspapers's proprietors also owned the Lahore-based *Civil and Military Gazette*, which had on its staff a young writer named Rudyard Kipling. Sinnett's *The Occult World*, published in 1881, and *Esoteric Buddhism*, which came out two years later, contained descriptions of HPB's marvelous activities in India and short versions of her doctrine. So much interest was aroused by these publications that Olcott and HPB decided to return to Europe and capitalize on it. But when they left India in 1884, a time bomb was ticking away, waiting to explode.

While the two leaders were enjoying great success in Europe and laying the foundations of a very large movement, a certain Madame Coulomb triggered a sensation. Madame Coulomb seems to have been an associate of HPB during a period she had spent, probably as a medium, in Cairo, before going to the United States. She had been born Emma Cutting, and she and her husband were employed at Adhyar, a generous response by HPB to an appeal for help from her former associate. After her benefactress's departure, Madame Coulomb, a rather sour woman whose heroine worship of HPB had for some reason turned to hatred, passed on a number of letters to the editor of the *Madras Christian College Herald*.

The editor of the *Herald*, a good missionary already worried by the success the Theosophical Society was having among Indian Christian converts, and seeing the *mahatmas*, no doubt, as heads of a conspiracy as wicked as the one discovered by the Abbé Barruel at the time of the French Revolution, was delighted. All could now be revealed, and the Antichrist destroyed. According to the letters allegedly written by HPB, most of the marvels which had so captivated everyone were blatant frauds. Madame Coulomb even admitted helping in the trickery. The occult airmail from the *mahatmas* had not been delivered by the astral post office but by Madame Coulomb through cracks in the ceiling. Furthermore, HPB walked around on moonlit nights with a model of Kut Humi on her shoulder to give the impression of walking with the *mahatma*.

The fallout of these revelations reached London through a correspondent of the *Times*, and caused a scandal. It also inspired the Society for Psychical Research to send out an investigator to India. This society had been founded in 1882 to examine "that large group of debatable phenomena designated by such terms as mesmeric, psychical and spiritualistic." Through its members, some academics, some scientists, even some politicians, it combined questionable scientific methods with the hope of scientific proof for occult phenomena. Among its leading men was William Crookes, scientific guarantor of Daniel Dunglas Home. All the members were in fact very much men of their time; they pretended to stand aside from the irrational when they were actually immersed in it.

The investigator, an Australian, Richard Hodgson, reached India before HPB. On evidence obtained in London, the society had seemed broadly favorable toward the Blavatsky phenomena, but Hodgson changed all that. There were further leaks from Madame Coulomb, and he was also shown a cedarwood cabinet in which communications from the *mahat-*

mas miraculously appeared. The believer who was displaying it slapped the cabinet to prove its solidity, and a secret door fell open!

HPB tried a counterattack. The revelations of trickery had been faked up by the missionaries, with the aid of a disgruntled Madame Coulomb. She even threatened a lawsuit but was advised that a magician would find little protection in the courts. HPB thought it wise to retire to Europe, where the scandal did theosophy no harm. In fact, the publicity only attracted more and more believers.

But the founder was dying, and she decided there must be another book explaining her gospel. This was *The Secret Doctrine*, a vast work two hundred pages longer than *Isis Unveiled* and containing the threat of a further two volumes which would come from the grave after her death. *The Secret Doctrine* was written with the aid of three assistants and a good deal of material cribbed, without acknowledgment, from other writers' works.

The ideas contained in the jumble of misunderstood Hinduism, Buddhism, and the occult traditions of East and West, were immensely appealing. *The Secret Doctrine* was yet another attempt to answer the nineteenth-century demand for a reconciliation of science and religion. Against Darwin's theory of evolution it placed spiritual evolution. If God had not created man in his own image, as Darwin insisted, then according to Madame Blavatsky man's task was to use the evolutionary process itself to attain that end. Personal evolution was controlled by the laws of reincarnation and *karma*, the Hindu doctrine that what is done in one life dictates the pattern of the next. This applied not only to individuals but to species and races.

There had been four races of man on earth before the present one. The first had lived on a continent called "The Imperishable Sacred Land." The second had occupied a territory at the North Pole. The homes of the third and fourth races had been Atlantis and Lemuria, and the fifth had originated in America. There were still remnants of the first four races around but they were rapidly dying out, "due to an extraordinary sterility setting in among the women from the time that they were first approached by Europeans."

HPB's evolutionary theory offered a more noble purpose to man than simply being at the end of the Darwinian cycle. He was on his way, as he had always wanted to be, to higher and greater things. Evolution continued until, perhaps after thousands of rebirths, a man or woman achieved *earthly* perfection. The highest of earthly creatures were, of course, the mysterious brotherhood of the *mahatmas*, who might voluntarily delay their further progress in order to help others. It was HPB's own, personal version of the Buddhist doctrine of the *bodhisattva*, the "Being of Wisdom" who, after "attaining the highest and final state of things, desires, heedless of his own efforts and toil, to teach his fellow men how to achieve tranquillity." [9] But HPB's version seemed startlingly new. Others were to take up the view of Spiritual Evolution, including Teilhard de Chardin, but HPB was there first and the climate was much more receptive. She appealed, as mesmerism, phrenology, spiritualism, and other occult movements had appealed, to the desire not only for assurance in a world of change but for confirmation that change could be good for man. Theosophy was firmly on the side of social reform, the "universal Brotherhood of Humanity."

Helena Petrovna Blavatsky died in 1891.

Now nothing would be nicer, nor more full of harmony
Than the first few months that followed the decease of HPB,
Till Judge of Calaveras produced a curious set
Of missives in red pencil what he said came from Tibet.

From these he reconstructed a Mahatma (very rare)
A nest of that peculiar kind pertaining to a mare
But Mrs Besant * found a rival message on the shelf
And said she fancied Mr Judge had written it himself.

* Madame Blavatsky's successor.

For in less time than I write it all the meeting got upset
With precipitating missives which did NOT come from Tibet,
And the things they called each other in their anger were a sin—
Till the public got disgusted and the temple roof caved in.

So Edmund Garrett, in *Isis Very Much Unveiled*, described the quarrels that divided the society after the death of its founder. Olcott was still alive, but living in Ceylon. William Quan Judge, who had been one of the original founders, had remained behind in America and probably felt that it was now time to assert his claim to leadership. He did so by producing confirmatory letters from the *mahatmas*. These were disputed, and in the end Judge led the American theosophists in a breakaway from the leadership of Olcott and Mrs. Besant, setting up their headquarters finally at Point Loma in California.

Mrs. Annie Besant had once been married to a clergyman of the Church of England, but the marriage had failed with her faith. In 1877, at the age of thirty, she had published *The Gospel of Atheism* and was unsuccessfully prosecuted for selling obscene literature—a tract advocating birth control. She was active in feminist causes and in 1888 became a member of the executive committee of the socialist Fabian Society. In the same year, she read *The Secret Doctrine*, met its author, and succumbed—rumor had it, on the rebound after being discarded by George Bernard Shaw, whose mistress she had been.

Olcott died in 1907, in the presence—it was said—of the *mahatmas*, leaving in undisputed control Mrs. Besant and a homosexual clairvoyant, C. A. Leadbeater. Under their rule, the society changed. Leadbeater, a former Christian minister, had been forced to leave the society in 1906, following allegations of misconduct with boys at the society's headquarters, but he was brought back by Mrs. Besant after Olcott died. Between them, they demoted the *mahatmas* and elevated themselves. They also discovered a new "world teacher," a Messiah in the form of a young boy named Jiddu Krishnamurti. He was, however, a reluctant messiah, and in 1929 broke up the organization founded to promote him.

Mrs. Besant may not have discovered the messiah, but she and the Theosophical Society did contribute to the creation of modern India. Cultural self-confidence is the first step to national self-assertion. The general contempt in which India's civilization had been held had been a valuable imperial weapon. But at the end of the nineteenth century, Indians had begun to rediscover—ironically, through the work of Western scholars—something of the wonders of their cultural heritage. The Theosophical Society's uncritical praise of Hinduism and Buddhism had helped in the rehabilitation, and the society had attracted the membership of many educated Indians. When the man who was to be independent Indian's first prime minister, Jawaharlal Nehru, was ten years old, Mrs. Besant suggested an English tutor to his father. The tutor, F. T. Brooks, was an ardent theosophist, and three years later Jawaharlal himself became a member of the society. He was initiated by no less a person than Mrs. Besant herself. After the departure of Brooks, Nehru forgot his occult interests, though not his association with Mrs. Besant, which was to be revived during the First World War.

Mrs. Besant entered Indian political life as a reformer, but a conservative one. She wanted to bring India and Britain together in a new understanding, as theosophy had brought India and the West. The outbreak of war in 1914 found Indian nationalism, after an upsurge of violence in the years following 1905, curiously quiescent. By 1916, in an endeavor to break this immobility, Mrs. Besant founded the India Home Rule League. She was opposed to violence, even to passive resistance, but not to agitation. She had in mind the classic British campaigns for reform, for the abolition of slavery, for the repeal of the Corn Laws, and for Irish Home Rule. Monster public meetings, newspaper articles, and pamphlets would, she believed, produce widespread support, and such agitation would compel the British to grant self-government. "British politicians," she maintained, "judge the value of claims by the energy of those who put them forward." Only in the dull climate of political thought in India in the middle of a war would such a statement have been considered revolutionary.

Yet it was. Mrs. Besant used the branches of the Theosophical Society to establish the initial cadres of the Home Rule League. Jawaharlal Nehru was attracted and formed a branch of the League in his home town of Allahabad six days after the authorities in Madras had arrested Mrs. Besant. In December 1917, the Indian National Congress—the main political movement, whose founder had been HPB's friend Allan Octavian Hume—elected Mrs. Besant president. Her views turned out to be too moderate and cautious, and she was not re-elected in the following year, but she had succeeded in changing the whole character of Congress. The moderate members began to leave, taking their ideas of slow constitutional reform with them. By 1919 the overwhelming majority of Congress members were young men and extremists, who found British concessions inadequate. Even those concessions owed much to the success of Mrs. Besant and the Home Rule League.

Mrs. Besant's legacy to the new Congress which discarded her was a countrywide organization and an agitational style. And it was a real *mahatma*, Mohandas Karamchand Gandhi, who appeared on the scene to lead it.

Four

MAGICIANS
AND MACHINE GUNS

Tibetan "protector" Za

1

The Revolt
of the Bird King

The Bird King, seated on his Lion Throne wearing the Five
Royal Accoutrements, in the presence of his five queens and
four ministers, watched his magical army march out against the
dragon. The preparations had taken many months. In jungle
villages there had been secret meetings. Mediums had gathered
and been possessed by spirits, and when the spirits spoke they
had all promised victory. The alchemists had produced the
elixir of invulnerability and the soldiers of the Bird King were
well protected. Magic diagrams had been prepared, with
symbols that would capture and control the elements or distort
the astrological field of the enemy, so bringing him to ruin. The
diagrams were tattooed on the skin, the elixir injected or drunk.
Magic gongs which, when struck, would cause the enemy to
wither away as his substance disintegrated, had been issued.
The gods of tree and hill and stream, the guardian ghosts of the
gateways of walled towns had been drawn into a magical
alliance, as they had been when the vast armies of Kublai Khan
had threatened the country seven centuries before. Then, the
spirit army had been defeated, but no one remembered the fact,
and again the spirits had been summoned with music and
dancing, with offerings of fruit and flowers, the singing of
incantations. Given such allies, even poor cultivators armed
only with swords and homemade shotguns were bound to win,

however well armed the dragon was. The astrologers had given their verdict. The time had come.

The year was 1930, and the dragon was the British, who then ruled Burma. Out of the jungle emerged the army of the Bird King. The magicians chanted their spells, the magical banners were held high, but the dragon did not die nor his soldiers wither. The Bird King's magical army disintegrated into small groups. Villagers were murdered. Looting and robbery engulfed the land. It took twelve months to suppress the rebellion. Two thousand men of the magic army were killed and the Bird King himself—a common criminal, said the British, named Saya San—was hanged in Tharrawaddy jail.

A magical rebellion, and not an anthropologist in sight to record it! Pitted against the guns of the alien conquerors was all the high technology of Asian magic. But the ghosts and spirits returned to their secret places, the magical banners were covered with mud, the mystic diagrams with some other tattoo, the incantations blown away in the gale of the world. Not, however, the ideas that had prompted the rebellion. The Burmese peasantry who had followed the Bird King or waited for his success wanted the complete restoration of Burmese sovereignty. When Burma finally got rid of the British nearly twenty years later, the men of the middle class who were their heirs could not persuade the people to accept even the slight diminution of independence involved in remaining a member of the Commonwealth. In that sense, traditional magic won.

The impact of the white man on non-white cultures in the late eighteenth and nineteenth centuries was similar to the impact of the Industrial Revolution on the white man's own culture, environment, and society. It threatened historical continuity, forcing the individual and the institutions that had sustained him and his ancestors into psychic and physical uncertainty. With the white man came economic and ecological pressures, exerted by an apparently superior magic.

The sources of that magic were difficult to establish. The white American, pressing across the Plains, brought Christianity and guns, the disappearance of the buffalo and the disintegration of the Sioux. Which was more important to acquire—Christianity, guns, or agriculture? The same problem faced the peoples of inner Asia as the Russians expanded their rule, and those of Africa, India, Burma, New Zealand, and many other places when the British brought their religion, their economics, their gunboats, and the whole package of what they so earnestly believed was a better way of life.

In the age of white expansion, the status of the magician and of the occult forces he claimed to manipulate depended on just what kind of war was being fought. When an overwhelmingly alien group was actually in control, a colonial regime apparently firmly established with all its strange technology of weapons and laws, the expectation of supernatural intervention by rebels was higher than in the case of a people experiencing defeats but not yet defeated. In a rebellion the magician was usually the leader, and his magical technology the main material of war. In a war against intruders the magician's major role was to supply prophecies of success, a magical infrastructure for military enterprise, and psychic support for the traditional leadership. Such a magico-military alliance is still sanctified, or at least accepted in the West when the name of God is invoked at the launching of warships and troops are blessed before battle by the ministers of that same God.

In the middle of the eighteenth century, the Indians of the eastern woodlands of North America found themselves caught between the rival imperialisms of Britain and France. The British, though they made no slaves, took the land, built cabins, cut down the forests, planted grain, and steadily expanded into the old hunting territories. The French sought to assure the Indians that they did not covet their land, and married into their tribes; with their quest for furs, their trading of a few trinkets for pelts, they did not disrupt old tribal ways as effectively as did the British settlements. In the 1750s, some thirty-three tribes declared on the wampum belt that the French were their brothers.

But the British pressed more heavily, forcing the Shawnees and the Delawares from Pennsylvania in 1759. Among the latter a prophet-magician appeared. At Tuscarawas on the Muskingum, the Delaware prophet made his revelation in 1762. Anxious to meet the "Master of Life," he had taken his kettle and his gun and traveled the land. One night he made camp near a stream, close to which there were three paths. He saw one of the paths grow brighter as darkness fell, but although he was frightened he did not move on. The next day he chose the widest of the three paths, but found his way barred by a great wall of flames. Retreating, he tried the next widest path, but there the wall of flames was even higher. On the third, narrowest, and straightest path there was no obstacle until he came to a vast and dazzling mountain whose sides were so steep that he could find no way up.

He was in despair, but then he saw a beautiful woman dressed in white. She told him to strip, bathe in the nearby river, and climb the glass-smooth sides of the mountain using only his left hand and his left foot. He reached the top of the mountain and there saw three villages. He was ashamed of his nakedness, but a voice told him to go on without fear or shame as he had washed in the river. At last, he met a young man who took him to the Master of Life.

The Delaware prophet was now shown many wonders, and given instructions from the Master to relay to his people. The animals had left the woods, said the Master of Life, because the Indians had used evil-smelling gunpowder instead of the bow and arrow, but if all would unite and drive back the white man the game animals would reappear. The Master gave the Delaware prophet a stick, on which were engraved secret signs containing his instructions. These, said the prophet when he returned to his people, were that they should drink water only once a day and never more than twice; give up the old custom of many wives and have only one; that Indian should not fight Indian, or sing the old medicine songs, as they were addressed to an evil spirit; that they should not buy or sell food but share what they had; that they should give up firearms and unite to drive out the white man.

The message of the Delaware prophet was a mixture of Christianity and Indian myth. He had a "book of learning," a kind of map on which he would demonstrate the position of the white man; he prohibited all magic except his own; even the Master of Life himself was a Christ figure.

The prophet prophesied a war, but it is not clear whether he claimed that the white man would be eliminated solely by magic or by a combination of supernatural aid and warfare. When his message was used by Pontiac, chief of the Ottawa, however, at a great council near Detroit in 1763, the supernatural was presented as an ally, though Pontiac defined the "white man" as the British alone. The confederacy of tribes that came into being after the council attacked along some five hundred miles of frontier, taking nine frontier posts and besieging Fort Detroit for fifty days. The romantic version of the "Conspiracy of Pontiac" can be found in the famous work by Francis Parkman—the warning of the Indian girl, the ball play on King George's birthday, and the massacre that followed, the sieges, and the bloody battles. The conspiracy failed, not because the magic infrastructure was inadequate but because Pontiac could not keep the tribes together, especially once the hunting season began.

The magico-military alliance appeared again at the beginning of the nineteenth century among the Shawnee. The Delaware prophet had his successor in Laulewasikaw. In 1805, after a life of stupidity and drunkenness, Laulewasikaw fell back one day, apparently dead. His friends gathered for the funeral, but he rose—from what may have been an alcoholic stupor—to announce that he had visited the Master of Life and received a new revelation. The young were now to aid the old and handicapped; there must be no further intermarriage with whites; flint and steel must be abandoned; and the white man's firewater treated as a poison. As a proof of his vision, Laulewasikaw had received the power to cure all sicknesses and mastery over death at any time or place including, specifically, the field of battle.

Laulewasikaw's claims produced a sensation and the burning of alleged witches and medicine men, but this stopped when one young man refused to allow his sister to be burned, saying: "The devil has come among us, and we are killing each other." Though this restricted the prophet's area of action, it did not prevent him from changing his name to Tenskwatawa, "Open Door," to symbolize his power over death. Doubt was silenced in 1806 when, learning somehow of the coming of a solar eclipse, Open Door announced that he would produce one by his magic power.

As his reputation spread, Open Door's predictions varied. In the form in which they reached the Cherokee, about 1812, they forecast the coming of a wind with giant hailstones that would kill everyone, whites and unbelievers alike. The only escape was to flee to the Great Smoky Mountains. Many Cherokees in Alabama and Georgia abandoned all their possessions and made their way to North Carolina, where most of their descendants still live today, having escaped, by this flight, the army's forcible removal of the Cherokee nation to territory west of the Mississippi in 1838-39.

Other statements by Open Door were widely accepted. The prophet had said that he had called all game animals away from the forests, and that they would not return until the Indians had given up their evil ways, particularly those they had copied from the white man. But, if the Indians reformed, Open Door would produce a two-day darkness during which he would free all the animals and restore all dead Indians to life. The effect of Open Door's prophecies on the local economy of the tribes was in some cases—as with the Cherokee—disastrous, but the disasters would have been confined to the Indian communities if the prophet had not had a brother who hated the white man. This was Tecumseh. His father had been killed in a battle with the Virginians in 1774, an elder brother in an attack on a frontier post, and another in 1794.

Tecumseh, though primarily a warrior, was not above displaying magical powers. Once, on a visit to the Creek tribe's town of Tuckhabatchee, where he found he was receiving little support, he said that he would leave for Detroit and when he arrived there would stamp his foot and bring down every house in the Creek town. On the morning when Tecumseh was expected to arrive in Detroit, the inhabitants of Tuckhabatchee were horrified by a great rumbling noise followed by an earthquake in which all the houses collapsed.

Tecumseh, while ordering his brother Open Door to avoid any breach of the peace with Governor Harrison of Ohio until he gave the word, spent his time making alliances. Open Door's promise to restore dead ancestors and his talk of the coming cataclysm in which the white man would be destroyed were beginning to take effect, and Tecumseh's success in forming a confederacy soon caused alarm among the white settlers. Governor Harrison believed, or pretended to believe, that the British in Canada were behind it all, and in October 1811 he precipitated open conflict by moving an infantry regiment to protect the town of Vincennes.

Tecumseh was not there at the time, and Open Door wrecked his brother's plans by taking premature action. The prophet was no soldier, and he offered his men supernatural protection without military expertise. He promised that the whites' bullets would drop harmlessly at Indian feet. But they did not, and the Indians were routed. Open Door later led a band of warriors west of the Mississippi, where he lived on a pension from the British from 1813 until his death twenty years later. Tecumseh commanded a group of Indians during the war of 1812—with the rank of brigadier-general in the British army—but was killed by American cavalry in 1813 during the battle of the Thames.

As white Americans pressed further and further west, encroaching more and more on the lands of the Indians, wars took place and prophets appeared, but most played little or no magical role although there was a continuing theme of invulnerability to bullets. But in 1870 a Paiute from Walker Valley, Nevada, whose name was Tavibo, "White Man," had a series of visions in which the Great Spirit told him that the whites would be swallowed up in an earthquake, though all their possessions would be left behind. When this was laughed at, White Man had another vision in which everyone, Indians and whites alike, would be swallowed up, though the Indians would return in three days. When this was also disbelieved, White Man revealed that the Great Spirit was so angry that only believers would be saved.

The news spread, and so did the first ghost dance, through which the dead ancestors were to be brought back to life. Various local prophets rose up with claims to invulnerability, but it was another Paiute, Wovoka, the alleged son of White Man, who was to produce, in the second, or Great Ghost Dance of 1890, the crashing climax to the collapse of American Indian culture.

Wovoka worked as a ranch hand for David Wilson in Mason Valley, Nevada. Wilson was a very religious man, and it is likely that he passed some of his Christianity on to his ranch hand. He also gave Wovoka the name by which he is best known, Jack Wilson. In the winter of 1888-89, Wovoka became ill with fever and during a solar eclipse in 1889—which caused considerable alarm among the Paiutes—claimed to have visited God. In the spirit world he saw all the people who had died long ago, happy and forever young in a land full of game animals. God told him to tell his people what he had seen, and to instruct them to love one another and give up war. He also taught Wovoka a dance through which reunion with the dead could be hastened. Further, he gave Wovoka five spells through which he could control the weather, there being one each for snow, mists, light showers, storms, and fine weather.

Wovoka's teaching and the ghost dance were swiftly taken up by Indians, though different tribes reacted in differing ways. Local prophets added their own interpretations. The Arapaho, for example, stopped shooting horses and slashing their arms in mourning. Believing the new world would follow a great flood, they made for the high mountains. The Shoshone, on the other hand, expected only a four-day sleep, after which they would wake up in a land renewed. Some Arapaho expected a great wall of flame which would drive back the whites, while sacred feathers would lift the Indians above the flame. Then a twelve-day rain would come and put out the fire, revealing the promised land. However, most tribes believed that the whites would be eliminated by magical means alone, and were later to blame the Sioux for attempting to bring about the new world by mixing the military with the magical.

In 1890 the Sioux were settled on several reservations in Dakota. A few years before they had been free, and as a free nation had inflicted a defeat on the white force commanded by Colonel Custer at the Battle of the Little Big Horn in 1876. By that time the great buffalo herds had gone, destroyed by the builders of the transcontinental railroads. Gold had been found in the Black Hills. This had attracted lawless white desperadoes, and in trying to defend their lands from them the Sioux had defeated Custer—but lost their lands just the same. In 1882 a white corridor was driven through their remaining territory. In 1889 they gave up eleven million acres for a promise of government payment, but it was slow in coming. So too were seed and rations that had been promised again and again, and in 1889 such crops as there were failed. Sick, hungry, bullied by Congress and incompetent agents, the ruin of the Sioux seemed complete.

But the Sioux had learned about the new magician in the west in 1889 and sent a delegation to visit Wovoka. Live in peace with the white man, was the magician's message, and wait, for the whites would be buried under a new land which would descend upon the old, and the red man would rule. The members of the Sioux delegation believed they had seen their own dead ancestors. They heard of a shirt through which no bullets could pass, and they also learned the ghost dance, that powerful magic that would raise the dead. Wild rumors were soon flying through the white population that lived near the Sioux reservations. Sitting Bull, who had returned from Canada where he had gone to escape the American army after the defeat of Custer, was living quietly at the reservation of Standing Rock. His name alone was enough to inspire unease among the settlers of Dakota; coupled with the ghost dance and rumors that the Sioux were preparing for war, it produced fear. And in no one more than in a certain inexperienced agent, a political appointee, at Pine Ridge reservation. He called for troops.

When the troops arrived, it was the turn of the Sioux to be frightened. Toward the end of 1890, a body of them left the reservation for the Badlands. Sitting Bull remained behind, and so did the ghost dance. When Buffalo Bill Cody was brought in to persuade Sitting Bull to surrender peaceably, the army countermanded the plan, and the agent at the reservation—who hated Sitting Bull—sent in Indian police to arrest the chief. Six policemen were killed in the struggle, and Sitting Bull was among the Sioux dead. But the final tragedy was not yet. On December 29, 1890, as a small band of starving Indians was moving toward the Pine Ridge agency, they were intercepted by a force of soldiers who demanded their weapons. While the soldiers were attempting to disarm the Sioux, a medicine man, Yellow Bird, protested that they were handling a woman much too familiarly and reminded the Sioux that they were wearing their ghost shirts, painted with the sun, moon, and stars, which made them safe from bullets. The question of who started the firing is still being disputed, but there is little doubt that the troops suddenly panicked and opened up with their Hotchkiss machine guns, killing many Indians as well as two of their own comrades.

The Battle of Wounded Knee was a massacre. Fleeing women, pregnant or with children in their arms, were shot down. Only a few of the band escaped, and they froze to death.

Indians were sure that Wounded Knee was a revenge for the Little Big Horn. The magician, Wovoka, was bitter, and those who believed in the prophecy of a purely magical offensive against the whites were convinced that it had been aborted by the Sioux. The ghost dance was performed for some years after Wounded Knee, but the dead did not return nor did the new land promised by the prophets appear.

On the other side of the world, in July 1904, Chot Chelpan, an Altai Turk of middle Siberia, had a vision. A man dressed in white and riding on a white horse spoke to him in a language he could not understand. But two other riders who were accompanying the man in white told him that the spirit had said: "I was and will be forever and forever. I am the chief of the Oirots, which I proclaim to you, as the time is near. You, Chot, are an evil man but your daughter is innocent. Through her I shall reveal to the men of the Altai my commandments." Chot's adopted daughter, Chugul, was visited by two young women as she shepherded the flocks, who told her that she must make her family leave her alone that night, when they would visit her again. When the time came, two women appeared out of rainbows and told Chugul to pray to the household idols; this she could not do, for it was not permitted to the women of the Altai. The two visions then made the idols topple into the fire.

Chot Chelpan's neighbors thought his daughter mad when they heard her story but, with a sudden clap of thunder, the magic visitors reappeared, promising punishment to any who would not believe and prophesying the return of the chief of the Oirots, whom Chot Chelpan had seen on his white horse.

Chot now began to go about among the Altai peoples preaching political unity and the revelation of a new god called Burkhan. The Altai had suffered from land seizures, and Burkhan would help them to recover what had been lost. Through Chot, Burkhan demanded that the Altai kill cats, stop smoking, and stop swallowing the blood of animals. Every night and morning, milk was to be sprinkled toward the four points of the compass and to the sky. The shamans' sacred

187

drums were to be burned, for their magic was evil. The Altai were not to eat with Christians, or with Altai who had been converted. No Russian was to be their friend, for "soon their end will come, the land will not accept them, the earth will open up and they will be cast under the earth." All available money was to be spent on guns and ammunition.

Burkhan would give the Altai protection against the Russians. "O my Burkhan," prayed Chot Chelpan, "deliver me from the Russians, preserve me from their bullets." Chot Chelpan's activities were seen as a threat to civil peace, and the Russians decided to arrest him. When they came to take him, however, they found three thousand Altai facing the east in prayer—but no Chot Chelpan. He had disappeared, though not for long. He was captured by Russian troops, and his disciples moved to Mongolia, where they continued to cause trouble to the Tsarist authorities.

After the Russian Revolution of 1917, the Soviet leaders hailed Chot Chelpan as a revolutionary figure. They changed their minds after 1930, when they alleged that his movement had been infiltrated by Japanese agents.[1]

All these anti-colonial movements, purely magical or magico-military, had at least one thing in common. Their magicians promised some form of invulnerability to bullets. It was natural that they should. Encounters with invaders possessing superior techniques and weapons demanded new forms of magical protection. Bullets were the principal agency of the white man's power, a manifestation of his superior magic. The medieval European alchemist had searched for the philosopher's stone in order to make gold as well as the drug of deathlessness. The anti-colonial magician looked only for a protection against death. The Bird King offered tattoos and an elixir; Wovoka, ghost shirts; and Chot Chelpan, prayer. The Hau Hau of New Zealand had another formula.

The Hau Hau movement arose among the Maoris of New Zealand in the 1860s, and again it was a question of land being the stimulus to action. Christianity had already penetrated the country before 1840, when the first British settlers arrived and the British Crown claimed sovereignty over the islands. In that year, the first British governor persuaded many of the Maori chiefs to sign the Treaty of Waitangi, which gave the British a first right to buy tribal lands. The Crown subsequently acquired land at a ridiculously low figure, and resold it to settlers at twenty times the original sum. Not surprisingly, the Maori felt cheated. The rapacity of the settlers, and the misunderstandings (at the very least) of government officials, led to steadily worsening relations between the colonists, the Maoris, and the government. A prophet appeared. Te Ua Haumene was a member of the Taranaki tribe and had learned the magic arts. He had also been educated by Wesleyan missionaries. In 1862 he claimed to have had a vision in which the Angel Gabriel spoke to him. As most Maoris took the Bible literally, they were quite ready for Te Ua's claims because they seemed to have biblical authority.

Te Ua, on Gabriel's instructions, was said to have maimed his son; the angel intervened and healed the boy again. Te Ua was also widely credited with having caused a British ship to run aground. He soon acquired close disciples who spread his message and also carried out an attack on a small body of British troops. They cut off the commander's head, and it became the oracle through which the Angel Gabriel subsequently spoke to Te Ua. One of the angel's first communications through the head was an order for the erection of a flagstaff, on which a number of flags were to be flown. Those present marched around it with raised hands, chanting. The words used were unintelligible to most of those who took part in the rite, but almost all the lines ended with "Hau," which referred to the wind and the angels of the wind, who descended by the ropes which were attached to the flagstaff. English words, parts of the church service, and military expressions were all incorporated in the incantations:

God the Father, Hau; God the Son, Hau;
God the Holy Ghost, Hau, Hau, Hau.
Attention, save us; Attention, instruct us; Attention.
Jehovah avenge us, Hau. Jehovah, stand at ease, Hau.
Fall out, Hau, Hau.
Father good and gracious, Hau.
Big rivers, long rivers, big mountains and sea,
Attention, Hau, Hau, Hau.[2]

Most important of all was the shout to be used at all meetings. "Hapa! Pai-marire, hau." This meant: "Pass over, good and faithful," and was a sure protection against bullets.

This magical protection was important, as the final struggle for freedom from the British was at hand. Victory was certain, and when the last of the Europeans "had perished in the sea, all the Maoris who had perished since the beginning of the world would leap from their graves with a shout and stand in the presence of Zerubbabel the Great Prophet. . . . The deaf would hear, the blind see, the lame walk; every species of disease would disappear; all would become perfect in their bodies as in their spirits. Men would be sent from heaven to teach the Maoris all the arts and the sciences known to Europeans."

Te Ua's attempts to bring together the tribes under his leadership led to clashes with the British in which the tribesmen were repulsed with heavy losses. Te Ua explained that the protection against bullets had not worked because he had not authorized the attacks. Some of his emissaries also took private vengeance. One, whose daughter had been burned to death by British soldiers when they razed a village, took an innocent victim—a missionary—killed him, ate his eyes, and used his blood for communion. The government responded with firm action, and Te Ua was captured early in 1866. He renounced his prophecies and was freed, but many of his followers were deported to some of the smaller islands.

Other devices supplied by magicians to counteract the bullets of the whites ranged from the "Talking Cross" sent by God to

190

the Maya people in 1761, to the human sacrifices of the Kiluawa in what was then the Belgian Congo, in 1961. The Yakan or "Allah water" cultists of the southern Sudan and northern Uganda placed their faith in water. In the 1890s the water was believed to have helped a number of tribes inflict serious defeats on the troops of Emin Pasha, a German whom General Gordon had appointed governor of the Equatorial Province of the Sudan. From this episode grew the myth of the water's effectiveness.

Among the Lugbura tribe of northern Uganda, the owners of the water were men of consequence, terrorizing their fellow tribesmen with threats that the life after death would only come to those who were members of the Yakan cult. The water, believed to be invaluable in time of war, was also believed to offer immunity to disease in time of peace. It was further thought to be helpful in bringing dead cattle and ancestors back to life. The water was kept in special temples, each with a guard of armed men. A large pole from a particular tree, with a piece of a shrub known as *inzu* fixed to it, was set up on a kind of parade ground near the temple. Here a sacrifice and dance took place after the magic water was handed over to a purchaser. The water had been mixed with a drug locally known as *kamiojo*, a powerful heart stimulant. The dance seems to have been based on military drill movements, the dancers carrying wooden rifles and going through a series of movements, aiming, ordering, and presenting arms.

This form of ritual was certainly appropriate, for the Yakan cult was an example of the magico-military alliance. Its reputation was diffused by fighting men, and though the cult occasionally lapsed it was revived, usually in revolutionary circumstances—when drinking the water offered a form of protection to rebels against the colonial power. The Yakan magic could also be used *against* the rebels, and at one time the British colonial government of Uganda employed a native soldier as the administrator of an "official" Yakan cult producing water for the government's native soldiers! As the government forces always succeeded in putting down rebellions, the water could be said to have been effective, if only—rather selectively—for one side.

The use of liquid protection against bullets was also found in China among the Boxers during their anti-white rebellion, which led to the siege of the foreign legations in Peking in 1900, and also in many other parts of the world. But there were also examples of magic which turned the enemy's bullets *to* water. One of the latest of these was that of the Radja Damai, or Prince of Peace movement, which arose during the Japanese occupation of Indonesia in the Second World War.

Forty years earlier, a magician in India had gone a stage further and promised to turn not only the enemy's bullets into water, but his weapons as well. In 1900, in the Vizagapatnam district of what was then the Madras Presidency, a member of a hill-cultivator caste named Korra Mallaya had a vision, and on the strength of it collected some five thousand followers. The police were not particularly worried until the leader announced that he was a reincarnation of one of the Pandavas, the five brothers of the great Hindu epic, the *Mahabharata*, who fought interminable battles and were generally considered as culture heroes of the first rank. Korra Mallaya's caste worshiped the Pandava brothers and their god-companion, Krishna. The magician announced, without any explanation, that his own son was the god Krishna, and that he had come to drive out the British and become ruler of India in their place.

The magician called upon his followers to prepare for the great battle. He issued them guns made from bamboo, and promised that when the battle was joined he would turn them into real ones and those of the British into water. As a first step, he announced that he would attack and loot a small village. This attracted the attention of the police, who sent two constables to investigate. They were beaten to death. When the police tried to recover their bodies, they found themselves outnumbered. The district magistrate called in reinforcements, and they, in arresting the magician, were compelled to fire on his followers. The bamboo rifles did not turn into real ones, nor those of the British into water. Eleven of the mob were killed, and many wounded. The magician and two of his closest aides were tried for murder, his other followers merely for rioting. The magician died in jail under mysterious circumstances; his two aides were hanged. When the infant Krishna also died, the rebellion ended and the Pandava brothers returned to their epic.[3]

Elsewhere in India, the desire to be rid of the British, though it was just as strong as that of Korra Mallaya, had been generally contained and was directed by members of the sizable educated and politically conscious native élite which had grown up under British rule. Most were westernized, in varying degree, and proud of it, in varying degree. The moderate elements usually emphasized the need for evolutionary reform, demanded constitutionally, and granted in the same manner. But, as the British were basically unwilling to give even the smallest of practical concessions, there was a spread of impatience that led to militancy and violence. With that militancy and, later, feeding it, there was the delighted recognition of India's great cultural achievements, a recognition considerably assisted by Madame Blavatsky, the Theosophical Society, and Western writers and poets.

The most important center of militancy and unrest around the turn of the nineteenth century was Bengal, that great sprawling province in which the British had first established their empire a century and a half before, and which still contained the capital of their Raj, Calcutta. Bengal had been on the receiving end of the conquerors' civilization for longer than any other part of India, and the people there had been the first to respond and react to what the West appeared to offer them. Members of the upper castes of the Hindu minority of the population of Bengal—which was a mainly Muslim area—had taken avidly to Western education, and because of the qualifications they earned had gained the lion's share of the new professional, administrative, and clerical jobs created by the expansion of British rule in the north of the subcontinent.

These Bengali Hindus became a status group known as the *bhadralok*, "respectable people." Socially privileged and consciously superior, the *bhadralok* dominated the legal profession, the universities, and local government bodies. Their ambition was to supply not only recruits for the lower levels of the administration which were open to Indians, but also for the almost exclusively British Indian Civil Service, whose members were the real rulers of the country. As Western education spread to other parts of India, however, the *bhadralok* monopoly began to contract. The new generation could no longer find places in the professions or in public service—the only employment that would permit them to retain their status. They felt themselves under threat, and particularly so when the government decided to partition Bengal in 1905.

This was the signal for violence. The decision to divide had been taken for sound administrative reasons—Bengal was too large—but the *bhadralok*, a minority within a minority, was convinced that the government wished to diminish its influence and power. Many Western-educated politicians and professional men began to listen to the propagandists of religious nationalism. There, perhaps, was a means of protecting their interests. Many of the younger men had already taken that path and joined one of a number of secret societies. Their inspiration was a mixture of mysticism, magic, and European revolutionary example. Some societies were modeled on the Italian Carbonari or the Irish Sinn Fein. Others took their model from the works of the Bengali novelist and ideologue Bankim Chandra Chatterji.

Bankim's writings gave a romantic view of the Bengali Hindu past and praised Hindu religious sentiments. He claimed that the period Bengalis were living through, a period of alien domination, was an essential prelude to the revival of Hinduism and a Golden Age. Such a revival would only come quickly if the young men of Bengal dedicated themselves without reservation to the motherland. In his novel *Abbey of Bliss (Anandamath)*, published in 1882, Bankim described the ideal of a selfless, dedicated existence in which men sacrificed family, property, and even life itself for the sake of the motherland. The story he told was of a band of holy men who rose in revolt in the second half of the eighteenth century against the tottering empire of the Muslim Moguls, and who were ruthlessly suppressed by the British in Bengal. The book had overtones of the magico-military alliance, for the holy men had acquired supernatural powers but still made use of more tangible weapons.

The young men took the novelist's ideas and turned them into reality. As the source of magic, they called in the black goddess, Kali, the destroyer of demons. The demons were now the British, and Kali the Mother of India. Her followers were: "Worshippers of the Mother ... in her incarnation of the sword. Lovers of death are they—not of life—and of storm and stress." And were there not many who would follow the Mother? "Are not ten thousand sons of Bengal prepared to embrace death to avenge the humiliation of the Motherland?" [4] For a time it seemed as if there might be.

The best organized and the most active of the secret societies was the Anusilan Samiti of Dacca, the city that is now the capital of Bangladesh. Its members were divided into three categories. There were boys under twelve years old; novices who took an initial vow; and an inner circle. Discipline was very strict. Nothing, not even the family, was to take precedence over the aims of the society. Traitors were to be killed. A member wounded in action was to be carried away or killed on the spot. Members took their vows at night on a cremation ground, after days of fasting before an image of Kali. Kali promised the devotee protection, though not, it seems, invulnerability. She blessed the bomb that was the main weapon of the terrorists.

The bomb would be more effective than magic by itself, as had been proved in the case of the magicians who alleged that they could reverse the government's decision to partition Bengal by marching through the gates of Fort William, the principal military installation in Calcutta. In the face of their power, wrote the revolutionary of the Second World War, Subhas Chandra Bose, "British troops would stand stock still, unable to move or fight, and power would pass into the hands of the people." [5] Unfortunately, the commander of Fort William refused to allow the procession to take place, and the magic was not strong enough to penetrate the massive stone walls of the fort.

Members of the Anusilan Samiti threw their first bomb in the provincial town of Muzaffarpur in April 1908. The target was a magistrate who, when he had been in Calcutta, had had a number of *bhadralok* youths publicly whipped for singing a nationalist song. The terrorists hurled their bomb into the wrong carriage and killed, instead, the wife and daughter of an English lawyer who held strong pro-nationalist views. The murders produced intense government repression and show trials of the leaders, some of whom were acquitted and others sentenced to life imprisonment in the penal settlements of the Andaman Islands.

But the assassinations continued, as did other terrorist acts, until in 1911 the British capitulated and announced the reunification of Bengal. At the same time, they revealed that they were moving their capital from Calcutta to New Delhi. The magico-military alliance of Kali and the bomb had achieved its first objective. Its second, the freedom of India, was finally brought about by somewhat different means. But even at that moment of triumph in 1947, when the secular nationalists seemed to have swept all including the British before them, and that other magician, Mahatma Gandhi, into the background, it was the astrologers who fixed the exact time of the transfer of power from Britain to independent India!

2
Chairman Mao and
the Lord of the World

Helena Petrovna Blavatsky had been wise to place the secret masters of the Theosophical Society in a mysterious country to the north of India. At that time, very little was known about Tibet, for it was closed to Europeans and few had crossed its borders. There were, however, tales of vast monasteries clinging to the sides of great mountains along the "roof of the world," of magicians who could keep themselves warm while sitting naked in the eternal snows, make themselves invisible, or move through the air at phenomenal speeds. Rumor made Tibet a powerhouse of occult forces, a magical state of the kind men had dreamed of, planned for, and even tried to bring into being. For once, rumor approached truth, for though Tibet was a religious state—a type of Buddhist Vatican—it rested upon a magical infrastructure of great social and political potency.

Buddhism had come to Tibet in the seventh century A.D. The scale had been small at first, confined only to the court, a courtesy to the king's Chinese wife who, legend says, had brought with her an image of the Buddha. Most of the countries surrounding Tibet were at that time Buddhist, but Tibet itself, a harsh, difficult region first colonized by nomads, was a place of spirit worshipers whose kings were divinities. The king who first permitted Buddhism into his court was also the man who introduced a new form of writing. The new script came from

India and made it possible for the great Buddhist texts to be translated into Tibetan.

At first there was some hostility to Buddhism. Later kings who did not have Buddhist wives were indifferent, others rejected it as foreign. But by the middle of the eighth century the first Tibetan monastery, said to have been modeled on a famous one in India, had been built with royal patronage and approval. A large number of Indian and Chinese Buddhist texts were translated into Tibetan and by the end of the century the supporters of Indian doctrines and the somewhat different ones from China were involved in arguments about which should be officially adopted. The verdict went to the Indian doctrine known as *Mahayana*, or "Greater Vehicle."

It did not mean that this particular doctrine, or even Buddhism itself, immediately acquired any great influence. Its royal patrons were not exclusively Buddhist, nor were the Buddhists particularly active in missionary work. Kings still believed that they were divine personages and were buried according to non-Buddhist rites.

Buddhists searched for common ground between themselves and the practitioners of such rites, for without compromise Buddhism was unlikely ever to achieve a mass following. The compromise had to be on an occult level, for the beliefs of the majority of Tibetans were very much concerned with the magical ordering of the perils and pleasures of the everyday world. This was less objectionable to the Indian Buddhist missionaries in Tibet than it had been to the early followers of the Buddha in India. There, the absorption of folk religion and magical beliefs had led to a dilution of the original message of the historical Buddha. But the now dominant Mahayana system was itself a product of the fusion of many traditions, not least the tradition of absorption, and had magical as well as more austere and intellectual schools. Representatives of the two schools in eighth-century Tibet were the magician Padmasambhava, and the gentle, intellectual monk Shantarakshita.

Of these two, the more lastingly influential was Padmasambhava, who became a culture hero for the Tibetans. He is said to have arrived in Tibet in A.D. 747 at the invitation of the king, and to have spent—according to his biography—111 years there, though other and more credible sources report the period as fifty years. Not that a stay of more than a century could be considered as extensive for the great sage. Padmasambhava was believed to have been born only twelve years after the death of the historical Buddha, which would have made him about twelve hundred years old when he arrived in Tibet. Whether the great teacher made these claims himself is not known, though his name gives a clue. Padmasambhava means "born from the lotus," not from the human womb. The historical Buddha, according to the Tibetan canon, did not teach the esoteric mysteries because, having been born of a woman, he was unfit to do so. At the time of his death, he promised to return in an unsullied form to reveal them. That form was believed to be Padmasambhava.

The historical Padmasambhava was undoubtedly a charismatic personality, but even his magic could not preserve Buddhism from politics. In A.D. 836 Buddhism's royal patron was murdered, and his death was followed by the collapse of his kingdom and the suppression of state Buddhism. Padmasambhava was not liked at court, and royal patronage was soon directed toward more conventional forms of Buddhism. The spread of Padmasambhava's teaching among ordinary people was believed to have undermined the king's divinity, making him accessible to assassination by creating indifference to his fate. His death brought more than a century of silence. Buddhism went underground, filtering into the minds and hearts of the people even though, publicly, it had almost disappeared.

Only in central Tibet, however, for Buddhist monks took refuge in the east and waited, preparing themselves and their followers for what they believed would be an inevitable return.

In the west, too, Buddhist rulers sustained the faith, building monasteries and temples, commissioning translations of texts, offering a place to foreign monks and scholars. From this reservoir of active faith the exiles returned to central Tibet in A.D. 978, and from then onward Buddhism was diffused throughout the country. Increasing numbers of scholars began to visit and stay at the great Buddhist "universities" in eastern India. Their intense desire for knowledge sent them to wherever there was a famous teacher, and they were willing to pay handsomely for instruction.

For centuries, Tibetans absorbed all they could from Indian culture. The great Buddhist "universities" of India had taught more than just the doctrines of Buddhism. Returning Tibetan scholars had brought home with them, among other texts, works on magic, medicine and astronomy, arts, and crafts. By skillful translation, an alien culture was naturalized. When Buddhist civilization fell in India at the end of the twelfth century, the Tibetans had no more need of it. Tibet now stood alone, for the Muslims who destroyed Buddhism in India had already destroyed it in the lands of Tibet's western neighbors.

While the Muslim invaders were laying waste the great religious establishments of northern India, the Mongols under the leadership of Genghis Khan were slaughtering the inhabitants of northern China, well embarked on the first stages of their creation of a vast Asian empire. It was not until the reign of Genghis Khan's successor, Ogotai—who became khan in 1227—that the Mongols turned their attention to Tibet. Ogotai's second son, Godan, sent raiding parties into the country in 1239 and some monasteries were plundered. Hearing, however, of the great influence wielded by the heads of the Buddhist orders, the grand lamas, Godan summoned a Tibetan representative to his court. The lama chosen was appointed regent and made responsible for passing on the khan's orders to Tibetan officials, but his activities did not meet with the complete approval of the other great religious leaders and their dislike hardened when the lama's nephew and successor established a close relationship with Kublai Khan, the future conqueror of China.

Kublai himself became a devoted patron of magical Buddhism, and Tibet entered upon a peculiar relationship with China which was not to end until the fall of the Chinese monarchy in 1911. The relationship was known as "patron and priest," for the ruler of Tibet was regarded as the religious adviser of the Chinese emperor, who in return acted as patron and protector.

The appointment of one grand lama as the virtual ruler of the country excited the ambitions of others. The great monastic orders tried to win the patronage of one or other of the Mongol chiefs, and to take advantage of the internecine quarrels that were characteristic of the Mongols. The lamas' success in attracting patronage brought them the support of conflicting interests in the Tibetan aristocracy. For more than twenty years there was intermittent war between the two greatest monasteries, a period of vicious and bloody deeds, of unscrupulous intrigue, in which men of religion played leading roles.

The decline of Mongol power in China ultimately led to Tibet's independence from China under a new dynasty of kings who were to rule for over a hundred years. A deliberate attempt was made by the founder to revive the old Tibetan royal traditions, but his successors could not maintain the impetus and were overthrown by their ministers. Then they too were displaced. Tibet remained under lay rulers until, in 1642, the fifth Dalai Lama gained control of the administration.

The grand lamas had not been inactive during the period of secular rule. They extended their influence both with the upper classes and with the people. As in other countries, the monasteries became important financial and economic institutions. But the most significant event was the establishment of a new religious order, commonly known as the Yellow Hats. This had its origins in the life and writings of a great fifteenth-century reformer, Tsong-kha-pa, and advocated monastic simplicity, religious devotion, and calm austerity—in notable contrast to the other orders. It attracted considerable support in the Lhasa area, and the founder's successors expanded its influence. Though the Mongols had been driven from China in 1368, some of their chiefs continued to exercise power in middle Asia. The new rulers of China, an indigenous dynasty known as the Ming, at first discouraged Tibetan intercourse with the Mongols, but later decided that missionary activity in that direction might reduce the Mongols' militancy. Few of the Tibetan orders were interested by now, but the third lama of the Yellow Hats met the most important of the Mongol leaders, Altan Khan, in 1578. They exchanged honorific titles, the khan receiving that of "King of Religion, Majestic Purity," and the lama that of "Ta-le" (Dalai), which was the Mongol word for "ocean" and implied in this case "Ocean of Wisdom."

From about the thirteenth century onward, certain of the monastic establishments had found their head lamas when they were still children, using the Buddhist doctrine of rebirth as a justification for the theory of reincarnation. After the death of a head lama, a child showing signs that he was a reincarnation of the dead man would be sought. There was no real religious purpose to this; the idea was to give a sense of stable continuity to the order.

The Yellow Hats also adopted this system, and with a sound sense of statecraft discovered the first Dalai Lama's successor, when he died in 1588, in a great grandson of Altan Khan. The arrival of this new Dalai Lama in Tibet in 1601 was accompanied by such a display of wealth and power that it aroused opposition. The arrogance of the Yellow Hats, who were now just as worldly as the older orders, even antagonized the lay rulers, who attacked their principal monastic establishment and put the Dalai Lama to flight.

In 1616 the Dalai Lama died at the age of twenty-five, probably from poison, and his successor, discovered in central Tibet, was escorted to Lhasa by Mongol troops. It was obvious to the religious orders and to the king that the bad old days of foreign interference were back again. But not quite, for though the king was defeated and killed and the other powerful orders humbled, the fifth Dalai Lama was not a Mongol puppet. For the first time, Tibet had a ruler who combined in his person both spiritual and temporal power, and at a time when the Mongols were in decline and the Chinese facing the first of the Manchu invasions. The Dalai Lama built for himself a great palace at Lhasa, known as the Potala (after the mountain sacred to the *bodhisattva* Avolokitesvara, the most popular of all Tibetan Buddhist divinities, the Lord of the World). The priest had now become the divine king, for it was accepted that the Dalai Lama was an incarnation of the god.

While the Dalai Lama was establishing himself in Tibet, a new foreign power was conquering China. In 1644 the Manchus drove out the Ming and founded the dynasty of the Ch'ing, which was to last until 1911.

The relationship of "patron and priest" continued, but by the beginning of the nineteenth century the Chinese central power was in decline and Tibet was able to cut itself off from the outside world, to become the Forbidden Land on the Roof of the World. By then, the Yellow Hat hierarchy was firmly in power. The Dalai Lama became essentially a symbol, the source of authority for the government and those who operated it. Though the lay nobility played an important role, the real power lay with clerical ministers. The bureaucracy was staffed by both lay officials and monks; provinces were governed by two officials, one a layman, one a monk; the influence of the monks was everywhere, for the monasteries were not enclosed foundations in the Western sense. Not all monks were scholars. Many worked in the fields and workshops, and it was not unusual for a monk to run a restaurant. The interplay between religious and secular became part of the essential texture of Tibetan life and created a deep sense of social unity. The government was authoritarian but not oppressive. Its sanction was the traditional acceptance of authority by the people. Tibet was a magical state, a theocracy ruled by a god-king in the service of millions of consenting theocrats who believed in magic.

There was a wide range of magic for Tibetans to draw upon. Everyday magic made use of magical appliances, for divination, the protection of crops, or the bringing of much-needed rain. There was even a kind of low-grade magical technology for bringing about the death of an enemy. But there was also a very high-level magic that did not depend on devices, though they were often used in an auxiliary capacity. The magician who could keep himself warm with psychic heat was able to do so only after long years of training, during which he would learn to capture the energy of a god. His training included periods of deep meditation, special postures, thought direction, the acquisition of control over the psychic nervous system, and physical exercises.

Very similar methods were used in acquiring the art of rapid transportation of the kind described by the Frenchwoman Alexandra David-Neel, who once saw in action a monk who had mastered the technique. "I could clearly see his perfectly calm impassive face and wide open eyes, with their gaze fixed on some invisible distant object situated somewhere high up in space. The man did not run. He seemed to lift himself up off the ground, proceeding by leaps. It looked as if he had been endowed with the elasticity of a ball and rebounded each time his feet touched the ground." [1]

High magic depended on the magician's taking control of a god or demon. This was not an easy process, involving the use of ritual, magic spells or *mantras*, and diagrams or pictures known as *mandalas*. A mistake in the ritual, a defect in the character of the magician, could lead to disaster. One famous story told of a monk who prepared for a ritual by spending a year in absolute isolation. As the ceremony began at last, everything appeared to be taking a favorable course. The lamps were alight with a constant and unflickering flame, the sacrificial butter was burning evenly. The terrible, grimacing face of the god emerged. Favorable omens became visible. The magic dagger began to shiver as an indication that the god was taking bodily form. Then the god's bodyguard began slaughtering large numbers of people, and his female partner appeared and demanded that the monk should expiate the sins of the bodyguard. The monk, who should have indicated agreement, replied that it was not his business—and by allowing himself to speak destroyed all he had prepared for. He did not know what to do with the piled-up corpses. The *mandala* clouded over. The sacrificial butter would no longer burn. The lamps began to smoke. And when the monk tried to escape, a great whirlwind blew up, tearing his clothes and hurling him to the ground.

Such things, naturally, were better organized at state level. The state oracle, who was frequently consulted on matters of high policy and whose advice was almost always acted upon, was very carefully chosen. The oracle was said to be possessed by Pe-har, a devil king supposed to have been brought to Tibet by Padmasambhava, who had conquered him by superior magic. The state oracle was established in the seventeenth century, and various tests were devised at that time to ensure that the medium was really capable. The tests, for obvious reasons, were rigorous and searching. The candidate was first presented with an immense sword, its blade made from the finest steel. With his bare hands, he was expected to twist this blade into a spiral. When he was in a trance, the saliva flowing from his mouth had to contain blood. When he was silent, his tongue had to be rolled backward with its tip pressed against the upper palate. An outline of the thunderbolt used by Padmasambhava to subdue Pe-har was expected to materialize on his newly shaven head. The last part of the test consisted of three questions about the past, present, and future. The tests were all carried out in private, and the only indication that a candidate had passed was that he was actually appointed state oracle.

The state oracle delivered his prophecies during the course of an extremely elaborate ceremony. According to modern observers, the procedure passed through the following stages:

The oracle-priest supported by his assistants takes his place on the throne. His eyes are closed. After the invocation prayer has been chanted by the monks, the medium's eyes suddenly open wide and appear to be bursting out of their sockets. The face of the medium turns red as the fit intensifies, and is contorted with pain and covered with sweat. He gasps for air and gesticulates wildly with his hands, trying to jump up from the throne, but is restrained by his assistants.

The medium rises, bows three times in homage to Padmasambhava, conqueror of the Pe-har, and begins a slow dance. The dance becomes wild and the medium's face turns red.

The questions are now put to the medium. His face becomes sad, cheekbones and the bones of the chin protrude sharply through tightly drawn skin. The medium speaks.

The ceremony ends with a wild dance after which the medium collapses, his eyes open with the whites visible. The deity has departed.[2]

During the four centuries of the institution's existence, the state oracle had a large number of successes. But there were also some startling and disastrous failures. In 1886, when the British then ruling India were active in the Tibetan border areas, the state oracle advised the occupation of a magic mountain that lay inside the frontiers of the state of Sikkim, then a feudatory of the British. The magic powers radiating from the mountain would prevent further troop movement on the part of the British and stop them from entering Tibet. This advice was taken, and a small party of monks went to live on the mountain. Some years later, however, the mountain was occupied by the British without opposition or repercussions of any kind. Again, in 1904, finding it impossible to negotiate solutions to outstanding problems with the Tibetan government at Lhasa, the British decided to send an expeditionary force to the Tibetan capital. The state oracle predicted that they would penetrate deeply into the country but would be defeated by the Tibetan army. Though the Tibetans—believing themselves invulnerable—fought with fanatical bravery, they were crushed by the British, who were making use of a magical weapon known as the Maxim machine gun.

The state oracle consulted before the Chinese invasion of Tibet in 1950 advised that the Dalai Lama, then a minor, should assume full powers. This advice was not followed at the time, and when the oracle was again consulted after Chinese troops had entered the country, Pe-har refused to take possession of the medium. But another deity that sometimes took possession of the state oracle was approached, agreed to enter the medium, and repeated the earlier advice. This time it was accepted.

The year 1950 was a time of great danger for Tibet. Within a few weeks of the establishment of the People's Republic of China under Chairman Mao Tse-tung in 1949, the new government had announced that the People's Liberation Army would shortly march into Tibet and resume the "special relationship" with that country that had been in force during the era of the Chinese empire. If that had been all, the situation could have been handled. But this time the Chinese would not be content merely with the relationship of patron and priest. Their religion, communism, was totally opposed to any other religion.

It was rumored that the state oracle had announced the collapse of Buddhism in Tibet and the imminent flight of the Dalai Lama. The omens were taken in monasteries and other places all over the country. They were not favorable. Signs and portents were observed, and interpretations circulated. The Tibetan government decided to undertake a magical offensive against the forces of Chairman Mao. It was one that had been used before at times of threatened invasion, and it had worked.

In this magic, the thread cross was used. In its simplest form, the thread cross is just two crossed sticks, their ends connected with colored thread which is wound round to form something resembling a spider's web. In the anti-Chinese magic, four thread crosses, each eighteen feet high, were used. Each was of a different color, representing the four continents of Buddhist geography. The crosses were set up inside one of the larger rooms of a Lhasa monastery, each resting on a substantial base nine feet square. The supports of the crosses were hollow, and before the ceremony were filled with bones, human flesh, and the blood of various animals and birds, particularly owls and crows, as well as the skulls—or at least portions of bone—of people of noble ancestry and men of the lower orders. To this mixture were added the fresh blood of a young man killed in a fight, the vagina of an especially notorious whore, weapons and other objects that had been used to kill people, the ear lobes, tips of noses, hearts, and eyebrows of men dead by violence, and the thigh bone and skull of a man who had died of a virulent contagious disease. The Tibetan government supplied fine cloth and silks from the state treasury; earth was procured from 108 cemeteries, and water from a similar number of springs. Leaves and twigs from certain shrubs and trees were added, with herbs and roots, large pieces of five different metals, the underwear, hair, and menstrual blood of prostitutes, and the skull, flesh, and blood of an eight-year-old male child.

The ceremony proper was conducted by a magician who had spent seven days in meditation and in attracting one of the powerful demons and forcing it to send a demon army against the enemies of the state. Other ceremonies went on simultaneously in other parts of the monastery, including readings from a special book. These ceremonies were designed to please the deity or deities the magician was attempting to coerce.

On the last day of the ceremony, the crosses and their bases were broken down into several pieces and taken outside, where they were set up again facing in the direction of the enemy. At a propitious time, worked out by an astrologer monk, the thread crosses and their bases were burned. If the ceremony had been successful, the enemy should have been destroyed. In 1950, according to one source, the operation was unsuccessful because the magician performing the ceremony committed a deliberate error, so nullifying its effect. Another source insists that the Chinese had the support of a magician of superior magical powers, who was able to protect the invaders from the demon army sent against them.

Another ceremony, said to have taken place at the moment of the Chinese attack, was the "sending of the *torma* of Kshetrapala." This deity, "the Protector of the Cemetery," was the principal minister of one of the great protecting deities of Tibetan Buddhism. He was usually depicted as being blue in color, with one face and two arms, his right hand raised in the air holding an axe which cut his enemies' roots of life. In his left hand there was a skull cup filled with his enemies' hearts' blood. The deity's open mouth showed four sharp teeth, and his three eyes, heavily shot with blood, radiated hatred. His facial hair was the yellow-red of fire, while that on his head stood upright and was yellowish brown in color. In his hair was a human skull; his loincloth was the skin of a tiger, and the upper part of his body was covered with the skin of a corpse. Riding on a black bear, surrounded by flames, he was a terrible and terrifying sight.

So too was his feminine counterpart. Like her consort, she had one face and two arms. Her dress was a kind of shift of black silk. In her right hand there was a polished mirror with which to blind demons, and a snare to catch them; in her left, a skull cup full of the blood of her enemies. Her hair was the same color as that of her husband. She laughed wildly as she reduced her enemies to dust.

Kshetrapala lived in a cemetery which was supposed to be near Bodhgaya in India, one of the sacred places of Buddhism. The cemetery was a place of overwhelming horror, where the laughter of demons shook the earth's foundations. Kshetrapala had a deadly enemy, a nine-headed demon who was said to give his support to China over matters concerning Tibet.

The purpose of the ceremony in 1950 was to dispatch Kshetrapala in the direction of the Chinese border. The central magical device of the *torma* was made from barley dough in the form of a three-sided pyramid. The *torma*, which was between eight and ten feet high, was colored bright red and represented the deity's palace. The sides were carved with flames to represent the flames surrounding the palace. One side of the pyramid was decorated on its upper third with designs in butter known as "white ornaments," and the entire *torma* was set in a large, flat, iron pan on a tripod which, in turn, stood on a rough black cloth. At the top of the pyramid a small human skull was placed, and on it a thunderbolt dagger. Above this was a small painting of the god, partly shaded by an umbrella of blue silk. Five streamers of different-colored silks, secured at the top, draped the sides of the pyramid.

On either side of the great *torma* were placed small *tormas*, and an enclosure constructed from the wood of a special thorny shrub and the inflated bladders of animals surrounded the whole. The bladders represented the "iron mountain" ranges which were said to mark the frontiers of the deity's dwelling place. Various offerings, representing Kshetrapala's treasures, were placed inside the enclosure with two skull cups, one containing beer and the other Chinese tea (although one source states that the latter offering was of blood). In front of the two cups a range of magical weapons was disposed, and in front of them were five vessels containing five different offerings.

The ceremony that followed the preparation of the great *torma* was designed to direct the power of the deity into the center of the *torma*. It lasted for seven days, and on the last day a path was drawn (in flour) from the tripod to the door of the room in which the ceremony had been taking place. The vessels containing the offerings were removed and the magical weapons ranged along the flour path. Outside the door, two men held a special kind of banner. The magical weapons were next taken outside, followed by the great and small *tormas* still in their iron pan.

The ceremony continued in the courtyard of the monastery. One of the participating monks carrying a smoking censer approached the great *torma*, followed by two monks bearing the "gold libation," an offering of beer mixed with grain. The monk with the censer took his place behind the great *torma*, and a pace or so behind stood the chief officiant with his assistant. To left and right stood the two "gold libation" monks. The libation ceremony was then performed by the chief officiant, after which the *tormas* and the magical weapons were carried out of the courtyard in procession. First came the two banners, then monks carrying the magical weapons, the two small *tormas*, and finally the great *torma* itself. Behind walked the monk with the censer, followed by the two libation monks and the chief officiant with his assistant. The rest of the monks who had been present at the ceremony in the courtyard followed in a single column, the first few carrying cymbals and the others drums, which were clashed and beaten as the procession moved toward a place a little away from the monastery, where, on a flat spot, stood a pyramidal structure made of dry grass, about ten feet high with a hole in one side. Here a further "gold libation" was offered, and in a long invocation the chief officiant again listed his demands to the deity. Some of the magical weapons were thrown inside the grass pyramid, while the officiant repeated the tasks Kshetrapala was expected to carry out with each of them. After this, the great *torma* and the smaller ones were set alight. When the great *torma* was all in flames, the monks clapped their hands to disperse any evil forces that might still be about, and the two banners were lowered as a sign that Kshetrapala and his army had started their attack. The final act of the ritual was the magical cleansing of the iron pan by the chief officiant, and the return of the procession to the monastery.

Kshetrapala's attack was not successful. Perhaps Chairman Mao had more powerful deities on his side as well as better weaponry than the Lord of the World. Certainly, the chairman's forces occupied Tibet without too much opposition, and the Lord of the World found it necessary to flee to India. Many of the magicians also fled, some of them to Europe and some to the United States, where they seemed to find a congenial psychic climate waiting for them. But the occult underground is still there in Tibet, erupting occasionally in magico-military guerrilla activity.

Five

WORLDS OF LIGHT AND
WORLDS OF DARKNESS

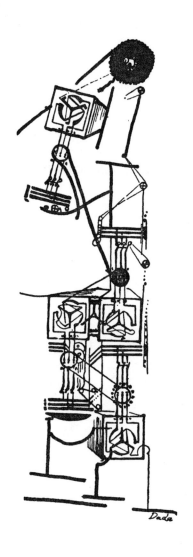

Max Ernst, *"die schammade"* 1920

1

The Surreal
and the Swastika

Between August 1914 and November 1918, the first modern war tore the heart out of Europe. Slaughter and destruction on an unprecedented scale wiped almost a whole generation of young men from the scene. Those who survived, hoping perhaps that a better world would emerge from "the sewer of blood, stupidity, and mud," [1] were disgusted to find that little had changed. Though empires had fallen and kings been hustled into exile, the society that had sent its youth so gaily into the valley of death was waiting at home for those who managed to escape, with the same old laws, moralities, and religions.

Disgust took many forms, and one of them was to lead Europe once again—and more than Europe this time—into the horrors of war. Another was to make an attempt to revolutionize the mind and society. Both drew upon the manifold resources of the occult underground.

A Machine for Capsizing the Mind

You can be sure it is the enemies of order who are circulating this elixir of the absolute. They sneak it past the guards in the form of books, poems. The harmless pretext of literature allows them to offer at a price defying all competition this deadly brew. . . .

Buy, buy the damnation of your soul. You will destroy yourself at last, here is the machine for capsizing your mind. I announce to the world this page one headline: a new vice has just been born, one madness more has been given to man: *surrealism,* son of frenzy and darkness. Step right up, here is where the kingdoms of the instantaneous begin.[2]

The extravagant claims of the surrealist leader Louis Aragon, in 1924, now seem commonplace, especially since the outrageous vocabulary surrealism introduced into literature, art, and even life has become part of the common language of the advertising culture of our time. Art historians continue to argue about whether surrealism was any more than a brilliantly planned hoax designed to promote the interests of its leaders, and historians of ideas about whether it warrants a significant place in modern intellectual history. Unbiased judgment is not assisted by a thick fog of theory and propaganda, left undispersed after the Second World War by the surviving surrealists. But all the backbiting, bluff calling, and Ph.D. theses cannot obscure the fact that the surrealists were the first important group of artists since the Romantics to attempt political action in order to change human society; and they shared a magical view of the universe derived from the occult tradition.

Surrealism was the creation of André Breton. Ironically, Breton, who died in 1966, is the least widely known of the surrealists, perhaps because he was a writer, a poet and not a painter. And yet it was Breton who ensured that surrealism would come to matter much more than any other *ism* in the turbulent history of twentieth-century art movements. In fact, he did not see surrealism as an art movement at all. For him, it was the crystallization of a notion of life. Not a new technique, but a new experience, and an experience firmly rooted in life rather than in the art schools and the literary coteries. The enemy at which surrealism directed its savage offensive was not an outmoded literary and artistic style but the society that nourished it.

In 1915 Breton became a medical assistant at an army mental hospital. His war was not to be the horror of the trenches but the tragedy of wounded minds, some of them impossible to repair. His interests were literary as well as professional, and one of the most important influences of that time was the poet Guillaume Apollinaire, who died of wounds two days before the armistice of November 1918. It was Apollinaire who invented the word *surrealism*, but he left Breton more than a word. He inspired him with the image of the poet as magician, and directed his attention to some of the magicians of the past.

For Breton, the most influential of these was not a poet but an unfrocked priest, expelled from the Church for heresy, a political activist who had tried to take the mysticism out of magic. Born Alphonse Louis Constant in 1810, he had set out by the middle of the century—under the name Eliphas Levi, the Hebrew equivalent of his two given names—to expound a magic suitable, he thought, for his times. Levi saw science as the foundation of magic, and knowledge, not faith, as the key to its mysteries. In this he was not altogether alone, in a century that considered science an instrument of both power and revelation. But where other writers on the occult in the second half of the century sought a reconciliation, even an alliance, between the supernatural and science, Levi insisted that there was no such thing as the supernatural. The marvels which mystics attributed to the supernatural were really parts of the natural universe awaiting discovery. The contrast between spiritual and material was only a matter of opacity, and man had the power to turn the opaque into the translucent. This power was imagination.

"Imagination," wrote Levi, "in effect, is like the soul's eye; therein forms are outlined and preserved; thereby we behold the reflections of the invisible world; it is the glass of visions and the apparatus of magical life." [3] With this statement, he placed himself firmly in the Western magical tradition. "To imagine is to see." And controlled imagination could not only see, but do, anything. The Renaissance magus, following on the Muslim alchemist, had been convinced of it. Cornelius Agrippa gave many examples in his occult encyclopedia, and Fabio Paolini wrote of those people who asserted "that the feelings and conceptions of our souls can by force of the imagination be rendered volatile and corporeal ... and will obey us in whatever we want." [4]

In the *First Surrealist Manifesto*, in 1924, Breton stated: "Perhaps the imagination is on the verge of recovering its rights. If the depths of our minds conceal strange forces capable of augmenting or conquering those on the surface, it is in our greatest interest to capture them." Those words disclosed not only the influence of Eliphas Levi but that of Pierre Janet and of Sigmund Freud, the magical tradition and the psychiatric revelation.

Most people have heard of Freud, few of Janet, though he was the teacher of that other towering figure of modern psychiatry, Carl Jung. From Freud, Breton took methods of exploring the dream; from Janet, the practice of automatic writing. Freud was the first to bring into the mainstream of psychological thought, and give scientific support to, the idea that the imagination was a realizing faculty, "images tending of themselves to impose on us and presenting themselves as real." [5] He was not, of course, writing of the imagination of the magical tradition, for Freud saw it as "real" only insofar as it had real effects upon the person; as far as the world was concerned, it was not real. Janet first put forward the use of automatic writing as a channel of therapy in the 1880s, but also saw that it could be used as a technique to explore the normal as well as the "sick" mind. He considered automatic writing as a corollary of automatic speaking in mediums. But not as a method of conjuring up the dead, for there was no place for the supernatural in Janet's thinking. Automatic writing was a means of exploring the psychic nature of man by breaking through mental inhibitions and letting the spontaneous workings of the mind emerge to view. Such a breakthrough took place, accidentally, in madness, but Janet thought that it could be induced without any exterior aid. Alcohol and drugs, in fact, tended to destroy the authenticity of the experience.

The influences of both Freud and Janet were clear in the definition of surrealism given in the manifesto of 1924:

> **Surrealism.** *n. masc.* Pure psychic automatism, by which an attempt is made to express, either verbally, in writing or in any other manner, the true functioning of thought. The dictation of thought, in the absence of all control by the reason, excluding any aesthetic or moral preoccupation.
> *Philos. Encycl.* Surrealism rests on the belief in the higher reality of certain hitherto neglected forms of association, in the omnipotence of the dream, in the disinterested play of thought. It tends to destroy the other physical mechanisms and to substitute itself for them in the solution of life's principal problems.[6]

When surrealism burst upon the scene in 1924, it shocked the Parisian artistic and literary establishment. They should have been prepared for it. Already there had been vicious attacks on accepted cultural standards and styles from the followers of Dada. This movement, which had begun in 1916 in a Zurich café not far from the one where Lenin could still be seen playing chess, was essentially destructive. "Let each man cry out: there is a big job, destructive and negative, to be accomplished: sweep, sweep clean." [7] The Dadaists poured ridicule on the accepted great writers and poets of the time, and even offered a new kind of poetry:

To make a dadaist poem
Take a newspaper

Take a pair of scissors
Choose an article as long as you are planning
    to make your poem
Cut out the article
Then cut up each of the words that make up this
    article and put them in a bag
Shake it gently
Then take out the scraps one after the other in the
    order in which they left the bag.
Copy conscientiously
The poem will be like you.
And here you are a writer, infinitely original and
    endowed with a sensibility that
Is charming though beyond the understanding of the
    vulgar.[8]

After the war was over, some of the Dadaists went to
Germany, where they were soon condemned by Adolf Hitler, in
Mein Kampf, as the carriers of a virulent disease that had to be
eliminated. Others went to Paris. Breton found the fury and
malicious humor of Dada appealing. He too was anxious to
sweep away the old. But Dada offered nothing in its place; it
was a demolition gang, a constructor of ruins. Breton wanted to
offer something constructive and new. After five years of
growing dissatisfaction with Dada, he decided that it was time
to release the creative revolution of surrealism.

Perhaps surrealism would not have been so shocking to the
establishment if its members had confined themselves to
writing unintelligible poetry and producing paintings full of
images obscure in meaning and symbolism. In that case they
could have been dismissed as a mere coterie. At the beginning,
the surrealists claimed: "We have no talent ... we who have
made ourselves, in our works, the deaf receptacles of so many
echoes, the modest recording devices" [9] of the liberated imagination. Many critics agreed about the lack of talent. But Breton
and his followers were out to change life and transform the

world. Their attacks were not merely on the outmoded formalism of art and literature, but on the *total* civilization of which, the surrealists maintained, its art and literature were merely symptoms of inner sickness.

"Western world, you are condemned to death," threatened Louis Aragon at a lecture in Madrid. "We are Europe's defeatists. . . . Let the East, your terror, answer our voice at last! We shall awaken everywhere the seeds of confusion and discomfort. We are the mind's agitators. All barricades are valid, all shackles to your happiness damned. Jews, leave your ghettos! Starve the people so they will at last know the taste of the bread of wrath! Rise, thousand-armed India. . . . It is your turn, Egypt! . . . Let distant America's white buildings crumble under her ridiculous prohibitions. Rise, world. See how dry the earth is, and ready like so much straw for every conflagration. Laugh your fill. We are the ones who always hold out a hand to the enemy." [10]

France was fighting a colonial war against the Riffs in Morocco under their leader Abdel Krim. The surrealists were strongly against war of any kind, and there were a number of demonstrations, including the breaking up of a literary banquet, which caused a major scandal. The newspapers, which had previously considered the surrealists good entertainment for their readers, turned against them, calling for legal action and the expulsion from France of those who were foreign nationals.

It was not the last time that the surrealists were to attract the active dislike of sections of the establishment. In 1932, Aragon was prosecuted on a charge of incitement to murder; the cause was a mediocre poem called "Red Front," which called upon its readers to shoot political leaders, the police, and social democrats. Nothing came of the affair, as even the French government recognized the absurdity of the charge. But this event did have one effect—it led to the departure of Aragon from the surrealist camp into that of the Communist party.

Breton and other surrealists had established an uneasy

relationship with the French Communist party in 1925. It remained uneasy, for though Breton understood and welcomed the political revolution of Lenin and Trotsky, he saw it as only part of a greater revolution, the revolution in the psychic personality of man. Unfortunately, the Soviet experiment turned out to be yet another experiment in orthodoxy, in which there was no place for the liberated imagination. The break with communism began in 1933, a significant date in the history of the world. Breton and the surrealists were quick to recognize the threat of Nazism in Germany; perhaps Breton was sensitive to its occult undertones. But, though the surrealists remained politically active, they had little if any influence. The working class did not understand them and, as a result, was suspicious. In any case, how could workers take seriously a group of artists and writers whose main supporters appeared to be rich collectors?

The surrealist magician was denied a place at the barricades. The polarization of left and right, of Marxist and Fascist, demanded a narrow, and narrow-minded revolution, not an expanding one. As war became more and more inevitable, no one wanted to be distracted by people like Breton, who was to survive the war, when it came in 1939, in exile in the United States with other leading surrealists, such as Max Ernst and Yves Tanguy. What he found there in the New World were traditions older than those he knew. On visits to Mexico and the far West, he discovered Indian folklore and the uninhibited forms of non-Christian myth and cultures. They helped to confirm his growing conviction that existing political formats were incapable of restructuring society, and that the revolution in the psyche must come first. Change the man, and he will then change his world.

The brilliance of the surrealist painters, the cosmopolitan genius of such men as the Swiss Paul Klee, the German Max Ernst, the Spaniards Juan Miró and Salvador Dali, the Italian Chirico, and the American Man Ray, have tended to obscure the essential message of surrealism. Painting is what most of the world knows of surrealism, and the world values that painting according to the standards of art critics and auctioneers. Surrealism did attract men of genius because it deeply reflected the sensibility of the times. But the ideas of surrealism, the ideas essentially of André Breton, are not restricted by time, not to be hung on the walls of museums and labeled "The Age of Surrealism." Breton picked up and carried forward the magical tradition. Surrealism restated and revivified the magical view of the world through which the liberated imagination reveals the infinite correspondences of man with Nature, in a universe in which neither man nor god stands at the center.

The continuing vitality of the magical tradition is one of the most astounding—and reassuring—of historical truths. Astounding, because its enemies have been many and are still with us. Reassuring, because the magical view is essentially optimistic. As Breton wrote: "The heart of a human being can be broken and books can get old, and everything must, outwardly, die, but a power which is in no way supernatural makes of this very death the condition of renewal. It assures all exchanges ahead of time, that nothing precious may be lost within and that through the obscure metamorphoses, from season to season, the butterfly regains its exalting colours." [11]

Occult Reich

While André Breton, in exile, was writing his hymn to life in 1944, the shadow of death which had once covered nearly the whole of Europe was contracting as the substance of the Nazi empire was burned away. The founders of that empire had also projected a magical view of the world, and had sought to impose it on others. They too believed in a harmonious universe, but it was the harmony of the sick, the tortured, and the dying.

When Hitler gained power in 1933, he knew that there was little to fear from the bureaucrats, soldiers, or scientists. And he was right, for with very few exceptions these classes supported the Nazi state until the end. But within a year the new rulers had moved first against fortunetellers and then against all occult groups, banning their books, closing down their organizations. Some commentators have taken this to mean that Hitler had no use for occultists or astrologers, whereas, in fact, he feared an occult conspiracy as much as the Abbé Barruel and the rulers of Europe had done after the French Revolution.

There is no doubt that, in the anarchy of German politcs after the end of the First World War, occult groups of various types had played a significant, if ill-defined, role. One was even linked with the very early days of the Nazi party. In January 1918, a small group calling itself the Thule Society was formed in Munich, apparently to study the occult significance of runes and runic characters, the letters which had been used in Europe in the early Christian centuries and were believed to have magical powers. One of the leading members of the new society was an adventurer who called himself Baron von Sebottendorf. During the revolutionary upheaval which shook Bavaria between November 1918 and April 1919, Sebottendorf made the Thule Society a center for extreme right-wing opposition. Among his contacts was Anton Drexler, founder and leader of the totally unimportant German Workers party, which Hitler joined in September 1919 and, after taking control, renamed the National Socialist German Workers party.

Occult groups were not associated only with right-wing terrorism, but also with the "Jewish-Bolshevik" subversion that most Germans felt was undermining their country in the postwar years. Certain occult organizations were said, too, to have been responsible for the "stab in the back" that had lost Germany the war, a myth that was to be carefully fostered by the Nazis. It was even alleged that Rudolf Steiner, founder of the Anthroposophical Society, in 1914 had mesmerized the German chief of staff, General von Moltke (one of his followers), into a state of military incompetence.

But though the occult groups had been dispersed and the

works of occultists banned, the *atmosphere* of the Third Reich was saturated with occult influences. Writers with some particular occult axe to grind have tried to make Hitler into a master magician, when essentially his outward relationship with his followers and the German people was that of the shaman with the hunters, the god-speaker who articulates the desires of the collective psyche. Hitler, however, was not an untutored mouthpiece with no resources other than the fantasies of his own paranoid personality. He had at his disposal, and was happy to draw upon, those strands in the occult tradition which emphasized the powers of domination and saw the treasures of secret wisdom as reserved for élites. Those strands were as old as the occult tradition itself, but the nineteenth century had added another, mainly in response to the theory of evolution—the idea of mystic racialism—and had given it all the authority of available science.

At the center of all Nazi thinking lay belief in the Master Race, the Aryan supermen who were the natural rulers of all mankind. Theorists drew upon a number of sources for their belief, not least of which was that occult perennial, the myth of Atlantis. The Greek philosopher Plato first wrote of the lost continent "beyond the pillars of Hercules" which had been destroyed because of the impiety of its people in the fifth century b.c., and it soon entered the occult tradition as a place whose inhabitants had once possessed the ultimate wisdom. But it had to wait for the nineteenth century to supply the Atlantis legend with the support of the dubious archaeology of the time. Toward the end of the century, the theory of cultural diffusion was put forward, and one of the early suggestions was that all culture had spread from one place—a thesis previously held by the authors of the Book of Genesis. But the theory could also support the claim that the Aryans had been the standard bearers of civilization, and that they had come from Atlantis.

In Germany after the end of the First World War this idea was in the air and was picked up by a number of people, including Alfred Rosenberg, who became the Nazi party's chief cultural ideologist (and who was hanged as a war criminal in 1946). In *The Myth of the Twentieth Century*, published in 1930, Rosenberg graphically described the waves of Atlantean people traveling "by water in their swan and dragon ships into the Mediterranean to Africa; by land over Central Asia to Kutschka, indeed perhaps even to China, across North America to the south of the continent." Rosenberg located the lost Atlantis in the north. So, too, did Professor Hermann Wirth, a German-Flemish specialist in prehistory who was appointed curator of the Deutsches Ahnenerbe in 1935.

This organization—the words mean, literally, "German ancestral heritage"—was a private research institute set up by Heinrich Himmler, the head of the SS and probably the most powerful person in the Nazi state after Hitler. The institute was not made part of the SS itself until 1939, but from the beginning it reflected the occult interests of its founder, which could also be seen in the structure of the SS itself. Among the many strange subjects allegedly investigated by the staff of the institute were the symbolism of the suppression of the Irish harp in Ulster and the occult significance of Gothic towers. The institute was also the official custodian of the glacial cosmology of Hanns Hörbiger.

Hörbiger was an Austrian engineer who had died in 1931. He had first thought of a "cosmic ice" theory in 1882, after deciding that a comet which appeared that year was actually made of ice, but it was not until a quarter of a century later that he considered his theory sufficiently developed to be worth discussing with an astronomer, even an amateur one like Philippe Fauth. But Fauth's main interest was in the moon, and the moon was crucial to Hörbiger's theory. The engineer convinced the astronomer, and together they produced a book outlining the "cosmic ice" theory.

The basis of Hörbiger's theory was that the universe was filled with cosmic building material in the form of hot metallic stars and light gases, certain of which combined into water in its cosmic form of ice. The interaction of heavenly bodies and ice could occasionally be explosive. One moon had been propelled into collision with the earth thousands of years previously; the event was still remembered in legend, particularly in the legend of the Flood. Another moon, according to Hörbiger, could also be expected to strike the earth in due course.

The cosmic ice theory appeared to have some relevance to the Atlantis myth, as it offered a convenient explanation for the disappearance of that fabled continent. Its proponents, therefore, received Himmler's support. Researches were instituted in such regions as Ethiopia and on the Himalayan peak of Nanga Parbat, and a special department of the Ahnenerbe was set up to produce weather forecasts on the basis of Hörbiger's ideas. Himmler's enthusiasm was such that high-ranking Nazi party members found themselves bombarded with cosmic ice literature. The influence of the cosmic ice theorists could hardly be ignored—not only did they have the support of the Reichsführer-SS, but of Hitler himself, who made it clear that when he built the great new city he planned near his birthplace he would erect there an observatory dedicated to Hörbiger.

The cosmic ice theory quickly became a factor in the internal politics of the Nazi party, and it was decided that in order to avoid criticism both it and the Atlantis myth would have to be cleansed of the more obviously lunatic occult interpretations. After a meeting in Bad Pyrmont in 1936, the leading exponents of the theory—including Hörbiger's son, Hanns Robert—issued a document known as the "Pyrmont Protocol," in which an attempt was made to give the cosmic ice theory a strictly "scientific" form. The document also hailed itself as "a really Aryan intellectual treasure." Not all those who had been present at Bad Pyrmont agreed with the protocol, and one occultist, angered at the appointment of Hörbiger as Intellectual Director of Cosmic Ice, denounced him to Himmler as a covert Freemason and Roman Catholic.

The Pyrmont Protocol seems to have legitimized cosmic ice

as one of the sacred ideas of the Nazis. In 1937 a pamphlet was produced which became one of the instruction handbooks issued to members of the SA, the brownshirted party militia. In it was the claim that cosmic ice represented a truly Germany scientific world picture. The actual influence of the theory in decision making seems to have been small—it contributed more to the intellectual climate of Nazism than it did to the determining of specific events. But it has been suggested that experiments with what was to become the V-2 rocket were held up because of doubts raised by some members of the Ahnenerbe that, if the rockets were released, they might affect the delicate balance between stars and ice in the universe and precipitate a calamity.

Cosmic ice was not the only theory of the universe that interested men of authority and power in the Nazi state. There was, in fact, some competition between cosmologies. In 1938, the department run by the cultural *Führer*, Alfred Rosenberg, was asked by a certain Johannes Lang for permission to lecture on the subject of "hollow earth." The idea of a hollow earth had been given its widest interpretation by an American, Cyrus Reed Teed, who called himself "Koresh." Teed, who died in 1908, maintained that we live on the *inside* of a spherical or egg-shaped universe, with the sun and the other planets at the center. The sky, he claimed was a cloud of blue gas, and the stars pinpoints of light within it. Lang was refused permission to lecture, and the hollow earth theory was publicly condemned by Rosenberg's department as "a completely unscientific explanation of the cosmos." But that was not the last of the hollow earth. In April 1942, at the height of the war, a team of scientists with quantities of radar equipment, then in short supply, was put to work on an island in the Baltic, with the aim of proving the hollow earth theory. They failed, but one of the Nazi leaders, at least, had thought it worthwhile to divert the attention of top scientific talent and scarce equipment for the purpose.

The Nazi empire died in 1945. Hitler shot himself in his

bunker in Berlin on April 30; Himmler, that supreme patron of magicians, crushed a cyanide capsule in his mouth a month later. Between them, these two men had created in Germany a magical state of a distinctive and horrifying kind. They had, of course, had allies. As the Plains Indians of North America and the rebels against colonial rule in other countries had brought together the magician and the warrior in a magico-military partnership, the Nazis united the magician and the civil servant in a magico-bureaucratic alliance. Without the completely dispassionate, utterly rational technicians, and the administrative automata like Adolf Eichmann, the Nazi state would not have survived for a year. That it lasted for twelve years and cost millions of lives should be a constant reminder that the potentialities of the occult underground can be terrifying as well as wondrous.

2

The Raising
of the Pentagon

Washington D.C., October 21, 1967. An official permit had
been granted for an attempt to raise the colossal building ten
feet off the ground. But permission was refused for the
technicians—the "witches, warlocks, holy men, seers, prophets,
mystics, saints, sorcerers, shamans, troubadours, minstrels,
bards, roadmen, and madmen" [1]—to encircle the building
completely, which sabotaged the machinery that might, just
might, have levitated the Pentagon.

That day, the global symbol and factual headquarters of
American military power was being besieged by some fifty
thousand people protesting against the war in Vietnam. And
there among the middle-aged liberals, the activist academics,
the pacifists, the sitters-down, the marchers, the tired rhetoric
of the radical tradition, was an even older tradition, that of the
"mystic revolution." The "mighty words of white light" hurled
against the "demon-controlled structure" [2] of the Pentagon
failed to raise it, perhaps because of official foresight in
ensuring that there would be a gap in "the circle of power."

On the whole, the media pundits dismissed the attempt as
yet another youthful extravagance, to be treated indifferently or
with contempt. But they were wrong. However crazy the whole
affair appeared to "rational" minds, it was an indication of the
re-emergence in our own times of the occult underground.

Black Magic Language

It is easy to catalogue and file away the "youth rebellion" of the 1960s as just another episode in the recurring cycle of generation conflict. More rabid, perhaps, more foul-mouthed, more widely publicized and, electronically, considerably more amplified than before, but still at bottom the same old adolescent infection for which the inevitable onset of adult responsibility is the only cure. Such a definition has much going for it—not least the comfort it brings to parents, and to those whose authority is wider, more pervasive, but no less vulnerable, the politicians and technocrats who rule our lives and design our destinies. But at the core of the rebellion, beneath the many-layered superficialities of the shocking, the blasphemous, and the merely silly, there lay an incoherent but no less real threat to the structure of contemporary Western culture.

The one common factor in the innumerable formulas of rebellion was the rejection of the fat-cat values of the technocratic society. Once again, the magical view of the world was ranged against the scientific, but with something of a difference. In the nineteenth century, the occult radicalism which showed up at the barricades drew strength and purpose from working-class deprivation, exploitation, and poverty. The occult radicalism of the 1960s, with its contempt for the material rewards of affluence and, worse still, for the wonderful technology that made them possible, could not relate to working-class movements dedicated to the maintenance and extension of those same material rewards for their members.

The traditional left, the unions, the Marxists, the old-style radicals who still remembered, with nostalgia, the Spanish Civil War, reacted unfavorably to the new radicals. It was hardly surprising. Leftist revolution was aimed at a redistribution of the goodies, not at their rejection. What was to be done with self-styled revolutionaries who posted up a manifesto on the walls of the Sorbonne in Paris in May 1968 which claimed: "The revolution which is beginning will call in question not only capitalist society but industrial society. The consumer's society must perish a violent death"? [3] Such statements offered a positive threat to the wholesome proletarian ambitions of at least one car in every garage and a color TV in every living room. And what did the rest of the manifesto mean? "We are inventing a new and original world. Imagination is seizing power." There it was again—the imagination. "A man could fell a camel, if he but demanded it with his imagination." And make a new world?

In France in 1968, the revolution—which had never, in any case, stood a real chance—was aborted by an alliance between the traditional working-class organizations and the state. In America, where in effect it had all begun, it was sapped by entrepreneurial subversion—by "clothing designers, hair-dressers, fashion magazine editors, and a veritable phalanx of pop stars who, without a thought in their heads their PR man did not put there" were "suddenly expounding 'the philosophy of today's rebellious youth' for the benefit of the Sunday supplements ... the feature to be sandwiched between a report on luxury underwear and a full color spread on the latest undiscovered skindiving paradise at which to spend the summer of a lifetime." [4]

But still at the core lay the threat and the magic—and the magicians.

Surrealism between the two wars, speaking only to a minority and with only a restricted media identity, could afford one magus. The "counter culture," because of its looseness of styles and ideas, the fact that its only conformity was that of nonconformity, had more than one and most of them counterfeit. But by no means all.

Allen Ginsberg was responsible for one of the most recognizable styles of dissent—that of "as it comes" naturalism, uncluttered with artifice. By the middle of the 1950s his poetry of protest, which until then had been in the main carefully structured and brief, had become rambling and ecstatic. The Surrealists had seen, in automatic writing, a way to the destruction of psychic blocks and mental hangups, a way of "listening to thought" and releasing the power of the imagination. Ginsberg too wanted "to just write . . . let my imagination go . . . and scribble lines from my real mind." To see "the universe unfold" in his brain. Like the Surrealists, Ginsberg belonged in an ancient and respectable tradition. Unlike them, however, he found a wide and essentially unlettered audience, who recognized that he was articulating life and not art, and that it was the kind of life they wanted to live. The rebel young of the 1960s demanded a lifestyle as different in as many respects as possible from that of their parents. Many found it in poverty, promiscuity, and drugs, and in the mindless vulgarity repetitively emphasized by the media.

This was not Ginsberg's message. Although superficially it might not seem so, his magic was not escapist, but of this world. He and others; following the path already signposted by the Romantics and other nineteenth-century disciples of the occult tradition, looked to the East for relief from the all-pervasive materialism of the West. Zen, Yoga, *Tantra* were imported, popularized, and generally misunderstood. Inevitably, there were criticisms both of the popularizers and of the misunderstandings. But it did not matter very much whether the young who avidly absorbed the works of Alan Watts and other less-responsible gurus got the authentic message or not. What was important was that large numbers of the young of the most affluent society in the history of the world were anxiously searching for a magical revelation to set against a scientific and technological reality they found unacceptable.

Because the new statements of dissent were suffused by an air of the exotic, some commentators—even the most perceptive—have expressed surprise that they should have been associated in any but the most peripheral way with radical politics. The weary old opinions have been rehearsed that ever since the Enlightenment the thrust of radical thought has been *against* religion, *against* God, and *against* the agents of God on earth—pope, bishop, parish priest. There has been knowledge-able talk of the "revolution" as being rooted in the militant, skeptical, secular tradition. But the first view is irrelevant and the second only half a truth. In the 1960s, the association was not between religion and radicalism, but between magic and rebellion. And the emphasis on the secularity of revolution ignores the role of the occult.

More dangerous than the surprise of some commentators was the suggestion—coming usually from the most impeccable of old-style liberal and radical sources—that the emergence of the "irrational" in youth politics could somehow be compared with the bloodstained madness of Nazi Germany. One thing was certain, adults, working-class Frenchmen, old leftists, police chiefs, and politicians could recognize a threat even if they had difficulty in defining exactly what it was. It was simple enough when protest was concentrated on the American involvement in Vietnam. There, the threat polarized and could be dealt with on the simplest basis, that of law enforcement. But in a very real sense the anti-war protest, in all its forms, was only part of a total protest against the kind of society that permitted such an involvement to take place. In particular, it was opposition to a society that hid the terrible truths, not only of war but of peace, behind such expressions as "body count" and "kill ratio," "war on poverty" and "the New Frontier," the vocabulary of what Ginsberg called "Black Magic language."

The war is language,
  language abused
    for Advertisement,
  language used
 like magic for power on the planet
Black Magic language,
  formulas for reality—

The Raising of the Pentagon

Communism is a 9 letter word
used by inferior magicians
with the wrong alchemical formula for transforming earth
into gold.[5]

Of course, the loss of confidence in the honesty of ordinary literal language, awareness of the gap between word and reality, was no new phenomenon exclusive to the second half of the twentieth century. Ever since the scientific revolution of the seventeenth century destroyed the foundations of centuries of accepted beliefs, that loss has been irreversible. With new idea systems eroding the old, absolute relationship between words and situations, men were faced with two possible courses. They could continue to believe that words meant what they said—but this would have involved facing the fact that there was no unchanging reality to which they could attach themselves, only an unpredictable flux. The alternative course was to accept the idea that the link between words and what they stood for was only temporary, which made it possible to assume that, while words and ideas might shift around, reality remained unchanged, a reality to which ideas and words might someday do justice. The second offered some kind of hope, and it was the course chosen. But it was a hope that has never been fulfilled.

At the same time, governments and politicians have never ceased to obscure their real meaning behind linguistic camouflage of one kind or another. The uniqueness of our times is the insistent claim that our vocabulary consists of clinically objective technologisms. No one should be surprised that against the black magic language of science the rebels have set a wide range of magical sounds and often meaningless *mantras*. There is something remarkably reassuring about the rumble of Sanskrit, even when mispronounced.

The war in Vietnam came to an end at last, though it is difficult to assess just how much the anti-war movement contributed to ending it. The great surges of protest subsided.

The word count of the black magic language increased, but the threat to what it represented seemed muted, if not moribund. There had been, nevertheless, a genuine rebellion, even if it had shown little interior or exterior coherence, a rebellion whose long-term significance is perhaps only now becoming clear. As the columnist Hugh Sidey wrote in *Time* magazine just after President Jimmy Carter's inaugural in January 1977: "Carter may be more the result of a changing national mood than the leader of it. The kids who swarmed over the Washington Mall a few years ago brought part of the message."

The Tao Inside

The cover story of the March 5, 1974, issue of *Time* magazine was "Boom Times on the Psychic Frontier," and boom times they seemed to be. Everywhere, in America, Europe, and even in the Soviet Union, the interest in psychic phenomena was proliferating research projects by scientists. At the Foundation for Research on the Nature of Man at Durham, North Carolina, J. B. Rhine, who first began his studies of the paranormal in 1927, was supervising work on the precognitive powers of animals. At the nearby psychical Research Foundation, they were finding evidence of human ability to "leave the body." At the University of Virginia Medical School the subject was reincarnation. With a grant from the National Institute of Mental Health, the Department of Parapsychology and Psychophysics of the Maimonides Medical Center in New York experimented in "thinking" the image of a painting into the dreams of a laboratory subject asleep in another room. In Washington, the Defense Department's Advanced Research Projects Agency, one of whose "wild schemes" was a mind-guided missile, assigned a team to investigate apparently authentic psychic phenomena at the Stanford Research Institute. At the University of California at Los Angeles, a leaf cut in half and then photographed by a special process produced a picture showing the "aura" or outline of the whole leaf. That was only a selection of the activities. Boom times, indeed.

In the Soviet Union, there also seemed to be an upsurge of research activity in the field of the paranormal. The photographic process which showed the amputated portion of the leaf at Los Angeles had been developed in the late 1930s by a Russian electronics engineer, Semyon Kirlian. By introducing a small amount of high-voltage, low-frequency current into the subject and recording the subsequent discharge on photographic film, the method produced a photograph showing the "energy body" or aura around the subject. For centuries, auras, "astral bodies," and "psychic energy" have been a part of occult thinking. Now there appeared to be some kind of "scientific" proof. A great deal of research had been done in Russia before the Second World War, but it had been interrupted by the war and its after effects. Research now seems to have been absorbed into the academic system and a general party line developed to cover it. The emphasis, as might be expected from an allegedly materialist society, is away from the occult and toward the scientific. In the West, research into paranormal phenomena has on the whole been directed toward trying to demonstrate the fact of their existence, and theoretical explanations are left to look after themselves in the future. Russian researchers stress that their main purpose is to discover a suitable physical basis to explain the phenomena.

The attempt by the Russians to formulate a unified theory to describe the basic energy transformations taking place in paranormal activity leads them to impose biological or physical limits to the explanation. The electromagnetic fields (the magnetic fluid of Anton Mesmer) revealed by the Kirlian process become "some sort of elementary plasma-like constellation of ionised particles." And the astral body becomes "the bioplasma body." [6]

Despite accusations, and sometimes proof, of fraud by researchers as well as "psychics" who offer themselves for scientific research, the desire by scientists to continue work on the paranormal seems undiminished. This is perhaps not so surprising when a poll of scientists and technicians taken by the London *New Scientist* revealed that 70 percent of those who responded believed in the possibility of extrasensory perception. At a time when the new physics suggests there are black holes in the universe, and has confirmed the existence of antimatter, quasars, and such exotic things as neutrinos that have neither mass nor charge, it would be churlish—even vaguely unscientific—not to accept at least the possibility of paranormal phenomena.

Nevertheless, some believers or partial believers are unexpected. Arthur Koestler, for example, discovers that modern scientists are merely "Peeping Toms at the keyhole of eternity," a keyhole that is almost completely blocked with bias towards rational and materialist explanation.[7] Abandon the prejudices of skepticism, says Koestler, and open the mind.

Most specific is the interest of the leading British behavioral psychologist, Professor H. J. Eysenck, in astrology. Eysenck, professor of psychology at the University of London's Institute of Psychiatry and a pioneer of aversion therapy (black magic language for therapy-by-terror), in 1975 published his opinion that there was "no doubt that the time of the year at which a baby is born, and his personality, are correlated."[8]

Professor Eysenck's astrology is not, of course, what Lyall Watson, a very successful popularizer of the "science proves magic" school, describes as the "glib, all-embracing predictions, in which everyone born under Pisces will have a good day, while another twelfth of the world's population will be busy meeting attractive strangers,"[9] the popular astrology of the newspapers. Eysenck's astrology is the real "writing of heaven" and the decipherers of the Linear B of the occult are Michel and Françoise Gauquelin.

The Gauquelins, working from the impressively named Laboratoire d'etude des Relations entre Rhythmes Cosmiques et Psychophysiologique at Strasbourg, have carried out statistical surveys based upon the time and place of birth of their subjects. They were fortunate that in European Catholic countries the precise time of birth has to be recorded on the birth certificate. The Gauquelins' results have been checked by the equally impressively named Belgian Committee for the Scientific Study of Paranormal Phenomena and there seems no possibility of fraud. Nor any doubt that certain types of personality were usually born under certain celestial circumstances—scientists under Saturn, actors under Jupiter, sportsmen under Mars. Not exclusively, of course, but quantifiably enough to convince Professor Eysenck and others. Research continues.

The way things are going, and despite great surges of dissent from the more "rational" members of the scientific establishment, we are witnessing the takeover of magic by science. There has been grudging acceptance by scientists and historians of ideas that magic was the precursor of science, even a necessary one. But now that science is finding proof for some of the basic ideas enshrined in the occult tradition, the general attitude is one of surprise—surprise of the same condescending kind as that bestowed on a nine-year-old prodigy who can play all Beethoven's piano concertos without a mistake but must be too young and ignorant to grasp their inner meaning. It must all, somehow, have been an accident, like Leonardo da Vinci and his flying machine, ahead of its time, ahead of its time's understanding.

At the beginning of the scientific revolution, magic and the new science were allies. The enemy of "modern science," then, was scholastic rationalism, represented by the theologians who refused to look through Galileo's telescopes because they were sure that they already possessed sufficient knowledge of the material universe. "If Galileo's findings agreed with Aristotle and Thomas Aquinas there was no point in looking; if they did not, they must be wrong." [10] The magician was willing to look. His sense of wonder and his view of Nature compelled him to judge what he saw with an open mind. It is time for magic and science to be allies again, before science and the technocratic society destroy us all.

It is not a matter of giving up central heating for psychic heat, or jet aircraft for "out of body" travel. There is probably a better chance of making rain by seeding the clouds with dry ice than there ever was by hurling spells at the sky. It is not the techniques of magic that are needed today but its cosmology, its way of looking at the world, its understanding of the interdependence of all things, and its sense of continuing wonder. That sense has never been, and should never be, the reflection of a conscious desire for ignorance, an unwillingness to understand, a preference for fantasy over truth. André Breton told the story of an occasion on which a distinguished psychologist and an anthropologist came to visit him. The three men were watching the behavior of Mexican jumping beans and Breton's friends were amused at his childish fascination with what seemed some kind of miracle, and at his postponement of opening the beans to find out what caused the apparent magic. Breton explained that his hesitancy was not due to any superstitious belief in magic—he was well aware that the physical cause of the movement was a parasitical insect lodged in the bean—but the sense of wonder was as necessary to his well-being as the knowledge and evidence of its logical cause. "Beauty demands that most often one should enjoy before understanding." [11] By "beauty," Breton meant the beauty of existence, the joy of living. The sense of wonder is something that seems to have been lost in the West, part of the price paid for the kind of society we live in.

Western man lost his sense of cosmic identity long before his sense of wonder. The early Christians deprived him of it, leaving it to the magical tradition to preserve the understanding of man's place in the harmony of the interdependent universe. What might be slightly surprising, considering the customary association of the occult and radical politics, is the unity of Christian and Marxist thinking about Nature. Both consider the history of man to be strictly unique. The Christians were the first to see human life and the march of events as moving from a fixed beginning to a definite end, and to argue that during the journey man won his salvation or earned his punishment. For the Christian, as for the Marxist, Nature had to be brought to heel. The first Christians had no love for the cosmos and awaited, with impatience, the imminent end of the world. When the world stubbornly continued, they institutionalized the belief that it was merely a vale of tears which had to be passed through on the way to the kingdom of Christ. If Nature was anything, it was merely a background to the drama of Christ's divinity. There were times, of course, when the occult underground broke the smooth surface of the Christian over-world—and then it was labeled heresy and brutally suppressed. In Europe, the guardians of the magical tradition were very careful what they said; the stake and the fire were never very far away.

The French Revolution, for a while at least, seemed to have killed off God as well as Louis XVI, for all the radical wanted from the priest "was his guts with which to strangle the last king." [12] But socialism, especially in the gospel according to Karl Marx, soon revealed itself as an enterprise designed to turn man into god, a secular religion with its own harsh orthodoxy and its own hatred of Nature. What was so significant about the radicalism of the 1960s, before it was transformed by the overreactive violence of law-enforcement agencies, was that it rejected both the harshness of ideology and the hatred of Nature.

Science, too, considered Nature fair game. And science too was soon revealed as an enterprise designed to turn at least certain men—scientists, of course—into gods. It is, therefore, all the more pleasing to find in the last quarter of the twentieth century a "subversive science" that not only seeks to point out what science has done and is doing to Nature, but that everything in Nature, including man, is endangered by it.

The magical world view has emerged anew in the science of

241

ecology, but to establishment science ecology is a heresy and it is under attack continuously and from many directions. The United Nations stifles it with international conferences, powerful industrial interests use the loopholes thoughtfully supplied by legislators in the superficially impressive array of conservation laws. The most subtle attack gives ecology scientific respectability by trying to turn it into a sophisticated systems approach to the conservation of natural resources, a device for manipulating Nature instead of battering it for the same exploitive ends.

These are dangerous times, and there can be very few people in the West, at least, who are unaware of it. Environmental collapse, world poverty, urban violence, the proliferation of nuclear capabilities, the fragility of sophisticated economies that shake at a few cents' rise in the price of a barrel of oil—all these are widely publicized and some of them personally experienced. The technocratic panacea that increasingly calls for some governmental or international agency to "solve" the problems arouses widening skepticism, not only among the young.

Of the two strains of social thinking in the magical tradition, one sought to transform society by revolution, the other by rejection. The revolutionary strain showed itself in the Naples rebellion of Campanella, the mesmeric radicals of the first French Revolution, the Romantics at the barricades, and the hippie magicians who tried to raise the Pentagon. The other strain can be seen in the Taoists' retreat from Confucian feudalism in China, the Fourier-inspired communities of the nineteenth-century West, and the experiments in communal living by the young and the not so young which began in the 1960s and are hopefully continuing today. It is also there, if not so consciously, in the desire of so many Westerners to leave the cities.

The city is the temple of technocracy, and its worshipers are deserting it. In the United States, where so many good things and so many bad things happen first, Louis Harris the pollster reported in March 1976 that: "Most Americans don't want more quantity of anything, but more quality in what they've got." [13] At one time, Americans, like Europeans, and now like the peoples of the so-called developing nations, flocked to the cities for jobs, education, and excitement. But today there is too much excitement; too many muggings, burglaries, and drugs; too little education, in overcrowded schools; and too many tensions on clogged and polluted urban motorways to make the jobs worthwhile.

This trend, of course, is no indication of some sudden spiritual awakening among the middle-class Americans who make up the majority of the new migrants. Self-interest is undoubtedly the largest factor in their decision to take up a new lifestyle. Most deserters from the cities are looking less for the often harsh realities of "back to Nature" than for the comfortable, physically secure small-town America enshrined in the work of the artist Norman Rockwell on the covers of the old *Saturday Evening Post*.

But if self-interest is the largest factor, it is not the only one. There are psychological ones, too, that most of the migrants would have difficulty in admitting to, far less defining. The magical world view was never an *intellectual* construction, but an intuitive, unreasoned, organic conception of reality. We may not hear the resonances of the harmony of the universe, but we do feel them. We may not recognize them, but we do respond. The Taoist philosophers, who were not crazy magicians "madly singing in the mountains" but men who hated the inhumanity of social tyranny and feared what it might do once it got its hands on the "science" they were developing, believed that the *Tao* was inside everything. By *Tao* they meant the order of Nature, the balance, the essential cooperation of its manifold components, and the understanding of it. In chapter fourteen of *The Book of the Master Chuang* (c. 290 B.C.) there is a superb piece of anti-Confucian satire which describes an imaginary meeting between the sage-philosopher and a Taoist named Lao Tan:

243

Confucius went to see Lao Tan. Lao Tan said: "I hear you are a wise man from the North; have you also found the *Tao*?" "Not yet," replied Confucius. "May I inquire how you went about searching for it?" said Lao Tan. "I looked for it in measures and numbers but after five years of effort I was still not able to put my finger on it." "And what did you do then?" asked Lao Tan. "I sought for it in the Yin and the Yang, but even after twelve years I did not find it," replied Confucius. "I am not surprised," was Lao Tan's response. "If the *Tao* could be offered from person to person, all men would present it to their rulers; if it could be served up on a plate men would all have given it to their parents; if it could have been talked about, everybody would have told their brothers; if it could have been passed on, men would certainly have willed it to their sons and grandsons. But no one was able to do any of these things. Because if you have not got it in you, no one can give it to you. . . ." [14]

Lao Tan knew that everyone, even Confucius, had the Tao inside—for it is the untamed, and so far untamable, element in man's spirit.

Notes

Where works cited are listed separately in the bibliography, only short titles are given below. PB = paperback edition.

Introduction

1. Thorndike: *History of Magic*, vol. 5.
2. Agrippa von Nettesheim: *Of the vanitie and uncertaintie of artes and sciences*. London, 1569.
3. J. G. Frazer: *The Golden Bough*. 12 vols. 1913-20. Abridged edition, London, 1923; New York, 1959.
4. C. Lévi-Strauss: *The Savage Mind*. London and Chicago, 1966.
5. La Barre: *The Ghost Dance*.
6. Jacques Ellul: *The Technological Society*. New York, 1964.

Prologue: The Morning of the Magician

1. La Barre: *The Ghost Dance*.
2. Holmyard: *Alchemy*.
3. Claudius Ptolemy: *Tetrabiblos*, vol. 1, in *Collected Works*, ed. J. L. Heiberg. London, 1898-1907.
4. R. Steele and D. W. Singer: "The Emerald Table," in *Proceedings of the Royal Society of Medicine*, vol. 21. 1928.
5. F. Max-Müller: *Ramakrishna: His Life and Work*. London, 1894.

Notes

Part One: Alchemical Arts and Natural Magic

1. Magisteries of Gold and Immortality

1. Albertus Magnus: *Libellus de Alchymia,* in Theatricum Chemicum, vol. 2. Ursel, 1602.
2. Taylor: *The Alchemists.*
3. J. D. Bernal: *Science in History.* London, 1954, Harmondsworth, 1965.
4. R. J. Forbes and E. J. Dijksterhuis: *A History of Science and Technology.* Harmondsworth, 1963. PB
5. C. G. Jung: *Memories, Dreams and Reflections.* London and New York, 1963.
6. Stanislas Klossowski de Rola: *The Secret Art of Alchemy.* London, 1973.
7. M. Berthelot and C. E. Ruelle: *Collection des Anciens Alchimistes Grecs,* vol. 1. Paris, 1888, reprinted, Osnabruck, 1967.
8. Fifteenth-century recipe quoted in Holmyard: *Alchemy.*
9. Needham: *Science and Civilisation in China,* vol. 5 part 2.
10. H. H. Dubs: "The Beginnings of Alchemy," in *Isis,* vol. 68, 1947.
11. *The Works of Geber,* trans. Richard Russell. 1678. Ed., E. J. Holmyard, London, 1928.
12. "The Book of Properties," ed., E. J. Holmyard, in *Proceedings of the Royal Society of Medicine,* vol. 16. 1923.
13. Avicenna: *De Congalatione et Conglutinatione Lapidum,* trans., E. J. Holmyard and D. C. Mandeville. Paris, 1927.
14. Roger Bacon: *Opera quaedam hactenus inedita,* ed., J. S. Brewer. London, 1859.
15. Quoted in Taylor: *The Alchemists.*
16. Quoted in Thorndike: *Michael Scot.* London, 1965.
17. Holmyard: *Alchemy.*
18. Needham: *Science and Civilisation,* vol. 5, part 2.
19. *Hai Nei Shih Chou.* c. 4th or 5th century A.D.
20. *Chhien Han Shu* [Pan Ku: *History of the Former Han*]. This version is by the present author, but see a partial translation of the work by H. H. Dubs and others. Baltimore, 1938.
21. *Ibid.*

22. Yen Kho-Chün (ed:) *Chhuan Shang-ku San-Tai Chhin Han San-Kuo Liu Chhao Wên*. Shanghai, 1836.
23. Ko Hung: *Pao Phu Tzu*. c. A.D. 320.
24. Su Yuan-Ming: *Thai-Chhing Shi Pi Chi*. A.D. 6th century.
25. C. H. Joosten: "The Text of John Dastin's Letter to Pope John XXII," in *Ambix*, vol. 4. 1951.
26. "Eirenaeus Orandus": *Nicholas Flamel, his exposition of the hieroglyphic figures, which he caused to be painted upon the arch of St Innocent's churchyard in Paris*. London, 1624.
27. All the quotations from Paracelsus are from T. P. Sherlock, "The Chemical Works of Paracelsus," in *Ambix*, vol. 3. 1948.

2. The Black Dog of Cornelius Agrippa

1. W. Fletcher: *The Works of Lactantius*. Edinburgh, 1871.
2. Agrippa von Nettesheim: *De occulta philosophia*, ed. with commentary by W. Schrödter. Remagen, 1967.
3. *De triplici ratione*, quoted in Nauert, *Agrippa* etc.
   4, 5, 6, 7. Agrippa von Nettesheim. See Introduction, Note 2, above.

3. The Pope's Magician

1. Campanella: *Astrologicorum*, Libri VI. Lyons, 1629.
2. Campanella: *Città del Sole*, ed. E. Solni. Modena, 1904.
3. Quoted in R. Lenôtre: *Mersenne et la naissance du mécanisme*. Paris, 1943.

Part Two: Subversive Magic and the Occult Underground

1. An Invasion of Demons

1. Gabriel Naudé: *Instruction à la France sur la vérité de l'histoire des Frères de la Rose-Croix*. Paris, 1623.
2. *Effroyables pactions faites entre le Diable et les prétendus Invisibles*. Paris, 1623.
3. A. Baillet: *La Vie de Monsieur Descartes*. Paris 1691.
4. *Ibid*.

2. *Monsieur Mesmer's Revolution*

1. *Mémoires de la baronne d'Oberkirch sur la cour de Louis XVI et la société française avant 1789* ... ed. Comte de Montbrison. Brussels, 1854.
2. *Journal de Bruxelles*, January 31, 1784.
3. *Ibid.*, May 29, 1784.
4. Erasmus Darwin: "The Loves of the Plants," in *The Botanic Garden*. 1789.
5. Restif de la Bretonne: *Monsieur Nicolas, ou le coeur dévoilè*. Paris, 1788.
6. *Journal de Paris*, December 8, 1783.
7. *Mémoires de la baronne d'Oberkirch*, see note 1 above.
8. Count Warnsted, quoted in E. M. Butler: *The Myth of the Magus*. London, 1968.
9. *Rapport des commissaires chargés par le Roi de l'examen du magnétisme animal*. Paris, 1784.
10. Jacques-Pierre Brissot: *Un mot de l'oreille des académiciens de Paris*. Paris, 1785.
11. *Ibid.*
12. Nicolas Bergasse: *Observations sur le préjugé de la noblesse héréditaire*. London, 1789.
13. Jean-Louis Carra: *Nouveaux principes de physique*. Paris, 1781-82.
14. Nicolas Bergasse: *Lectures*. Ms. in Bergasse archives at Château de Villers, Villers, Loir-et-Cher, France.
15. Nicolas Bergasse: *Lettre d'un médecin de la faculté de Paris* ... The Hague, 1781.
16. Humbert: *The day of Jean-Baptiste Humbert, clockmaker, who was the first to climb on the towers of the Bustille*. Paris 1789. Trans. Reay Tannahill in *Paris in the Revolution*. London, 1966.

3. *The Magician at the Barricades*

1. Abbé Fiard: *La France trompée par les magiciens et les demonolâtres du dix-huitième siècle*. Paris, 1803.
2. Marquis de Luchet: *Essai sur la secte des Illuminés*. Paris, 1788.
3. Jacques-Pierre Brissot: *Rapport sur l'affaire de MM Dhosier et Petit-Jean*, in *La Revolution Française*, vol. II. Paris, 1882.
4. Quoted in A. Viatte: *Les Sources occultes du romantisme*, vol. I. Paris, 1928.

5. Marie Antoinette: *Correspondence,* ed., von Arneth and Geffroy. Paris, 1874.
6. Abbé Baissie: *L'Esprit de la Franc-maçonnerie dévoilé, relativement au danger qu'elle renferme.* Rome, 1790.
7. *Vie de Joseph Balsamo, connu sous le nom de comte Cagliostro. Extrait de la Procédure contre lui, à Rome, en 1790.* Paris, 1791.
8. Charles Louis Cadet-Gassicour: *Le Tombeau de Jacques Molay ou le secret des conspirateurs* . . . Paris, An. Iv (1795-96).
9, 10. Quoted in K. Epstein: *The Genesis of German Romanticism.* Princeton, 1966.
11. *Oeuvres complètes de Charles Fourier,* vol. I. Paris, 1841.
12. Quoted in Darnton: *Mesmerism.*
13. Victor Hugo: *Choses vues.* Paris, 1887.
14. AE (George Russell): *The Living Torch.* Second ed. London, 1937.
15. Lewis Spence: *Freedom for Scotland.* Edinburgh, 1927.
16. Fiona Macleod: "Celtic," in *Contemporary Review.* 1900. Reprinted in *The Winged Destiny.* London, 1904.

Part Three: Industrial Revolution and Scientific Magic

1. *The Medium and the Message*

1. S. T. Coleridge: *Literary Remains.* London, 1836.
2. Honoré de Balzac: *Ursule Mirouet.* Paris, 1831.
3. Quoted in Giustino: *Conquest of Mind.*
4. *Ibid.*
5. Charles Bray: *Phases of Opinion and Experience.* London, 1884.
6. George Combe: *Elementary Phrenology.* London, 1881.
7. Alexander Bain in a letter to John Stuart Mill, quoted in Giustino: *Conquest of Mind.*
8. E. W. Capron: *Modern Spiritualism, Its Facts and Fanaticism.* Boston, 1885.
9. Quoted in Nelson: *Spiritualism and Society.*
10. Capron, as note 9 above.
11. M.Levaillant: *La Crise mystique de Victor Hugo.* Paris, 1954.
12. Leonard Huxley: *Life and Letters of T. H. Huxley.* New York, 1900.

Notes

13. Oscar Handlin: *The Americans.* New York, 1963, and London (as *The American People*), 1963.
14. Andrew Jackson Davis: *A Voice to Mankind.* Boston, 1848.
15. Quoted in Nelson: *Spiritualism and Society.*
16. Viscount Adare: *Experiences in Spiritualism with Mr D. D. Home.* London, 1870.
17. The Imperial Archduke Johann of Austria: *Insight into Spiritualism.* London, 1885.

2. Wise Men from the East

1. Quoted in Hesketh Pearson: *The Smith of Smiths.* London, 1934.
2. T. B. Macaulay: *Minute on Education 1835*, quoted in Michael Edwardes: *British India.* London and New York, 1967.
3. James Gawthorne: *Essay on Taste.* London, 1786.
4. Quoted in Michael Edwardes: *East-West Passage.* London and New York, 1971.
5. Swami Vivekananda: *Complete Works*, vol. 4. Almura, 1923-36.
6. Rudyard Kipling: "The Sending of Dana Da," in *Soldiers Three and Other Stories.* London, 1895.
7. E. J. Buck: *Simla: Past and Present.* Calcutta, 1904.
8. S. Ramaswami: "How a Chela Found His Guru," in *The Theosophist.* Reprinted in *Five Years of Theosophy.* London, 1885.
9. Ashvagosha: *Saudarananda*, trans. E. H. Johnston. London, 1932.

Part Four: Magicians and Machine Guns

1. The Revolt of the Bird King

1. Lawrence Krader: "A Nativistic Movement in Western Siberia," in *American Anthropologist, vol. 58. 1956.*
2. Quoted in S. Barton Babbage: *Hauhauism: An Episode in the Maori Wars 1863-66.* Wellington, New Zealand, 1937.
3. E. Thurston: *Omens and Superstitions of Southern India.* London, 1912.
4. *Jugantar*, quoted in B. B. Majumdar: *Indian Political Associations and Reform of the Legislature.* Calcutta, 1965.
5. Subhas Chandra Bose: *An Indian Pilgrim.* Bombay, 1965.

Notes

2. *Chairman Mao and the Lord of the World*

1. Alexandra David-Neel: *Magic and Mystery in Tibet*. 1931. New York and London, 1970.
2. René de Nebesky-Wojkowitz: *Oracles and Demons of Tibet*. The Hague and London, 1956.

Part Five: Worlds of Light and Worlds of Darkness

1. *The Surreal and the Swastika*

1. André Breton: *Entretiens*. Paris, 1952.
2. Louis Aragon: *Le Paysan de Paris*. Paris, 1924.
3. "Eliphas Levi": *Transcendental Magic. Its Doctrine and Ritual*. Trans. A. E. Waite. New York, n.d.
4. Fabio Paolini: *Hebdomades*. Venice, 1589. Quoted in Walker: *Spiritual and Demonic Magic*.
5. Ferdinand Alquié: *The Philosophy of Surrealism*. PB Ann Arbor, 1969.
6. *First Surrealist Manifesto*. 1924.
7. Tristan Tzara: *Dada* No. 3. Zurich, 1918.
8. Hugo Ball: *Dada* No. 2. Zurich, 1916..
9. As note 6, above.
10. *La Révolution Surréaliste* No. 4. Paris, 1925.
11. André Breton: *Arcane 17*. New York, 1945.

2. *The Raising of the Pentagon*

1. *The East Village Other*, New York. Nov. 1-5, 1967.
2. *Ibid.*
3. Report from Paris in *The Times*, London, May 17, 1968.
4. Roszak: *The Making of a Counter Culture*.
5. Allen Ginsberg: *Wichita Vortex Sutra*.
6. S. Ostrander and L. Schroeder: *Psychic Discoveries Behind the Iron Curtain*. Englewood Cliffs, New Jersey, 1971.
7. Arthur Koestler: *The Roots of Coincidence*. London, 1972.
8. H. J. Eysenck: "Planets, stars and personality," in *New Behaviour*, London, May 29, 1975.
9. Watson: *Supernature*.
10. Needham: *Science and Civilisation in China*, vol. 2.

Notes

11. André Breton: *La Clé des Champs*. Paris, 1953.
12. As note 4, above.
13. Quoted in *Time*, New York, March 15, 1976.
14. This version is by the author, but see also Lin Yutang: *The Wisdom of Lao Tzu*. New York, 1948.

Bibliography

Many thousands of works in many languages have been published on occult and allied subjects. Listed below are the few recent titles (all but one in English) which have been found helpful in the writing of this book.

BALAKIAN, ANNA. *André Breton: Magus of Surrealism.* New York, 1971.

BONELLI, M. L. R. and SHEA, W. R. (eds.) *Reason, Experiment and Mysticism in the Scientific Revolution.* London, 1975.

COHN, NORMAN. *Europe's Inner Demons.* London, 1975.

DARNTON, R. *Mesmerism and the End of the Enlightenment in France.* Cambridge, Massachusetts, 1968.

ELIADE, MIRCEA. *The Forge and the Crucible: The Origins and Structures of Alchemy.* New York, 1972.

FEUCHTWANG, S. D. R. *Anthropological Analysis of Chinese Geomancy.* Vientiane, Laos, 1974.

GAUQUELIN, MICHEL. *Cosmic Influences on Human Behavior.* London, 1974.

GIUSTINO, D. DE. *Conquest of Mind: Phrenology and Victorian Social Thought.* London, 1974.

HOLMYARD, E. J. *Alchemy.* Harmondsworth, 1957.

HORTON, R. and FINNEGAN, R. (eds.) *Modes of Thought. Essays on Thinking in Western and Non-Western Societies.* London, 1973.

LA BARRE, WESTON. *The Ghost Dance: Origins of Religion.* Cambridge, Massachusetts, 1970, and London, 1972.

Bibliography

LINDSAY, JACK. *The Origins of Astrology in Graeco-Roman Egypt*. London, 1970.

MAUSS, MARCEL. *A General Theory of Magic*. London, 1973.

NAUERT, CHARLES G. *Agrippa and the Crisis of Renaissance Thought*. Urbana, Illinois, 1965.

NEEDHAM, JOSEPH. *Science and Civilisation in China*. Vol. 2: *History of Scientific Thought*, 1956. Vol. 5, Part II: *Chemistry and Chemical Technology*, 1974. Cambridge, England.

NELSON, G. K. *Spiritualism and Society*. London, 1969.

PACHTER, H.M. *Magic into Science. The Story of Paracelsus*. New York, 1951.

ROBERTS, J.M. *The Mythology of the Secret Societies*. St. Albans, 1974.

ROSZAK, THEODORE. *The Making of a Counter Culture*. New York, 1969, and London 1971 PB

———. *Where the Wasteland Ends*. New York, 1972, and London 1974 PB.

TAYLOR, F. SHERWOOD. *The Alchemists*. St. Albans, 1976 PB.

THORNDIKE, LYNN. *A History of Magic and Experimental Science*. 8 vols. New York, 1923-58.

TREVOR-ROPER, H. *The European Witch-Craze of the 16th and 17th Centuries*. Harmondsworth, 1969 PB. And in *Religion, Reformation and Social Change*. New York, 1969.

VERNANT, J.P. (ed.) *Divination et Rationalité*. Paris, 1974.

WALKER, D.P. *Spiritual and Demonic Magic from Ficino to Campanella*. London, 1958.

WATSON, LYALL. *Supernature*. London, 1974 PB.

WEBB, JAMES. *The Flight from Reason*. London, 1971, and New York (as *The Occult Revival*), 1973.

WILSON, BRYAN. *Magic and the Millennium*. St. Albans, 1975 PB.

YATES, FRANCES A. *The Rosicrucian Enlightenment*. St. Albans, 1975 PB.

Index

Index